The Girl On The Bus

An autobiographical story that
will take you beyond Kismet

By

Alexander Milnz

Copyright © Alexander Milnz 2023

Alexander Milnz has asserted his right to be identified as the author of this work in accordance with the Copyright, Design and Patents Act 1988.

All rights reserved. No part of this publication including artwork may be reproduced, stored in a retrieval system, or transmitted in any form or by any means, without the prior permission in writing of the copyright owner.

BOOK ONE – part one

CHAPTER	1	From A 'Very' Early Age	1
CHAPTER	2	My Father Did Not Deserve This	6
CHAPTER	3	Work, The Bus Ride, My First Time, Isla	17
CHAPTER	4	Gillian, Patricia, and My Brother	25
CHAPTER	5	Love, Marriage, Babies, Dancing	33
CHAPTER	6	Little Trials And Tribulations	37
CHAPTER	7	The Cottage, Balloons, and Things	43
CHAPTER	8	An 'Innocent' Indiscretion	47
CHAPTER	9	The 'Happy Balloon' Starts To Deflate	53
CHAPTER	10	A Very Dark Decade	59

Chapter 11 onward is to be read in conjunction with Book Two

CHAPTER	11	The Millennium Years	65
CHAPTER	12	The Phoenix, and Will-O'-The-Whisp	69
CHAPTER	13	Kitten And The Truth Drug	75
CHAPTER	14	Coincidences Or Kismet, No Secrets	81
CHAPTER	15	Ironworks, The Girl and A Gamble	85
CHAPTER	16	Tosca's and the Station Of Dreams	91
CHAPTER	17	Immeasurable	97

BOOK ONE – part two

CHAPTER	18	Beyond The Station	99
CHAPTER	19	The Request	103
CHAPTER	20	Mo'Daka, Singosari, and Reiss	105
CHAPTER	21	Into The Kitten's Lair	111
CHAPTER	22	Joining Hands and Everything Else	117
CHAPTER	23	A Sensitive Relationship	127
CHAPTER	24	Pizza, Coffee, and A Hair Day	133
CHAPTER	25	Chinese Tigers	141
CHAPTER	26	La Dolce Vita, Breakfast, and A&E.	147
CHAPTER	27	A Few Deep Thoughts	155
CHAPTER	28	Dinner With (Unexpected) Dessert	161
CHAPTER	29	Boobs, My Body Or Me, A Phone Call	167
CHAPTER	30	A Different Way To Serve Soup	173
CHAPTER	31	No Sex ? No Chance ! The Beginning Of The End	179
CHAPTER	32	The End Of The Line	188
CHAPTER	33	Any Path Taken Can Be A Wrong One	191
CHAPTER	34	Clinical Chats and Spats	195
CHAPTER	35	France, Bombshells, Decisions	201

CHAPTER 36   The Airport, A Birthday, More Plans   209
CHAPTER 37   Karma   217

The connection with Book Two is now complete. Book Two continues independently, with Cancer Update #2, page 313.

CHAPTER   X

    1. Epilogue: 225
    2. Aftermath: 231
    3. Conclusion.. *if there really is one.*   261
    4. And So, To The Final Line + 'Spoilers'   265
    5. The Real Beginning?   269

In May 2021 the author assumed this part of the book had gone as far as it could go. In effect, it was now completed, finished.

But, a 'muse' followed. And exactly twelve months later (a coincidence surely?) came not a conclusion, but a series of incredible revelations that gave clarity to almost everything that had gone before.

    6. Afterword: The 'What If'   273
    7. Food For Thought:
        a - A friends view   277
        b - Revelations & realisations   281

BOOK TWO

    My Seven Year Itch... with Cancer   305

***

Acknowledgements and In Memory   345

Foreword

The book is of two stories, both completely different and yet inextricably linked. Book Two has to be read in conjunction with Book One from Chapter 11 to Chapter 37 (inclusive).

As far back as I can remember, I have always had an inquisitive mind. A seeker of knowledge, and of truth, if you will.
This knowledge seeking has always been for personal satisfaction, though in later years, it held me in good stead within my academic learning and profession as well as other endeavours.

More than once people have said that I am reading too much into something or reading into something that is not even there (a very ambiguous phrase I have found) and even, that I am delving too deep and in doing so, could open a 'can of worms'. Sometimes I have stepped back whilst other times I have ignored the 'advice' and gone on to seek out the truth. This has, on occasion, been met with verbal confrontation from people who have their own interpretation and possibly their own agenda.

Over the years I have also found that I, like many other people, have been able to recall personal events in detail. Though this in turn, can have its drawbacks.
Whilst having a retentive memory can often be a blessing, it can also be a source of great irritation to others.

I am not a writer, just a recorder of memories. No other person, professional or other has been involved in the writing of this book, and I have no doubt it will show within its composition.
This is a narrative non-fiction book. An accurate account of events, in time-line form (with the odd tangent), created through memory, many scribbled and typed notes and also documented evidence, as it was seen, heard and even felt at the time.

To write a full autobiography would take in truth, a lifetime, and this book could very well have been over a thousand (mostly boring) pages long, even by now.

But there are those times, events in all our lives that are more memorable than others. These events shape our lives and for many, shape us individually into the person we are today.

And this book contains such.

There are a number of such memories, hopefully mostly positive to the reader, but some they may find traumatic and from which a few readers may find even harrowing. For that I cannot apologise but that as they say 'that's life' and yes, wouldn't it be blissful without conflict or misunderstandings. Alas it never is and reality truly can bite, and bite hard.

But there is one particular memory that lasted over forty-six years and when it was unlocked, a complete opposite of *Pandora's box* emerged. But there were also mysteries within the box, waiting to be unfolded. And they were.

Sometimes we hold secrets, that even we didn't know existed.

Some readers may become sceptical of events within this book, and in turn become inherently cynical. All that I can say to that, is, this book is not about converting or influencing anyone. I will not attempt to convince the sceptics, or those in two minds, otherwise. My only hope and wish is that one day they experience something that will allow them to see things a little differently.

The full realisation of its contents may not however, at first become fully apparent. And to that end all that I suggest is that you may have to read it more than once to understand and fully realise the emotional, psychological and 'spiritual' impact created.

In October 2021, two-hundred copies of a 58k version of this book were privately published. A dozen were given to close friends, with the rest to independent private booksellers.

Within three months, they were all gone. Such was the interest.

I am pleased, and relieved that it was not sent to a publishing house at that time, because so much happened in the following eight months it made my head swim.

Also, events and thoughts previously deemed too personal have now been added, and in all, has now created a book containing 103k words.
It has also allowed me to correct some continuity, time-line and descriptive mistakes from the previous and shorter version of this book.

This book now includes totally unexpected revelations from less than twelve months prior to publication date, and that a very recent revelation could be hard for many readers to comprehend and at the same time, believe possible.
These revelations have proved to be so enlightening as to create a form of closure not only for myself, but also to a part of the book, I say 'part' because life still goes on, and who knows what lies ahead, and future events may turn everything within this book, on its head and therefore complete closure is a distance away.
A real, never ending story in fact.

You can never change the past through words or deeds, but by learning from them, you can help shape a clearer and better future not only for yourself, but for others close and far, as well.

And you can never allow yourself to stop learning. It will continue to enrich your life by creating an even better understanding of everything and everyone around you.

One can ask, should this book ever have been published?
There may well be gasps from those who recognise themselves; But yes, I am personally glad it is published whilst the memories are still vivid to me, and hopefully to others. It has been a long journey and I am so pleased to have met those who have changed my life for the better.

Note: *As English is a recognised universal language, I have used within this book, the currency and distance-measures as pertaining to, and as used in England, the United Kingdom, for consistency.*
As exchange rates fluctuate – check rates as per event year

~ March 17th 2023 – Alexander Milnz

Although this book is based on real people and real places,
all those names and places have been changed
to protect their anonymity.

BOOK ONE

The Girl On The Bus - part one

CHAPTER 1
FROM A VERY EARLY AGE

It was either 1980 or 1981, that, whilst decorating the lounge area of my house with my Father, I asked him,
"Why did my Mother show me so much aggression, when I was younger?"

Out of the blue, my Father threw me a curveball. Though it stunned me initially for about a minute after he started talking, everything began to fall into place, and my heart went out to him. For the next two hours, he opened up to me.

He started by telling me that after my Brother Patrick was born, my Mother wanted a girl to 'complete the family'.
When I was born, my Mother, though disappointed, showed me love and affection for about a year.

Then everything changed. I had begun to walk.

My Mother occasionally dressed me in girl's clothes whilst in the house. She also refused to let my hair be cut for a long time.
My Father also told me that she used to call me Alexandra when she thought no one else was in the room or house.
When he talked to the family Doctor about this, he was informed that,
'Sometimes having a baby of a different sex than what was longed for, can traumatise the woman. It will eventually lessen, and go away completely between eighteen and twenty-four months after birth.'

On finding some old photographs, it seems it took around three years with me, though my Father did say, I never went out of the front door with girl's clothes on.

Even before I started school at nearly five years of age, I clearly remember my Mother always sitting me in the chair at the kitchen table whenever she was cooking or baking. She would recite the same words,
"Look what I'm doing. You will need to do this when you get older."

When she was doing the washing, I had to help by catching the clothes and stacking them up after my Mother put them through the Mangle.
It was also around this time, I remember making my first (unbaked) 'Milk Loaves' (or something that resembled them from the photos of the Be-Ro book). I took them upstairs to my Mother. She *'loved them'*, as Mothers do.
This 'training' continued until I was almost five years of age, soon after I had started at infants/primary school.

Then everything changed again. I became the Devil's spawn.

I recall that my Mother would often get a neighbour to take me, along with her own daughter, to school. And then my Mother or Father would pick me up at 3pm.

Quite vividly, I remember that I was often shouted at for the least thing, and often 'nudged' out of the way, whilst in the house.
My Father even told me that when he came home early one afternoon, because he was sick. He said he noticed that I had very little food on my plate. He asked my Mother if that was right, and she replied that I *"did not eat much,"* but Patrick chipped in that *'Alex sometimes cries because he is still hungry."* My Mother never denied it, nor admitted it.
She just told Patrick to *"stop telling fibs"*.

Quite often I would hear my Father get up to go to work in the very early hours of the morning and I would go downstairs, where he would greet me, and then make me a milky cup of tea.
I must have got up late once, only to hear him close the front door.

Too late for my usual drink.

I must have panicked. I managed to open the front door.
I must have thought to myself *'I must catch him, I need my tea'*.
The bus was waiting at the starting stage for its journey to Hamilton city centre, two or three-minutes' walk past the other side of the croft. Facing the old 'Family Welfare' house
It was still dark. I remember as I did a short-cut over the croft, looking to see if he was still walking on the pavement around the outside. That there was a sudden sharp pain in my right foot.
It hurt so much, and I could not run, so I limped to where the bus that took my Father to work, was waiting.

I saw my Father, already sat down on the bus downstairs. I must have called out because I saw the Conductor inform my Father, who got off the bus, to talk to me.
He saw my foot, which by now was quite bloodied, and left red footprints on the pavement.

The concerned Conductor obviously said he would wait, so that my Father could carry me home and then return.
He took me into the house and must have called my Mother to come downstairs. My Father seeing I was safe, made his way back to the bus.

I had three holes in a triangular fashion in my right foot.
I think it was later that day, that my Mother looked for, and discovered, a piece of wood on the croft with three nails going right through it.
The Doctor came sometime the same day (I think), bandaged my foot, and gave me a needle in the arm, so no Hospital.

But, not long after, I did end up in Hospital, for corrective eye surgery.

I had a strabismus, commonly known as a turn or squint and from all accounts (and photo's) a very bad one.
They had to wait until I was at least six years of age before they would operate. I still have a slight detection of a turn and it does sometimes bother me, but I was fortunate enough, to have had concerned parents.

And whilst still in 1957 at the age of six, both my Mother and I travelled from our house to my Grandmothers (her Mother) in the east of Hamilton. A journey of about ninety minutes and two buses.

It was the return journey from the City centre to home that would forever stay in my mind and as clear now as if it was only yesterday

As we approached Billington just outside the city centre on Princeton Road. My Mother became very agitated.

She needed 'get off the bus'.

I think she told the conductor she was feeling sick and I remember he frantically rang the bell for the driver to stop the bus at the next stop, which was at a Vet's – *Veterinary Surgeon.*

It was dark and fine rain had started to fall as we got off the bus and started on our journey walking home. We walked and walked, buses passing us by but my Mother stubbornly carried on walking with me holding her hand, sometimes letting go and she would stop to tell me to hurry up.

Finally, near a public house called the Rose and Thorn about three miles from home and for whatever reason, we stopped at the bus stop and waited for the bus to arrive. When we did finally get home, I distinctly remember my mother telling me *'if anyone asks including Daddy, tell them that the bus had broken down'.*

[Some years later I worked out the distance my Mother and I walked – it was five miles and it must have taken about three hours]

In late spring 1958, my Grandfather, on my Mother's side, died of either cancer or tuberculosis.

My Mother took it bad, really bad for what seemed like an eternity.

[This may have been the catalyst that led to a later, more traumatic period for my Mother and the family].

It was also the very last time we ever went on holiday together.

[more on this in a later chapter]

As the years went by, the severity of the treatment given out by my Mother had eased.
And by the time I was eight, any ill-treatment had virtually stopped, and we became an everyday family, or so it felt like.

Another mishap, which **did** cause me to end up in Hospital, happened on Whit Sunday 1959, when I was eight.
I was wearing a moss coloured suit (short trousers of course), a white shirt and a tartan tie. Funny how you remember such detail.
Anyway, near home I threw a quarter-brick into the air.
It landed on my head. It hurt, but I was ok.

Ok that is, until my Mother opened the front door, saw me with a face covered in blood, dripping onto my shirt and suit, and screamed. Four stitches were needed, and they could not use a 'freezing agent' because of where the cut was (?). And that really did hurt.
But no lasting damage (physical or mental – though some may tend to disagree...ha-ha). And once healed, the good times continued.

Though I enjoyed my early education, including my one and only school play at Christmas in 1958, I have to say it wasn't always so good at school.

My 'arithmetic' in my early years was less than average.
And my teacher at the time would scold me constantly.
Using a ruler to strike me on the palm of either hand, when I could not recite the twelve-times table from mid-point.
Each time I went back to my desk, he would ask me what the answer was again. I couldn't, so I had to go to the front of the class and receive my punishment. After a continuous sixth time, I remember tears formed in my eyes. This at least, stopped the others in class from laughing.
When I got home I told my mother, and the next day she took me to see the Headmaster and informed him. My mother got an apology from the Teacher. And I was never hit like that again.

The following year or was it 1960, but at the tender age of nine, I had my first girlfriend, and my very first 'kiss'.

Her name was Sandra.
She lived on the top floor of the three-storey block of flats/apartments, next to my parents. And it was outside her front door that I gave her a (very quick/peck) kiss on the lips.
I then walked down the concrete stairs of the block, feeling very happy and yet, sort of embarrassed.

I was almost eleven, just before I started in the 'big school' (Seniors/High/Secondary), my Mother, a once serious amateur dancer, decided it was about time I learned to dance. Dance as in Ballroom and Latin.
She taught me the rudiments of many of the dances used in competition and social, except the Jive because, try as she might, I just could not get the co-ordination required. I remember this really frustrated her at the time.

Also, during this time, she also started to introduce me to some of the problem's women have to go through, often referred to as 'women's issues'. Rather it than repulse me or make me feel awkward, I found myself quite interested, which pleased my Mother no end.

[Had she finally got the girl she wanted?]

Later, from early 1961, I was often taken by bus by my Mother, to the 'Lamar Dance School' in North Hamilton.
A full sixty minutes plus and two buses away, to continue my dancing from professional instructors.

It was a very long day, especially after finishing school. Lessons started at 7pm prompt until 9 or 9.30 pm meaning we had to leave our house at 5.30pm and not arrive back home until 10.30 to 11pm.
When going by bus, and even though my Mother smoked,
she made sure we were always sat downstairs where smoking was, by then prohibited.
Little did my Mother realise that by the time I was fourteen, and still at school, I was already smoking,

[and continued smoking for the next forty-five plus years].

CHAPTER 2
MY FATHER DID NOT DESERVE THIS

Looking back, there were many occasions when my Father had every justification to walk out of the front door, and leave my Mother for good. But he didn't.

He told me that my Mother would *'scream the house down'* if he even so much as put his arm around her. And as for 'Sex' (my Father surprised me with his openness) that stopped after I was born and never 'happened' again.

[And I have no doubt right up to his death from Cancer, in 1991, that's a LONG time to be celibate and worse when it was not your choice].

My Mother persecuted him and made his life Hell for many years simply because I was a boy, and not the girl she wanted. But other reasons may have also come into play.

It was in Spring 1958 that my Grandfather died. My Mother did not take it well.
She became that distraught, her actions both mental and physical became irrational.
She was put on drugs to calm her, to sedate her. They worked, until they wore off. She then was put on drugs to 'make her happy', to give her a lift and drugs to calm her down. Commonly known as 'uppers' and 'downers', which were stimulants and depressants.

Many times over the next three or four years she would forget to take the prescribed drugs and World War Three always ensued.
But even when there was a lull we were all on tenterhooks.

Before the 'modern holiday' began, there were the 'traditional ones.
All the family in a caravan at the sea-side for a week, and it was in the late summer of 1958 that became the last time my family went on holiday together.

It was to be a holiday with a bad start and even worse ending – but happy memories in-between from what I can remember.

Whilst we were all waiting for the coach to pick us all up to go on holiday, my Mother had what was to be later called 'an episode'.
The 'episodes' seemed, in my mind as a seven-year old, to have started after my Grandfather (on my Mother's side) died earlier that year, just after the Munich air disaster)

My Mother suddenly started to become very verbal (aggressive talking) with my Father, stating that she had changed her mind and that she did not want to go.
This carried on even when the coach arrived, but eventually, my Mother calmed down and got on the bus.
The holiday carried on and we were a 'family'. But then after a week and on our way home on the coach, my Mother had another episode.

This time she was panicking and becoming very verbal once again. She wanted to get off the coach there and then. This time it was possibly claustrophobia or motion sickness (like she may have had that time on the bus a year earlier).
It was lucky, as in those days coach drivers often pulled into rest stops along the way and one was not too far away – much to the relief of other passengers who could obviously hear my Mother
.
I remember clearly my Mother and Father sitting away from the other passengers (who were obviously talking about the 'incident on the coach). By the time the coach left, my Mother had thankfully calmed down and the rest of the journey continued without any 'episodes'. My Family holidays finished that day.

[It wasn't until 1975 that those holidays resumed – with a new Family]

Then in 1963, her Brother, the youngest aged twenty-five, died tragically in Australia. That did it, she had a nervous breakdown.
The full effect of that lasted over two years, with the repercussions, even longer. A period like no other, and it also became a learning period for me.

8

From 1961 to late 1962 I missed a lot of schooling due to the fact I had to stay at home on many occasions, because my Mother begged (for her) not to be left alone.

This was never mentioned by my Mother when the school board downgraded me to a lower stream due to my absences. I was confused, shamed and made to feel guilty.

During this period, rather than my Mother being grateful, the opposite happened. Any little thing I did that she did not 'approve' of she would inform my Father when he got home from work.

And if she shouted at him for long enough, which was often the case, he relented and I ended up being 'punished'. And this I feared more than anything.

My Father would call me, and I knew what was going to happen.

He would go into the cabinet draw and bring out his army belt.

I tasted the salty tears that were already forming, before he even struck me across my buttocks and top of my legs, four-five-six times. Never hard, but enough to 'smart' for quite a while.

Then later, usually when I was in bed, he would come to me and say he was so sorry for what he did, but if he didn't *'your Mother would have made life a lot worse'*. It was of little consolation at the time, because he hurt me for no reason other than because my Mother told him to.

But, it was around this time (maybe a little later) that I was beginning to realise through talks with my Father that it was not my Mother's doing, and that the fault lay with her illness, the drugs and the treatment she had to go through. My learning and understanding period was still in effect, and there was more to come.

It was not long before my Mother's illness and irrational behaviour became that serious, that my Father had to take extended leave from work, to look after her full time. Before this he would phone in work many times to inform them (I don't know what he actually told them as to the reason) that he could not make work that day.

He did this for just over a year, until a specialist carer called Erin, was allotted to my Mothers case.

Prior to Erin coming, and whilst my Father was looking after my Mother full time, there was very little money coming into the house.

My Father had to use his 'Superannuation' (a form of works savings), and he also sold his car to make ends meet.

We also had the stigma of having our electricity meter changed to a one shilling slot meter (a 'Pay-As-You-Go' and only the 'very poor' had those), because we got behind with the quarterly debit payments.

At least this allowed us to have light for most of the day.

But still, to work within a budget, if the electricity went off at six or seven in the evening, it stayed off until the morning.

We learnt to be resourceful, and very frugal.

As any income was meagre, my Father could only budget for one bag of coal a week to heat the house, so both my Father and I resorted to 'logging'. My Brother had just started work after leaving school in 1964, so he was excused of extra duties by my Mother.

I had to accept what I saw as the unfairness of that.

My Father and I would take turns to go into the nearby woods during my Easter and summer school holidays and many times after school, to collect as much deadwood as we could find, stack it in a pile near the woods' edge, to be picked up later. This we did (my Father mostly) when it went dark. And when lit, it had to be mixed with coal to lessen the embers lighting up the sky at night from the Chimney and gaining the curiosity of people nearby.

The neighbours soon worked it out what had happened, but such was their understanding, bless them, we were never reported.

And so, as soon as Erin arrived, my Father was able to go back to work, and within a couple of weeks, we had light (and tv) night and day and a healthy supply of coal to heat the house. This was good news because it was September, and it was becoming colder. Any extra monies were still meagre though, as my Father had to repay debts to friends, from whom he had to borrow from.

And so, the 1960s wasn't all 'Sunshine and play', and we lived in the more 'modern' and, some say, prosperous Woodhouse Green area of south Hamilton.
Hamilton, by the time of my teens was one of the largest cities in the country and covered an area (with suburbs) of around sixty square miles with a population of over three quarters of a million. And a length of over twenty miles, North to South (where we lived).

[By the Millennium, the City and suburbs had grown to cover four-hundred square miles and with a population of nearly three million]

Because of her nervous breakdown and the treatment she received, my Mother had numerous violent and verbal 'episodes' during this period, and it is right to say that both my Father and I took the brunt of this.
To me, this violence could only be attributed to the medical treatment my Mother received. It was common practice at the time to use 'Electric Shock Treatment', a cruel treatment that was, thankfully, stopped a few years later.
My Brother was never abused as such, and I do mean, never.
A little later my Mother spent a month to six weeks 'convalescing' (we were told) at a nursing home near Clearwater on the coast.

[I found out later it was the Priory near Rosemount, a place that was to have a very different connection, some fifty years later],

This, we were told, was to 'review' her medical condition.
She became, in their eyes 'cured, but was still kept on the same medication (be it a lower dosage?) for several years afterwards.

It was just before going to 'Clearwater' that my Mother committed her last violent action against me. And one I cannot ever forget.
I was in the bedroom I shared with my brother when I heard my Mother starting to shout, almost scream, loudly whilst at the same time banging on the (upstairs) landing window.

She was annoyed at some boys playing football on the croft across the road. This they did many times, but this time, for whatever reason, it set my Mother off on an 'episode'.
Fearing she would smash the window and injure herself, I tried to pull her away, she screamed, *'get off my hand'*,
And as I did, she grabbed my hair and pulled me down, kneed me in the face, and then, pushed me down the full flight of stairs.

I was bloodied, but nothing was broken.
I just went outside into the back garden and sat down, both numb and emotionless.
It later, made me even more acutely aware that a person's mental illness is not always their fault. And this in turn allowed me to become more understanding. Strange isn't it, how things turn out.

For what seemed like many years, both during and after my Mother's illness, came a form of agoraphobia.
This restricted her road to recovery. The only way she would go anywhere was when my Father drove her, but also, even to the main shopping centre, the car had to be loaded with personal belongings. This left little room for any shopping.
She would really panic if she thought she had forgotten something and they had to return home to collect it.
It was pitiful to witness, to see and hear the relentless one-sided tirade that followed.

[This continued, even after my Father's accident (next paragraph) and into the 1970s and 80s].

Just after my Mother finished her 'treatment' and was on the road to recovery, my Father was struck down by a hit and run driver very early in the morning. He was crossing the well-lit Royalty Way (a local main thoroughfare) into Hamilton to get on a 'works bus', which was waiting for work-men.
His leg and hip injuries were so severe; they kept him off work for almost three years.

This man suffered so much in his lifetime, mentally and physically.

His upbringing, though he often told me was fair, was quite strict, and wasn't helped because of the area he was brought up in, the east of Hamilton city centre. A place where people lived, by today's standards, in poverty and squalor in 'two up-two down', 'back to back' houses.

I often visited that house of my Father's Mother when I was a youngster. You see life and surroundings very differently when a child, but even so, the 'smallness' and closed-in dark atmosphere of the house, was felt even then. But I didn't care.

In late1940, when he was eighteen, he volunteered to join the army, and then, in May 1943, into the newly formed Parachute Regiment. He saw the horrors of the war, both in Europe and South-East Asia. He was 'mentioned in dispatches' on three occasions, one of which stated that although injured from grenade shrapnel, he led two successful attacks on enemy machine-gun posts.

Had he been an officer and not a corporal, as he was at that time, those dispatches would have led to medals. Throughout his life, he never fully recovered from those injuries. He always said to me, that each time he jumped out, into the unknown, he saw some things he hoped to God he would never see again, but he did, time and time again.

In December 1947, a quickly arranged marriage to my Mother, being three months pregnant with my Brother, Patrick took place.
It was something he, nor my Mother, expected or possibly wanted.

My Father was still a reservist (for up to ten years or 35 years of age) after the war. As a NCO (non-commissioned officer) parachutist within the Parachute regiment, he was 'called up' as an Instructor. Even in peace time, whilst training other Parachutists, he watched the horrors come back again, when Parachutes did not open and the young men failed to use their reserve 'chute.

A few years later, came my Mothers illness, and the start of his unstinting devotion to her.

The wedding vows, 'In sickness and in health' meant just that to him, though I feel it was never truly reciprocated by my Mother..

The day before my Father left the hospital in plaster and using crutches, his sickness benefit stopped. You have to remember, you got no 'sickness benefit after six weeks in those days; you were basically 'on your own'.

His 'Superannuation' was already dried up from when he took time off to look after my Mother previously.

Then a minor miracle happened.

A week or so after he returned home, the car that hit my Father had been seen by a fellow worker at the time, when it slowed down.

He had taken a partial number-plate and what type of car it was.

The police were able to find the man who drove the car, and later prosecuted him for causing the accident and failing to stop.

When charged, the man's insurance company had to pay my Father compensation. It's so different today.

My Father was given two choices, either a lump sum or a monthly amount until he could return to work. My Father, against my Mothers wishes chose the latter.

Though a meagre amount at the time, that decision proved to be the most financially rewarding.

In early 1966 and whilst my Father was still recovering from his injuries, my teacher asked me if I was staying on at school as I showed tremendous promise in Technical drawing and the arts, and that I showed an extraordinary work ethos by joining 'night school'.

I had to tell him was that I would not be staying on. I did not tell him that I was 'told' in no uncertain terms by my Mother that I had to get a job instead, and *'bring some money into the house'*.

[I was so happy that both my parents were alive, my Father, especially, to witness my achievement, and my joy, when, much later in life, I attained the BSc with honours, and later my Masters, but sadly for my Father, not my PhD – but my Mother did]

My Brother was working as an apprentice, since leaving school a couple of years before. And although his wage was low, he was not asked or told to get a job that paid more.

You could not help finding a job in the 1960s; it was a 'boom time'. I went into Hamilton in the morning and came home with a job.
It was working at the main wholesale Fruit and Vegetable market. This meant me getting up very early in the mornings to catch the 3.30am bus to get to work for the 4.30-5 am starts.

The wage being £10 a week, of which my Mother took £8 for my keep.
I never missed a day, except when I was 'poorly' (*see next chapter*).
Shortly after, I was fortunate enough to land a second job, one that fitted in perfectly, with a one-hour break, with my morning one.

My Father, never once, gave or offered a reason as to why he stayed with my Mother, such was the humility of the man. And I never asked him either, even on that day when he was helping me decorate the lounge of my house, a few years later.

I felt then, as I still do now, though he was often brow-beaten through my Mothers actions and words, and his love for her was sorely tested, he never gave up hope.
Hope for her recovery, hope for a better life together. His devotion to her never seemed to falter. He could never leave her side. And to his last breath, he never did.

He wasn't a Martyr, he wasn't a man of faith, but he was a humble man who accepted the challenges life, and love, put before him.

CHAPTER 3
WORK, THE BUS RIDE, FIRST TIME, ISLA.

Whilst still at school in late 1965, I joined a couple of evening classes. One for cooking and the other for photography, both of which I had a strong interest in from an early age.
With the cooking, I was adding to one of my school period choices in place of Woodwork.

As I had not left school and therefore deemed 'underage' to join the 'evening classes', they initially rejected my application, but after talking to one of the subject teachers, they made an exception in my case due to the fact that my interest was high, they knew me (obviously), and class numbers were moderate.
Those classes in photography helped me secure my 'second job' after my 'enforced' leaving of school and a month after getting my first.
I say 'second' job, it would be more accurate to call it my second and a half.

In late 1966, whilst at my very first job working at the wholesale fruit and vegetable market, a friend who started to work at a club about ten miles south from where I lived, told me the club wanted a DJ for Saturday nights using their equipment and records. My friend knew me as being 'chatty' and knowledgeable about music and suggested I go for it. He would give me a lift there and back if I got the job and I could even take my own meagre collection.
I went for the audition, messed it up a little as I was both excited and nervous, but the management liked what they saw and heard, and offered me the position.

My (proper) second job was as the third and assistant photographer at Ace Studio, and this fitted in perfectly with my early finish job at the Market. And it even paid better. For 25 hours a week I was paid £12 and other than £2 as extra for my keep, I was allowed to keep the rest.
Woohoooo, I was rich!!

I never really stopped to realise that I was actually working something like sixty to sixty-five hours a week. And that was without my DJing, my dance lessons and competitions.
Yes, life was certainly looking good though I was getting little sleep, my body (and mind) were adjusting.

It was a Professional, well-known studio that worked with many of the models (male and female) from the local model agencies in Hamilton.
All the models (both male and female) were older than me (mid-twenties mostly), and were so 'with it' fashion-wise and very professional.
They modelled clothes, hair, makeup etc. in both studio and public surroundings, appearing in catalogues, journals, and newspapers.
I certainly don't remember any other type of 'modelling' taking place, though I did hear rumours of a couple of the female models doing work for another studio in the capitol.
A number of the girls became very well-known, not only locally but internationally as well.

Occasionally, as part of my job, I was to go on 'shoots' with them, mainly local, but I recall, at least three or four times, abroad, which was brilliant, but that meant I had to make up a 'fake' illness to the bosses at my other job – belated apologies to those guys.
I was even introduced, and later chatted to the American actress Cicely Tyson whilst I was taking a break on a 'shoot' in Baleford. Baleford is a popular Spa Town some sixty miles south of Hamilton. A really nice Lady who was genuinely interested and friendly, and not a put-on show for her personal photographer.

Whilst socialising with the models and female outfitters on one particular occasion, I joined in their conversation about 'women's issues' and talked about it knowledgeably (thanks to my Mother).
They were a more than a little 'embarrassed' at first, but then decided amongst themselves that I was probably 'effeminate', a polite term in those days for someone who was either homosexual

or on their way to being one. I never felt that I was 'effeminate'; I certainly had no interest of any kind, for boys.
Maybe it was because I was around women all the time. Remember, I was starting to live without restrictive 'taboos' from an early age. And I can only thank my Mother (again) for that.
My Mother was quite open, but I never found out the reason why for another ten years or more.
Besides, I really fancied two of the models. Who wouldn't?

They also loved the fact that I could *'dance proper'* (which seemed to fit in comfortably with their 'effeminate' tag), and I was asked more than a few times to give them some basic lessons.
In return, they would buy me a popular dance record they heard whilst on location or 'passed on' a bizarre article of clothing (which actually cost the male models nothing) and even the odd bottle of wine; I actually got quite used to 'that', (the wine) and the taste for it is still with me.
The occasional records came in handy as well, as it helped boost my meagre record collection, as I had already started to earn a little extra income from DJing in the autumn of 1966 and by late 1967 started working at a well-known (and later legendary) club in Hamilton.

It was quite possibly in early August 1968, and I also recalled it being a bright warm day, that I took a bus trip just short of Hamilton city centre, into Billington, and John and Marsha's record shop on the districts bustling, main road and shopping areas.
I made some purchases for both myself and 'Diggles', a youth club disco where I was a DJ, and later helped to run.

I am sure it was in the August, as 'Diggles' was to re-open on the first full Friday of August after its annual six-week summer recess. I had to purchase quite a large amount of new 'danceable' records for the re-opening.

I made my way back to Princeton Road and to the bus stop in front of the SAVD (Sick Animal Veterinary Dispensary), a well-known charitable organisation that we often called 'Saved'. By a

strange coincidence, this 'Vets' and this bus stop were the very ones that were mentioned back in 1957 in the first chapter.
The number 76 bus, which dropped me off almost outside my house, had its stop about ten minutes further away but like as not, if I started to walk to the stop, one would pass me by.
But, from here, at the SAVD, I had a choice of two buses, the 75 or the 77; either still meant I had a ten minutes' walk home after I got off anyway. But at least I wouldn't miss it.

Within a couple of minutes, the 75 arrived.
I jumped on and made my way upstairs and to the fourth or fifth set of seats on the left.

[For many years after, I had always assumed it was on the right-hand side. But recently I realised that even now if I travel by bus I always 'sight-see' and sit on the left, And it made sense regarding as to where I remembered putting the records].

I placed the records upright on the seat against the bus side panels, and as I was sitting down I noticed a dark-haired girl in the seat behind me.
I can't be sure as to who struck the first words of contact. It may have been me, as I was brought up to say *'excuse me'* when turning your back on a girl or woman, in this case whilst sitting.
To me, that was common courtesy, but I certainly remember the words this girl spoke,
   "Are you the DJ at Diggles?"

I turned around, and there she was, and she was talking to ME.

For many years after, all that I could remember of her physically was that she was a brunette with hair done in a style of the day, though not as short, and her beautiful eyes. Eyes are the first thing I notice about a person, and oh boy, I could not take my eyes off hers. Perfectly formed (to me anyway) bright and alert. It was as if I could 'see into them'.
What a strange description, but that is how I saw them.

And when she later stood up to get off the bus, I put her height at around five-foot four or five-foot five inches.
   The bus journey lasted maybe thirty, thirty-five minutes. But during that time, a constant non-stop chatter of random, tangent questions, answers, repartee, and retorts burst through from both of us.
It knocked me out. It was so 'different'. And yet so casual and weirdly, it was also a little scary. I just opened up.
It was all random chatter, but we seemed to 'know' what each of us was going to say, and we had an answer for it, like twins separated at birth.

Whilst this was going on, I looked behind her and to the other side of the bus, and people were smiling; our chatter seemed to make them smile. They may, of course, have been thinking, '*what the Hell are they on about*', or maybe they saw something neither of us saw.

When the girl got off the bus, I always assumed it was at a row of shops called The Minister Parade. I later found out it was the stop before the Parade, but I'm jumping ahead of myself here.
Anyway, trying to act cool and nonchalant as the bus moved away from the stop, I moved across to the other side of the bus to try and see her again. I didn't.
And we never even exchanged names.
But, oh well, it felt good whilst it lasted.

I think, at that time, it was about the longest I had ever spent talking to a girl and a total stranger at that. I'm not shy, I do talk to girls, but thirty minutes?
I just never had that much confidence before, how strange was that.
And no, I never went looking for her after that day.

[It is very true to say that as time, and years flowed by, people have quite often remarked on my quickness with the repartee and retorts. I have always answered them with the words, and strangely, I always seemed to have a lump in my throat as well, when saying them.
   "But there was one, who was better and quicker than me."

and I would go on to mention in a couple of sentences the non-stop bus ride chatter.
I must have done this so many, many times over the years.
But why, every single time did it create a lump in the throat?
So confusing. Why was it such an emotional thing?

And so, for many years, this girl was still there, still occupying a reserved space in my life. Was it the unexpected connection, the intense openness that remained with me all these years? Whatever the reason, I can truthfully say it is one standout experience I could, would never want to forget. A sort of 'forever memory' I guess].

The rest of autumn and into the winter of 1968 was uneventful, I had finished at the Club in Hamilton in the Spring, but by the time Winter came another opening for a DJ came along, and just around the corner from the club in Hamilton.

This was also the time I had my first 'full-on sexual encounter.

I was 'knowledgeable' of a girl's body from the age of fourteen, having gleaned the 'Adult' Magazines and a couple of 'fumbling experiences' with an older girl called Helen, in the wheat fields a few minutes' walk from my parents' house. But yes, until December 1968 at the grand old age of 18 and through circumstance, not choice, I had remained a 'virgin'.
It was a one-night stand at the annual Haletop Hospital Nurses Christmas Disco. I had arranged the disco for that year. The sexual experience was, you could say, an (almost) complete failure.
I had very little experience even really talking to girl's, except for that time on the bus, and as for being intimate, that was a totally foreign word to me.
It took me a couple of months to even mention it to my dance partner, Isla. And when I did, she just said that it was,
   "Nothing to be worried about, the more experience you have, the better it will get. My first serious boyfriend did the same when I was fifteen."

Believe me; those words were so comforting at the time.

Isla was so supportive of me.
We had more than the odd argument, but only ever, over our routines.

Later, when on the circuit, taboos were broken down when we would share a room to keep our expenses down. There were many occasions when we would bump into each other whilst changing or bathing and see each other either partially clothed or fully naked. And not an eyelid was blinked.
My parents would have flipped if they had ever found out. And I only met Isla's Mother once, when she travelled from the north
of the Country to witness our first Amateur finals, and she was fine with the arrangements.
Even though she was a lovely, fabulous girl, and one that yes, under other circumstances, I would have made a play for and possibly dated. But having a relationship could have caused too many issues.
Dancing came first, and so we happily endured a Brother-Sister type relationship.

By the end of 1968, the year was just about the same as the previous year, not that eventful. Well, as far as I, an 18-year-old boy, was concerned, it was. No more mysterious girls and certainly no more 'sexual encounters. Both were memorable though.
I didn't have much time to myself really, much like the last couple of years, since my Father's accident. I had two jobs, so I worked from 3 am (well, awoke) to 6 or 7pm, five and a half days a week, and the occasional, though, sometimes regular (five or six times at same place) DJ work.

As my parent's paid for my early dance lessons, even when money was tight. I took it as a sort of 'payback' and carried on doing the same for almost three years until my Father was fit to resume work in late Autumn 1969.
I had carried on with my dancing during this time, with late evening training. This sometimes made me so tired that I fell asleep on the bus going to work in the early hours of the next day. Luckily for me, that was the terminus in town. More than once, those extra minutes of sleep made all the difference.

Then there were the weekends, with the circuit and occasional dance competitions, and a lot of work juggling
So, by the end of the 1960s and the *'swinging sixties'*, everything was hectic, but 'cool'.
Music and love were the key to happiness for many.

Though dating full time, was for me, was a virtual non-starter, I did have the odd dates with girls, but that was it.
I did not really have the time to give them the attention they possibly deserved anyway.
As for music and dancing though – what a fantastic period to grow up in. It truly was for many, the swinging sixties.

And I, like thousands of others, were so fortunate to grow up and have their teens in this decade.
And take advantage of the truly awesome, forward-thinking education system we had then, south of Hamilton.
Many years later I found out just why we were so privileged.

New build areas south of Hamilton were deemed the gateways to the future and resources were funnelled into these areas, and in many cases to the detriment of other areas around Hamilton.
So yes, we were indeed fortunate back then. As it put me in good stead, after a ropey start, in achieving my later professional and academic qualifications.

CHAPTER 4
GILLIAN, PATRICIA, and MY BROTHER

With the two jobs and the DJing work, I managed to save a little each week. With my Father back at work, I was still doing the two jobs for another couple of months and so, was able to buy my first car, a five-year-old 1964 blue Mini 850 for £95 in the August.

In the July of 1969, I had also started dating a girl called Gillian who worked in the local sub-Post Office.
She was my first real girlfriend.
In a way, it was she who asked my Mother about me. My Mother liked her and thought we would be a *'good match'*. Mothers do that sort of thing don't they, but I gradually felt so as well. It took a while getting to that point, but an engagement? Nooooo, far too early.

After about four months, near to my birthday I think, I took her to meet Isla at one of our training sessions.
Isla was ecstatic that I had a steady girlfriend at last – welllll, longer than a couple of weeks. And it was her first chance to actually see her.

Gillian, though, was *'not so pleased'* after seeing me perform the Rumba with Isla. And she let me know as we were driving back to her house.
She thought we danced far too close to each other. I remember her words,
   "It was disgusting, it looked dirty".

I tried to explain that the Rumba is a passionate dance, and had to be danced like that.
She replied that her,
"Mum and Dad dance together, but never like that'. And *'if you want to keep seeing me, you will have to stop doing dances like that, especially with 'her'."*

Well, that sealed the end of what I hoped would have been a lasting, or at least, longer relationship less than a week later.
It upset me, yes, but not unduly. But what happened a few months later, really did upset me and made me feel very guilty.

At the end of October 1969, work disaster.

Just after I bought my first car, my early morning job was lost through another company's takeover. Then less than two months later, in February 1970, my job at Ace Studios was gone. They had too many staff, and in those days, it was a case of 'last in, first out'.
I was 'gutted' about losing the studio job. How can I put it – it was 'me'.

Suitable jobs started to become harder to find. But soon after, I managed to get a job as a 'progress chaser' at a local refrigeration and air conditioning company. And low and behold, the secretary was Sandra, my first 'girlfriend' and the first girl I ever kissed. She was expecting her second child. She left her position the following Friday
Five months later, the company decided to relocate to larger premises some five miles away.
This became very awkward as I had sold my car shortly before, to a friend, ironically because the company I worked for was so close to my home. As was the dance studio.

I bought a bicycle and cycled to the new premises for a few months. But the long hours were beginning to affect my dance training with Isla, though she also had distractions... a new boyfriend.
I left my job and started to DJ 'full time'.

In the Summer after Gillian and I finished, I was shocked, mortified when I heard that she had been killed, along with her Father, in a car accident, only a few months later in 1970.
Her Mother survived, though severely injured. My immediate thought was that if I had still been her boyfriend, still dating her, she in all probability would not have been in the car.

My Father consoled me greatly by saying that I should not carry that weight of guilt on my shoulders. And that it was fate for me not to have been in the car as well.
[I have since, visited her grave several times and laid flowers each time. The last time being in October 2020 for the belated 50th anniversary (belated due to my treatment and also the pandemic restrictions) and laid a special bouquet. As there were no other flowers to be seen, I could only assume that her Mother had also passed away at some point].

Because of my natural flair for being able to communicate with the party goers I became like a different person.
Full of confidence, even slightly extrovert. I have always put this down to the microphone. That's was my defence shield.
That and the fact that with my pro-active working attitude I had, by now, a larger and more varied record collection, I was getting more work.. and more money. Woohoo, I was laughing.
And it was in the late summer of 1970, and I was working, as a DJ, with well-known male model and DJ, Bobby Smooth, and his friend, and fellow DJ, The Raving Loon. Bobby also had a friend called Lynn Cohen whose Father owned a successful clothing factory in Hamilton. Lynn, in my opinion could have become a fashion model, blonde, tall and had long slim legs that seemingly went all the way to her armpits when she wore 'Hot Pants'. Lynn also had a look of Raquel Welch, and could have become Hamilton's very own. Both snappy and warm, I quite liked her (seriously, and who wouldn't have?).
It was also, at this time, that I met Patricia.

Patricia was the cashier/receptionist at a Jamaican club in Broadstairs, where Bobby, the Raving Loon and other DJ's often worked. She was two years older than me, and (as I soon found out) with more sexual knowledge and experience than me, which wasn't that hard as I only had a solitary experience, and that being a failure.
She taught me a heck of a lot about the joys of fore and after play as well as the beauty and enjoyment for both whilst actually making love.
We even spent a couple of nights together when her parents were visiting friends and staying over.

From what I told them of her, both my parents thought she might be *'a future Daughter-In-Law'* and wanted to meet her; and this time I had similar thoughts.
Was I in love with her? I'm not really sure.
But my Brother, with his wicked sense of humour, put an unfortunate and very nasty end to that vision or any future with Patricia.

I had told Patricia about Gillian, and her dislike of my dancing, and also about her death. She felt so sorry for me.
My Parent's already knew of course, as did my Brother as they had met Gillian two or three times.
Patricia and I chose February 14th, Valentine's Day 1971 as being the day for her to meet my parents, for the first time. We were both looking forward to it, as were my parents.

A short while after Patricia arrived; I had to get a bottle of Mateus Rose wine from a shop a few minutes' walk away, for Sunday lunch. My mother loved the bottle as she used to put candles in the neck (when empty of course).

Unknown to my parents, who were busy preparing the Sunday lunch for us all, Patrick, carried out his cold, heartless prank.
He told Patricia that it was a *'family secret that I had really got Gillian pregnant and refused to marry her, and because of that she killed herself and the unborn baby'*.

My parents rushed into the room when they heard Patricia sobbing. They couldn't control her, and didn't know the reason for her crying. Patricia ran out of the house, into her car, and drove away.
I came back with the wine, noticed her car was missing, asked my parent's, *"where was she?"*
My Mother was distraught. And Patrick just said,
   "It's not my fault she can't take a bloody joke."

For what seemed like an eternity, I tried to find out what happened. Then Patrick opened up. He told me what his *little joke* was.
My Mother was almost hysterical, and I was devastated.

My Father told Patrick to
"Get out of the house and stay out for the rest of the day".

About an hour later I tried phoning Patricia's house, but each time, the person on the other end put the phone down. I needed to drive to her house.
My Father advised me not to drive to Patricia's in the state I was in, but I did all the same. He then relented and gave me his car keys.
When I got to Patricia's, her Mum refused to let me even talk to her.
"My daughter does not want to see or speak to you ever again, and neither do I"

…. and with that, closed the door in my face.

I could not even remember driving home that day. And once again, my Father did his best to console me. I never spoke to my Brother for over twelve months after that.

Whilst only two young Ladies have been mentioned (and named), I have had maybe two or three other short-lived girlfriends by the time of my twenty-first birthday.
Though each were of short acquaintance, (a few weeks), no way could you say, or I, even claim, to be a Ladies-Man. I just wasn't that confidant, brash, pushy or whatever you wish to call my demeanour.
I often kept my guard up, just why I don't know. An inbuilt thing I guess. I did however; treat them with respect, as they always should be. I just wasn't that vain; to constantly need to parade a girl on my arm.
And again, work always seemed to come first.

      Later in 1971, as did my Brother two and a half years earlier, it was time to celebrate my twenty-first birthday.
When my Brother had his, it cost my parent's, well, my Father, a lot of money (in those days) to hire a room, entertainment and a full buffet.
I did not want them to go through that expense again, so I concocted a story about me working on the day of my proposed

birthday party (a Saturday, with my actual birthday being the day after).
I wasn't, obviously, and I guess my Father realised that too, but did not say anything.
So, on the night in question, I just got into my car (another Mini) and drove to the Airport, parked up, watched the planes take off and land, walked around the public part of the airport, had coffee, listened to music on the car radio and cassette player for nearly five hours.
I arrived back home just after midnight. My parent's both asleep.

For the life of me, I cannot remember getting any 'presents' the following day. I think I received two or three cards, one containing some money (how much I cannot recollect either) from my parent's.
I can honestly say, it did not bother me a great deal because I felt I had done 'the right thing' in not celebrating at someone else's expense. A guilt thing, Hell knows. What was done was done.

Then rather crazily, I decided to 'reverse' the birthday thing, and buy my parent's a present each, as a humble 'thank you' for putting up with me for the last twenty-one years.

I bought my Father a cream Baracuta G9 'Harrington' jacket, and my Mother, a brown and red three-quarter length coat from an upmarket fashion shop in Hamilton. I knew the coat she wanted, as she had mentioned it to my Father about six weeks before, but he could not afford to buy it. It left me little in my bank account, but to me it was worth it.
The colouring and pattern of the coat (like a honeycomb effect I think) reminded me of another time. I was sure I had seen something like it before. At the studio, in a film, was that girl on the bus wearing one like it? It really did seem familiar, maybe from a newspaper or catalogue? Or maybe it was just the case of it being popular around that period.
After I gave them their gifts, I don't think I ever saw my Mother wear her coat even though it was winter.

I learnt around two months later that she did, in fact return it to the shop from where I had bought it from. They must have

accepted it back without the receipt as it was one of their own exclusive brands and obviously, had never been worn. Once refunded she used the money for something else, just what I do not know.
Yes, of course I was annoyed, but it was her present, and her choice to do with it what she wanted. It still peed me off though.

As mentioned earlier, I really missed my job at the photographic studio, but occasionally over the next two or three years I saw and spent time chatting with the other photographers and some of the models when I saw them in the centre of Hamilton, either on a shoot or just socially walking around the centre.

[I even kept in regular contact with the main photographer, up until his death in 2021]

But time moved on at a rapid pace during this period, with both my DJing work and dancing (competitive and training) both keeping me very busy six sometimes seven nights a week.
Interestingly (or not) it was during this period I found that all I needed was four or sometimes five hours of sleep a night. At the week-ends even less, as I didn't get in from (DJ) work until 3 am, I was up, wide awake at 6 am. Totally mad I know, but it was due to my body clock of which I had no real control over.
When I did sleep, it must have been a quite deep one.

With having three jobs for a lengthy period of time, it seems my body slowly got used to the short hours of sleep. There weren't even any side-effects that you hear about, such as 'sleep deprivation'. I felt perfectly fine and alert for the rest of the day.

[Nothing has changed even up to the present day… up at around 5 am, even when on holiday. No lay-ins. Now, how really sad is that, ha-ha].

CHAPTER 5
LOVE, MARRIAGE, BABIES and DANCING

Time continued to march on, as they say. And whilst working as a DJ in a club (the Lamplight on Poland Street, in the centre of Hamilton) in November 1972, I met, and later, fell in love with my future Wife, Claire.

I said to my friend (and future Best Man) Peter Bromley whilst looking at Claire along with her friend, on the dance floor.
"That girl I'm gonna go out with ... better than that, that Girl I'm going to marry."

Peter just replied, *"Not a bloody chance of either"*

He ate his words, not only a couple of weeks later when we all rolled into The Bangladesh restaurant in Hamilton, and Claire sat beside me. But also, when I asked him to be my Best Man for my marriage to Claire in June 1973.

Originally, we both decided on a longish engagement of at least two years so that we may get to know each other better and also to save up not only for the wedding but also a deposit for our first home.
We were engaged in early March, to many people's surprise, including my parents, who had not even met Claire at that time.
I feel the reason for that, was the memory of Patricia and what had happened that day.
They, thankfully, all met the day after our engagement, at my parent's' house and (again) for Sunday lunch.
My Father was concerned and asked if Claire was pregnant.
I wasn't taken aback by his question and I believe he was relieved when I answered, *'No'*.

[I suspected much later, that my Father was thinking of how he started married life, with an enforced marriage to a pregnant bride]

But, as often happened in the 1960s and 70s, Claire 'got caught' in late April, and in Winter 1973, she gave birth to our Son, Graham-Anthony.

Graham-Anthony arrived during a snow blizzard that was almost horizontal, in the middle of December, and during a black-out which was due to the power workers strikes at the time.

Claire gave birth in a delivery room with only a single light bulb for the delivery staff to work with, no heating and to help create a sterile environment, the windows being wide open, all this whilst it was dark outside and a snow blizzard in full force.

After speaking to Claire, I went outside, intending to go home, get something to eat and phone the Family. I took one look at the car and the snow and though better of it..

The snow was over two-feet (60cm) deep, I could not risk driving the car out of the hospital car park, which was on a downward slope. And so, after telephoning Family members, I spent the next two days, mostly in the waiting room and seeing both Claire and my newly born Son.

My Father, I so cherished that man, managed to get to the hospital early on the second day. He parked his car at the bottom of the hill and walked the rest of the way with a large snow shovel.

Luckily, it had stopped snowing, but the snow in the car park was still up to the top of the wheel arch of the car.

He gave me some money to buy some food from the hospital canteen whilst he dug the car out. This took him a good two hours.

From day one, no Granddad could have loved his Grandson more, and that love remained to the day my Father died in 1991.

In early 1980, Claire had a devastating miscarriage. The Doctor trying to comfort Claire whilst in Hospital, said:
"You will be back here in twelve months with a baby."

What a prophecy.

And in the Spring of 1981, Zoe-Ann was born, and was heavier and longer than her Brother, the complete opposite to what they are now.

When Zoe-Ann was born and all through her early childhood, my Mother showed a veiled resentment toward her. Because I was the boy, whom she wanted to be a girl and whom then produced a girl as a second child after having a boy.
But, thankfully in later years, and until her death in 1998, she warmed to Zoe-Ann, possibly realising, finally, it was too long a time for jealousy to fester.

By the time of Zoe-Ann's birth, I had given up Ballroom and Latin dancing, not once, but twice.
Isla had married in 1971, and settled down in her native Scotland.
It was hard to find another partner, so I 'retired' from dancing in mid-1972.
This may not have been a bad thing because I doubt Claire would have been too pleased in the knowledge that her husband was sharing rooms with his dance partner AND walking around naked. Not many Girlfriends or Newlyweds would have tolerated that. And besides, both Isla and I lost many points due to my terrible Jive.

[A pattern repeated over forty years later when I went back to raw basics and found a new partner, Caitlin. Though, even that stopped after about a year, due to Caitlin having personal issues to resolve. Or was it me, being too eager on the dance floor?]

It also didn't help because Claire has an abhorrent dislike of Ballroom and Latin dancing, and, as I later found out, ANY form of structured (Choreographed) dance. She has always said (and still does),
"What's the point of dancing like that, there's no fun in it."

You can't really argue with an emotive statement like that.

I tried to get back dancing in the mid-1970s.
I found a new partner, Christine. But due mainly to a very personal past-dancing issue where someone (who later became a celebrity dance adjudicator), did not do their homework. And thus, created a very embarrassing and heated situation regarding nationality. My comeback was short lived.

Though quite some time later, the matter was resolved with an unreserved apology and reinstatement, the damage had been done.
Both my Mother and I stated we would never dance competitively or other, again in this Country. And we never did.
And so, after three years I finally did retire from dancing.
I had lost confidence with, and in, the system.
Even though as mentioned before, I got 'back to basics' some forty years later.

When two people live together, differences start to show.
In a number of ways and situations it was obvious that Claire and I were brought up differently, a case of opposites attract I suppose.
Nothing major, just little things. But there was indeed a North-South Hamilton divide, from education to lifestyles.
And rather than talk about the differences and find a mid-point for mutual understanding, I allowed myself to be slowly drawn, into Claire's 'World'.
For better or for worse. I didn't really have a problem with this. I was prepared to fully adapt.

And in doing so, little did I realise then, that I set in motion the self-inflicting erosion of my own identity and more so, my confidence.

CHAPTER 6
LITTLE TRIALS AND TRIBULATIONS

Through the ups and downs, as in most marriages, the strain of 'differences' started to fray the edges of a once (for the most part) happy marriage. I wasn't the 'perfect husband', and Claire wasn't the 'perfect Wife', (is there really such people in the world) but we worked on it, and yes, we tried the best we could. And, for the most part we succeeded. We had got used to each other's 'quirks' and together it became an 'ok' marriage'. We were happy with that.

There were 'trying moments' of course, such as the first meal Claire cooked, the day after we got married (we never did have a Honeymoon, or even an engagement party), a traditional Sunday roast with Chicken.
What follows I learnt a few days later;
Claire put the Chicken in the oven, prepped and started to cook the vegetables.
Later, when she checked on the Chicken, she realised she had not turned the oven on. She turned off all the vegetables and switched on the oven. Dinner would be running late.
She finished off the vegetables, cut up the Chicken, and placed it on the table.
Then, in real time;
We both ate, with me showing how appreciative I was of her cooking skills, but I did not see Claire serve herself any Chicken.
The following day and for the next fortnight I suffered from a severe care of food poisoning.
I had to stay off work for a whole two weeks.

A couple of days into my sickness, Claire did explain about the Chicken. It happens. No shouting from me. The joy and forgiveness of being newlyweds.
Then of course there was the infamous (but humorous) 'flying Scholl sandal' incident in 1978.
Which still creates wide eyes and laughter when told.

I was engrossed in reading a hardback book, 'Now Voyager' which became a classic and cult film, (and I still have the same book today), but Claire wanted help with some curtain hanging. I said,
"Ok, give me a few minutes."

But that few minutes went into thirty, Ooops.
Claire stormed into the front room of the house and furiously, snatched out of my hands, the book I was reading and proceeded to tear pages out of it. And then threw it aside, hitting the wall.
I just sat there and waited for her to finish her tantrum.

I then picked up the book, and calmly walked past the curtains she wanted hanging and into the kitchen. I got the sticky-tape out of the drawer and proceeded to calmly stick all the pages of the book back (about two or three, I recall).
After this, I calmly looked at the book, flicked through the pages and said,
"Now, where was I?"

Big, BIG mistake.

From the corner of my eye, I saw Claire take off one of her Scholl sandals and launch it at me.
I moved my head to the side as it flew past, missing my head by inches and then straight through the sitting room glass window.
Claire was mortified, and I just said,
"Oh, Great!"

The next day I purchased and replaced the window pane, and life carried on. You could now call the book, a true Glassic' (humour).

And there were 'moments' even before we were married.
    I collected Claire from work, the week before we got married. The girls from work did their usual customary 'job' of getting her dressed up and then taking her to pub after pub during an extended lunch break.
When I went to pick her up to take her to her house, it would have been about 2pm. I realised then that there would be nobody at home to 'look after her'.

She was in a very drunken state.
So I took her to my flat (they call them apartments now) in Hasden, carried her up a flight of stairs, which nearly killed me, got her into the flat, and put her onto the bed.

And NO !!.... I didn't.

I had **[and still have]** an unwritten code that says, *'you never take advantage of a woman who is drunk'* because, let's be honest, there can never be any real pleasure to be had, by either one.
My friends often laughed at this and thought I 'had a screw loose', but that's me and I'm proud to be 'me'.

So, I thought, *'get her in the shower, to try and sober her up'*.
So I undressed her, and managed after one heck of a struggle to get her into the shower, and upright.
I had to keep hold of her as I turned on the shower.
The water cascaded down onto her – and a fully clothed, me.

It was also the very first time I had seen Claire fully naked.
When we made love previously, it was always in the dark and under the bed-sheets. And not through choice either.
As soon as the cool water hit her, her eyes opened wide, and she started to shout, nay, she screamed:
   "You're drowning me, I don't want to die."

Yes, it was comical and I couldn't help but laugh.
But after a good five minute 'soak', she had sobered up enough to be able to walk.

She had 'survived'.

And after which, I think I created a salad for us both to eat, and then later when fully recovered (or close enough), drove her home.
   I have been blessed, honoured and privileged to be present at the birth of both my children. And I never want to forget it.
Witnessing, both the pain and the beauty of a new life being seen, and held for the first time is so emotional and breath-taking.

And I smile looking back at this:
When our Son was born and we took him home (to the cottage).
It suddenly dawned on both of us that we needed a washing machine.
Previously we hand-washed our clothes in the sink – no big issue, but now... with the new baby, a washing machine was a 'must have'.
This was before disposable nappies were everywhere, and the order- of-the-day was, Terry Towelling Nappies.

As our credit score was zero, due to having no debt and only recently bought the cottage and furniture with cash **(see next chapter)**, and crucially never having HP (Hire Purchase agreement) before.
We had to scrape together some money for the washing machine and pretty damn quickly. Luckily both our parents came to the rescue and between them and what spare cash we had, within four weeks a brand-new washing machine delivered.

But before the luxury of a washing machine, I became the 'washer'.
The nappies had to be de-soiled and soaked, then washed, by hand. This was a duty of mine, as Claire would literally throw up (be sick) as soon as she even looked at, never mind smelt a soiled nappy.
I quickly learnt to breathe only through my mouth (and not my nose), and I never allowed the sight to bother me during the de-soiling or the washing.

[And what I learnt, I still practice today and it has come in handy at least twice, once our own and the other time, a neighbours, toilet became totally blocked and needed a 'hands on' or should I say a 'hands in' job of clearing the U bend.. a total yuk!].

When the washing machine arrived, we had to use the kitchen sink tap to load the washer with water for the first couple of weeks until I plumbed in a cold feed and waste. Yes, I know... it should have been done earlier. My excuse being, that it was all new to me.

It was all part of the learning curve many couples go through, not only with their children (should they desire them) but also through their time together.
There were also annoying times, but we get over them, we had to. But one has always stuck, vividly in my mind.
It happened in late 1989, a time period covered in a later chapter.

Claire was visiting a wool craft fayre along with her Sister, about ten miles from home, and to the north-east of Hamilton.
Her sister told me on their return that Claire had seen a cardigan, which she thought and exclaimed that it was *'absolutely beautiful'*, and it fitted her perfectly when she tried it on.
It was a little expensive and though she had the money on her, she thought it was 'not really worth it' and it became one of those reluctant 'sigh' moments for her, according to her Sister.
Now this was the same craft fayre that Claire and I, along with Zoe-Ann in a push-chair, visited five or six years earlier and when I, in a daft 'daddy' moment purchased a furry 'ET' hand/arm puppet.

[a puppet which in later years, created so much fun and amazement at some of the venues I came to work at whilst DJing, for a few years after. And a puppet that I still have to this day].

Unfortunately, Zoe-Ann took a instant dislike to the hand puppet when I returned from the craft stall with it on my arm. No way was she going to tolerate it. It had been paid for, I liked it and so her gift became mine.

I naturally asked Claire about the visit, and asked about the cardigan that her Sister had told me about and also why didn't she buy it.
Claire extoled the virtues of the cardigan, the colour, the fit, the style, everything. But she didn't think it worth the price the Lady seller was asking.
Was this a subtle hint to me? I suspected it may have been. And that she really did want it.

And so, unbeknown to her, I took an extended lunch break from work the very next day and drove some twenty-miles to the Craft Fayre and back to purchase the cardigan. Hell, it wasn't cheap either, but I managed to haggle a slightly lower price, with both the seller and myself happy with the result.

I presented the cardigan to her a couple of days before Christmas, but her response stunned me.
"What have you bought this for? I don't like it, take it back"

I replied, confused
"But you said you liked it very much",

Claire looking angrily at me gave the strangest answer.
"Yes I did, but I wouldn't have bought it".

A woman's logic?
A woman will give many reasons for this and every single one of those reasons only makes the man even more confused, bewildered.
And very annoyingly, my twenty-first and the present of a coat which I gave to my Mother instantly came to mind – déjà vu?
No one is immune to life's trials and tribulations, and we all have many of those, throughout our lives. And that being the case, all we can honestly do, in a rather forlorn hope of learning from our experiences, is to just 'get on with it' and with any luck remember some of them, hopefully though rare with a warm and knowledgeable smile.

When you are married or have a long-term partnership there is an extra element to consider, and that is quite literally, the other person. We all have quirks, and different ways at looking at something.
We are no longer single and our egos have to be eased back to accommodate that other person. Because with that someone, we hope will make our lives complete.
But even *that* is a gamble, if truth be told if that partner is not into the fair sharing of compromise.

I digress yet again. Time to get back onto the correct 'time-line'…

CHAPTER 7
THE COTTAGE, BALLOONS, and THINGS

A couple of months after we were married, I heard about a late 18th century (1794) cottage on offer in Hawksmere, about three miles north of Shodden.
I took one look at it from outside, and extraordinary, strange feelings came over me in an instant.
Feelings of contentment, security, warmth and a haven from the outside world. All wrapped together, a wonderful, calming feeling. It was indeed a magical, almost spiritual feeling.

Once inside, it was evident it had not been in use for a number of years, and needed a lot of TLC.
It also needed some essential work doing, such as a bathroom and WC. But the asking price?
It was an absolute bargain and within a month I had used my savings and with a very small loan from my Father for furniture, bought the Cottage, and set about the renovations.
The cottage was one of four in a small courtyard with a lovely little brook only twenty metres away. And a view to die for, overlooking acres of moorland.

Claire was not impressed, though.
She doesn't do '*change*' well, and she was a '*townie*'.
Many-a-day I would come home from work to find a note saying *'At mothers, pick me up'* or somewhere else. It was a twenty-plus mile round trip each time before I got back home to something to eat.

I was offered the cottage next-door by the same person I purchased my cottage from. The asking price was very reasonable, but I had to pass because it became evident after our Son's birth, Claire wanted to move back to *'where she knew'*.
Though it made a good profit, I was so sad to leave that cottage, and the feeling it gave me, which never faded.
There was just '*something*' about it that place. I cannot truly put it into words.

[Many years later (around 2013), I drove down to the now gated courtyard to see the old place. So much had changed. The stream had been culverted due to new houses being built. And the moorland was filled with flimsy boxes called houses almost to the cottage doorstep - ridiculous. The cottage was slowly becoming 'cocooned' and had sadly lost that strong '*spiritua*l' warm, inviting feeling. And I doubted that feeling I first had, would ever come back again.
I went back again in 2022 and I was totally shocked, I could not believe what I saw. It would take too long to describe, but I know for certain it would not have been allowed to happen if I still lived there. It was heartbreaking to see]

And so, in October 1974, we bought a house about three miles north of Hamilton City centre. Twelve miles from the Woodhouse Green suburb where I grew up, and only a few minutes' walk from Claire's mother house. And Claire was happy once more.

In Spring 1975, I decided that my late 1968 Canadian export Ermine White model Ford Cortina Mark 2 needed a spruce up, to *' brighten things up'* a little bit.
All the paintwork was prepped up and then out came the Dulux paint (only the best) and the car went from Ermine White to ...'Foxglove'.
It certainly was an 'eye-catching, jaw dropper' where I lived and received many a double glance wherever I drove it.
Most people said *'A PINK car?* Morons!! it's FOXGLOVE.

My first holiday, with my new family came about in 1975.
It felt good, especially for me as it had been seventeen years since I took a holiday of any description.
Though it was for only a week, it certainly was a most memorable holiday as it was the first time I had ever donned a pair of roller skates at the age of twenty-four, and I learnt to skate that day without falling over once. And I felt really pleased with myself.

For our anniversary in 1976, I decided to use some 'novelty' balloons for our party. Mixed in with small clusters of other balloons, I added... condoms.
Wow, they took some 'blowing up'.

But when they very slowly went down during the party, you could hear the screams of laughter from both the men and women, except for my Mother-in-law, but I did see a 'sneaky' smile appear across her face a couple of times.

A year later (1977) and our last full year in that house, Claire went out to the city centre to do some shopping and window gazing. She came back about six hours later to find the internal hallway wall knocked down, the stairwell blocked off on one side, and where the built-in wall unit was, a gaping 'hole' that now acted as a walkway between the front to the back rooms.

After a week, with the plastering all done and a smoked glass vestibule built, it looked really good, modern and created a lot of interest with the neighbours, as the Ladies kept nudging their husbands and later, three couples in the road where we lived, altered their hallways in the same fashion.
It was pure logic really, as it created a warmer house and added extra space to the front room.

Though I say it myself, ours was the best looking, as the others made the vestibule wall blank. Ours, with its 2m by 1.5m smoked glass made it feel less enclosed.

OK, I was biased. Shoot me.

CHAPTER 8
AN 'INNOCENT' INDISCRETION?

In August 1977, I was working in a club (Luigi's) in the centre of Hamilton, and Susie reappeared.
I had previously dated Susie a couple of times whilst working in the Lamplight Club back in early 1972, a few months before Claire came on the scene.
Susie was only about five feet tall, with very wavy short blonde hair. And with her dark small round glasses on, she was almost the double of Bonnie Bramlett, an American Rock and Blues singer (whom I interviewed along with her husband, Delaney, and Bekka, their daughter for a local radio station in 1971).

I humorously gave her the nickname '*Mighty Mouse*' due to her stature, and the fact she never appeared to keep still.

Susie appeared very drunk that night. Her friends said that she told them she '*knew me and could I take her home after I finished work?*' because they were going on to a party after the club, and Susie was too drunk to make it.
I agreed, and why not? She was in need, and I knew her – simples.

They gave me the location and number of her house, which by good fortune was on the way to my home.
Susie got herself into the car, and as we were driving to her house, she started quickly to sober up, which I thought was a bit odd, but maybe she didn't want to stagger in the house, if anyone was waiting, and create a scene. Quite natural I thought.

She asked me to stop just short of her house, which I did.
And then she started talking about her husband and how he was in prison for drug dealing, and her little boy, who apparently was at home with a babysitter.
She recalled the good times we had together whilst I was at the Lamplight and how she would love those times back.

This rambling talk went on for maybe ten or fifteen minutes. I did not try to stop her, because she was remembering a good time, and maybe I should have, but…
She held both my hands, stroking them, kissing them.
I should have realised by then what was happening and backed away, let her out, and drove home, but again I didn't.
I kissed her, and she kissed me back. We hugged each other (as best you could in the front seats of a car). She then gave me a love bite (a hickey or whatever you wish to call them). It felt good at the time, but then, at the same time, it was so wrong.
After this, she just said,
    "*Thanks for the good times.*" and got out of the car.

[Other than seeing her in passing less than a handful of times over the years, I never saw, nor spoke to her again].

Getting ready for bed, and as I washed I noticed the love bite.
OMG! How can I explain this?
I was panicking; the coldness of fear hit me.
I tried to cover it with some (foundation) make-up of Claire's.

But the next day Claire spotted it. The expletives from her mouth were, shall we say ... extensive and very colourful.
She also hit me many, many times, with her fist and open hand.
And though I pleaded to stop, I knew I deserved it.
Stupidly, I said it
"*Wasn't a love bite,*" and that I had "*banged the side of my neck whilst at work the previous night*".

Like honestly, how stupid and unconvincing did that sound?

Claire was in tears and said she was leaving me, stormed out of the house and went around to her Mother's for consoling. I was frantic, my heart was racing.
I couldn't tell her that other than being given the love bite, nothing sexual happened, which it didn't.
But the fact that I had the mark on my neck was all that that what was needed for Claire's imagination to run amok.

She must have been 'gasping for breath' at the shock of discovering it. There was nothing I could do. I was 'caught red-handed' as they say.

One of her Sisters who was visiting from Canada and staying at her Mothers, consoled her, as did her other Sister, **[which was a little ironic, as we found out only a short time later that she was having an affair with another man, both Sisters being married]**.
I was fraught with guilt, and I was scared, petrified of losing Clair.

I pleaded with her to forgive me, and I suspect her elder Sister (from Canada) may have also asked her to reconsider about leaving me.
It seems the intervention from her Sister, thankfully worked.

Over the following days, and Claire having returned home, a very dark cloud and suspense-ridden atmosphere lingered and continued for a very long time after. It was dreadful.
I was walking on eggshells all the time.
I was occasionally hit, often at the most unexpected time, but thankfully, always in the house, and I just had to accept it.

I knew then, that I could have retaliated verbally and quite easily. Bringing up the number of times she went out with friends, then coming back home, drunk, alone, and banging on the door at two, three and even once, gone 4 am, because she was incapable of putting the house key into the keyhole.
If I allowed myself to think in such a way, I could have easily accused her of having the opportunity to have any number
of indiscretions, assuming that she hadn't done so already. But I didn't.
After about three months, a form of neutrality and 'normality' returned to the house.
But Claire would always have the memory of her 'unfaithful husband'.
I could never tell her that nothing sexual happened, **[even to this day]**. There would be no point. I had to accept my fate, so to speak, and learn from it, because it doesn't matter what sort

of slant you tried to put on it… I had allowed myself to slip, and badly.

[Susie died some twenty-five or so years later of a heroin overdose. I did not find out until a year after her death.
I felt more than a twinge of sadness. I also felt guilty and yet had no reason to. I liked the girl quite a lot. She was always on the move, couldn't keep still. And yet so positive on the moment. Was she doing drugs at the time? There is that possibility.
Her husband was in prison for them, maybe that's the connection between them. In later life and the continual use of even maybe stronger types and higher doses led to her demise. I simply don't know? It is often a natural human trait to think and wonder, *'if only'*.
I don't even have to close my eyes, even now, to still see her.
So sad, really sad, a total waste of a lovely, warm spirit.]

A tangent:
It was also in August 1977 that I followed my Fathers 'footsteps' (sort of) and became a (civilian) parachutist. When I was twelve or thirteen my Father took me on the Parachute ride at a local fairground. He told me that the speed we descended with each circular rotation of the ride was the speed that you actually landed in a real-life situation. You either took to it or you didn't, there was no middle ground.
It gave me a hell of a 'tingle'.

[And so, it started off as a single jump for a children's charity and over the years that single jump extended itself to over one hundred and eighty (according to the log at the association).
To me, it was an easy way to raise money/funds for that single charity and believe me, I had butterflies with every single jump. Be very wary of anyone saying they have never had them.

With my 50th jump, some twelve years later my Father (unknown to me) arranged a small gathering of eight long time comrades from his old battalion at a local public house in Woodhouse Green.

There, I was presented with a beret, and the colour of that beret was the same as the Parachute Regiment.
Though not gained within service of the regiment, they believed I had deserved the honour because of my many charitable jumps. My Father also presented me with his very own cap badge. A very humbling moment in my life. And a very special bonding moment with my Father.

      During our time together, both before and after I married, he gave me guidance on many aspects on how to conduct my life, with honesty, integrity and humility and also with diplomacy – though I still struggle with that latter part on occasions. He also taught me not only how to defend myself, but also how to suppress those intent on physical aggression.
Both proved useful later, when I worked for the Governments Homeland Security department.
      During the 1980s I would accompany my Father to many of the annual reunions of the battalion, but with each passing year, the number of the survivors dwindled to the point that at the last one I attended with my Father in 1990 there were less than twenty in attendance, with the rest of the gathering being made up with (like me) direct family members.
With the entitlement of being his son, I wore the beret, along with his cap badge for his 'final' reunion, when I represented him in December 1991, three months after his passing].

Apologies again (but you were warned in the book's foreword).
Now getting back to the books time-line with Chapter 9

CHAPTER 9
THE 'HAPPY BALLOON' STARTS TO DEFLATE

In 1978, a larger house came up for auction, not far from where we were living. Only a five-minute walk in fact.
It had potential, lots of it. Not for expansion (there was very little for that), but what you could do inside. And the inside was indeed a mess.
It required new windows throughout, a complete electrical rewire and plumbing, floorboards replacing, new bathroom and kitchen. Plus of course, completely redecorating.

Because of finances, there would be only me doing all the work. But I had a vision of what it would look like. I took a gamble.
And so, in the November I placed my 'fixed bid'.

A bid of just £1.00 Sterling over the auction starting price.

I just had this gut feeling.
It paid off. At the end of November, the house was ours.
So whilst we were still living in our existing house, I started work on the latest acquisition.

And so it began. Within an hour of finishing my usual daytime work, I started working on the new house, ending each night at around 11pm or just after midnight. And with many hours at the weekends throughout December to and including March the following year.
The only sections I brought help in, were, the window frames and the electricity distribution box.
But by the end of March, four months after starting, we were moving into our fully decorated and 'up to standard' house.
And here we have been ever since.

The back 'garden' area, which was an eyesore and kept getting flooded when it rained, saw a complete transformation over a short time. The whole of the floor area was covered entirely with rough brick face, then gradually, giant Yuccas, Bamboo, and a

Pergola, with hand-carved seating areas and, yes, the obligatory four-burner flatbed Barbeque. Let's say, the whole of the rear of the house was unique for the area we lived in [**and is still is**], enjoyed by family and neighbours alike when they visit.

There is nothing like a Barby on Boxing Day when it's minus -0c and even minus-14c once, I am not jesting, it's a wacky tradition that has lasted many years.
Close neighbours brought over their Christmas left over's in the morning. I would put them in a couple of different marinades, and after two or three hours, they were ready for the afternoon Barby, no matter the weather.
If the weather was terrible, 'they' stayed in the house whilst occasionally peering through the patio windows to see how I was doing. But it was good fun and a great socialiser of an event.

Besides my day work, I was also enjoying a reasonable income from DJing. Private functions as well as night clubs and it was at one such night club residency, just outside Shodden, where I was the 'party animal' DJ on the ground floor (a three-floor disco – basement, ground and first floor with a restaurant on the top floor) for three years.
During my time there I was 'headhunted' in 1983 by one of the owners of an up and coming venue on Ibiza.
The money offered was better than excellent and a two season (sixteen month) contract. I turned it down. I was still in a happy marriage with two young children, and I wanted it to remain that way. Going away for eight months at a time may have been catastrophic for the marriage.

[By 1987, word was out that Ibiza was THE place to go for 18-30 years olds and really took off after 1990]

But with the extra income I was already getting, it paid for house improvements.

[Over the next thirty-five years or so, the kitchen had a 'complete' makeover six times in design, build and install including services and appliances.
It was hard work, long hours, tried my patience more than

once and you learnt new skills, but the finished product is how 'you' wanted it.
And of course, you can save a lot of money by doing it yourself, but, be prepared for a partner who expects, nay demands they want it all finished by the time they get up in the morning, and no mess.
It doesn't matter if it was their suggestion in the first place.
I'm lucky and thankful, to have had enough confidence left to do it, but again, I'm jumping the years a little.]

When we were first married, and for the next ten years or so, Claire and I had regular, if not expressive or animated, sex in the bedroom, it was always a 'no-no' anywhere else in the house.
Just why that was, I have never understood.
Claire would not even discuss it. In fact our conversations, even the general ones, were getting sparser as time went on, and sometimes became quite snappy.

Claire always enjoyed a social drink, sometime a little too much, but never any real issues. Then after a few years she started to drink more and more and once that happened, it often was a case of 'look out, this is gonna get messy' along with verbal abuse and sometimes aggressiveness. I was getting brow-beaten and I was actually accepting it, because there was little I could do. My confidence was being shot away.

By the early 1990s, our joint sex life was almost totally lost in the mists of time, no matter how, or with what I tried to please her during the day; a 'turned back' was often what greeted me when getting into bed.
I started to realise that the relationship, our marriage, was truly on the wane. But maybe still salvageable.
Just to hold your life-partner, feel their love, is so precious

   The catalyst for the deflated 'Happy Balloon' came in the early summer of 1994 when Claire was 'pushed' down some front doorsteps whilst at a party she was attending.
She went to hospital 'plastered' (drunk) and came home the same way, but 'in' plaster.
Her ankle being broken and pinned together.

Even after twelve weeks when the ankle was healed and the plaster came off, she still complained it hurt, and especially when I became (even a little) amorous.

I had no reason to disbelieve her, but after a year I realised she did not want to have any form of love making, not even any foreplay or any shows of passion anymore.

Bloody Hell, a loveless, passionless, sexless marriage after twenty-one years, for crying out loud, that's no time at all.

I did not go looking for '*outside comforts*. I just resigned to the 'for better or worse' part of the marriage vows.

From that period onward, Claire started to change, becoming more irritable, demanding, and argumentative to the point of being irrational. She was forty-five, and her hormone change was kicking in. And like a willow in the breeze, I leaned with her as best I could.

But I was slowly crumbling away, dying.

Until you actually experience it, it's more than hard being a partner, a husband during this period in a woman's life.

She started to drink even more, and excessively at times, and that of course did not help the situation one little bit.

From this point, and for the next ten years, it just got worse.

It was almost like she was revelling in the disharmony she was creating. It was destroying me, and there was nothing I could really do.

On more than one occasion she had me in tears, and I mean really sobbing. My confidence was shot. I had nothing left to give, to offer. Nothing satisfied her.

I kept trying to bounce back, but I was getting weary. My feeling of self-worth was fading as fast as my confidence. The bouncing back too was fading fast, too fast.

Other than working during the day, my only two 'escapes' from the reality from all this disharmony were my DJ work, and my dancing.

I still loved dancing, and creating dance routines.

But she even became 'annoyed' even with that small pleasure.

I was ridiculed every time I tried to do any dance practice in the house. And I don't mean playful ribbing.
Hateful, bitter remarks like
　"You look fucking stupid" followed by sneering laughter.

I couldn't afford to hire a room to solo practice on an ad-hoc basis, so I had to practice at home.
And to even prevent that, she would rearrange the house furniture so that it restricted my workspace even more.
She would also complained that she could not hear the tv whilst watching in another room. A no-win situation.

And so, I had to switch off the music that I was using to practice to, and had to wait until she went out to friends where she always seemed to have a few drinks, or went to bed.
It was not uncommon for me to turn the music on low and practice at 6 am in the morning.
It wasn't just the dancing that became 'issues'; it became anything I was doing that she didn't 'approve' of.
Even an everyday conversation became a 'warring, verbally offensive act' if Claire was 'not interested' or didn't 'grasp any points'. She often retorted that,
　"You should not have married me if you thought I was not good enough for you."

and also,
　"Why didn't you marry any of your 'posh' friends, then I would have had a happy life."

This type of unwarranted verbal recrimination also happened on odd occasions at a party, especially if she had a few drinks.
It was a ridiculous situation for me, for anyone in fact, to find themselves in. It was soul-destroying. I had to pick up the pieces (quite literally on one occasion) and apologise to people when this happened. She wanted to out drink everyone there and ender up staggering across the room and falling onto a quite expensive nest of small occasional tables.

Claire would get up the following day and conveniently not remember anything.

I was gradually being 'muted'. I was being strangled, suffocated, and stripped of confidence, yet I didn't move out for two reasons:
1, I was scared of the 'unknown'; the confidence within myself was almost zero.
2. Even though the mortgage was fully paid up, I thought, why should I have to go looking for somewhere else, having the burden of those bills and still be stuck with bills etc, for the house I was living in at the moment.
Even if separated, I would still legally bound to 'keep a roof' over my Wife's head. Until such time as a divorce took place (after three years of separation) and the assets are negotiated and split.

I became numb, blanked it out, and accepted my position, and I stayed in the marital home. Literally 'for better or for worse'
So, in effect, I became so much like my Father, and in more ways than one.
And that frightened me. It was a vile depressing time, and one that injured me, deep inside and kept hidden away from the prying eyes of others, even my Son and Daughter.

CHAPTER 10
A VERY DARK DECADE

Watching a family member slowly fade away with an illness, before your very eyes, especially when it is Cancer is not good, it's not good at all.
You realise you are in a hopeless situation, one that you can do nothing to remedy. And when it's your Father, someone who you admired for so many reasons. It can numb you on the inside for a long time. And so it did with me in 1991.

Three years earlier, in 1988, I took my Father to hospital for an appointment to see a specialist. I was totally unaware at the time he was suffering from lung cancer.
I sat for maybe a couple of hours in the hospital waiting room as he did not want me to come in with him when he saw the Doctor. When we left, no words were spoken, until we neared his home.

He looked at me and said slowly to me that he *'had Lung Cancer and that they are going to operate soon'*.

I asked him if Mum knew he had Cancer, and he simply answered, *'yes'*.

I left him at the house, knowing that he will need to speak to Mum alone.

A few weeks later, just before his operation, and whilst at my parent's' house. I asked him
   "Is an ambulance coming on the day or do you want me to take you".

My Mother jumped in, somewhat angrily,
   "What does he need an ambulance for?"

   "For the hospital... the operation for his cancer" I replied, rather puzzled.

   "Who told you he had Cancer?" retorted my Mother.

"Dad did, when I brought him home last time" I replied, even more puzzled.

"You had no right to know about his cancer" she shouted at me.

It was becoming obvious that my Mother could not, would not, accept that her husband had Cancer, and that the prognosis did not look good for the future.
All those years she persecuted him, and now the reality that he may die and leave her on her own, was hitting her, very hard.

My Father came through the operation, and for two years led as normal a life as possible, but he knew, and he confided in me, that it wasn't to last and he felt he did not have long to live.
The last six months of his life was both heartbreaking and yet, inspiring to witness. His fighting spirit and jokey ways were still there, though his body was slowly disappearing before our very eyes. He passed away in September 1991, aged sixty-nine. Less than a month from his seventieth birthday. No age at all.

In late 1991 after my Father's funeral I went on only my second 'solo' holiday since being married.
It ended up being a not-so-happy experience.
I was involved in a RTA (Road Traffic Accident).
One which caused the car I was driving in, and whilst waiting at the traffic lights, to be shunted from the rear, across a four-way (crossroad), road junction, being hit by two other cars and with only the roof, front seats and part of the front of the car I was driving, remaining intact.

Though I had a number of abrasions, I had no broken bones. I did however; end up with my mouth being in too close a contact with the steering wheel, losing nine teeth and a three, part fractured jaw which needed extensive surgery but, other than that, I was still very much alive. Too close a call, somebody or something wants to keep me alive it seems. ha-ha
Later, seeing what was left of the car, even the police and emergency crews said they could not believe someone walked (not quite – stretchered to be precise) away from it.

I spent the rest of the holiday, plus an extra week in hospital, in a head and neck brace. And for almost two years after that, minor corrective surgery was still required at a hospital close to me.

On my return it was evident that my Mother was still in shock and disbelief regarding my Father's death. She was becoming very bitter and I truly believe she did not like what she was becoming, but she became a fatalist.

As a family, for the next three years we continued to go on holiday together. Sometimes twice a year. But our last was soon to be around the corner.
Our last family holiday together (with our Daughter, but minus our Son) came about a couple of years later in 1994
Earlier that year, on Valentine's Day, and in the company
of Claire's Sister and her husband, I produced two air tickets
for her and Zoe-Ann to go to Australia. They had been twice before. And I, once.

She was beaming, elated, for two minutes, until I said,
 "Let's make it a 'Family' holiday," and produced my air ticket.

Her face dropped in a micro-second, and she made it verbally 'very' clear that she didn't want me to even go with her; it was embarrassing.
Anyway, we did go, and even though she complained for a lot of
the time. I feel that she was grudgingly pleased I did go, as her ankle was still hurting (she never had the pins taken out as I suggested many times) I was there to help her get about when she couldn't put pressure on the foot.

Since that time, we 'decided' to always take separate holidays.
And with Claire, that started the following year with her going to her friends in Malaga and Barcelona, and me going to see the French members of my Family in Lyon and Le Thor.

By 1996, my Mothers outlook on life hadn't changed since the passing of my Father. And as if that wasn't enough heartbreak, she was to receive a final, unrecoverable blow just five years from then.

Her firstborn Son, my Brother Patrick was found to have an incurable growth in his brain.

The surgeons would not operate on him as the mortality rate was, in their opinion greater than ninety-five percent, and even if they were successful they feared that Patrick would be in a vegetative state for the short time he remained alive.

It was at this time that his, quite noticeably domineering, live-in girlfriend decided that they should get married.

She (later) stated that it was Patrick's idea, as he *'wanted her to become beneficiary'* to the lovely house he had bought.

In his innocent eyes and mind, keeping a roof over her head.

I only found out about the marriage in early 1997, when I drove down to Patrick's house and saw all the wedding cards on display.

I was stunned, and very angry deep inside to say the very least.

Not with Patrick, but with his scheming new bride.

Obviously, none of my Brothers family were informed and only members of the Bride's family were in attendance. And the actual wedding was presided over by a Priest, who happened to be a close friend of the Bride's family'.

Although in shock of seeing the wedding cards, I knew instinctively something was not 'right'. I pretended not to notice them and calmly asked the new Bride where Patrick was.

She just replied that;

"Patrick is still in bed, he is too exhausted to come down and see you"

Even so, I went upstairs to his bedroom and had a short talk with him, I congratulated him on his marriage and his reply shocked me more than a little. His words were.

"I enjoyed your wedding, was it last year? look after her, I may be joining you soon"

This is the mind and the words of a man who is supposed to have said his vows of marriage only a couple of days before.

What happened to a declaration of being 'of sound mind?'

Something was wrong, very wrong.

I went downstairs, to find one of Patrick's friends? who had arrived and made himself at home whilst I was upstairs.
The 'new Bride', my Sister–in-law, was making him a cup of tea.
I wasn't even offered one when I first walked in.
The new arrival then started talking to the 'new bride' about where and when 'they' were going for groceries.
I looked outside and didn't see another car on the roadway or the driveway. They were obviously going to use Patrick's car to go shopping.
Soon after, and as they were seemingly waiting for me to go, I left.
.
Later, I recalled that previously, because Patrick was incapable
of driving, I took him in my car on occasions to some of his old haunts, and also be able to see some of his friends at the place where he worked for such a long time
And also not forgetting of course, the place where he spent a lot of time doing charity work for children.

But, as time progressed, and too quickly, he became more confused as to his whereabouts and too soon, became virtually bed ridden.
But he still arose from his bed and recited his vows for the wedding.
Yes, something is so wrong.

Patrick died two weeks later on January 13th 1997, aged forty-eight.

My Mothers heart was broken, her fellow Gemini, her first-born had joined his Father.
But if anything worse could happen... it did.
My Mother along with my Father, knew by her actions and words from the moment they were both introduced to her, Patricks (Bride to be) was nothing more than a 'gold-digger' with a very fake American-Irish accent.
Two days before Patrick's funeral it was made known to my Mother that there was to be no Limousine made available for the Mother of the deceased. The only one will be for the Wife and the Wife's mother.

I had to make a number of phone calls to find a Limo', which I did. But the insult was not to finish there
It was already known that I was to read a eulogy. Only about twenty sentences.
As we entered the Church I reminded the Priest who told me that 'There are to be no speakers at the service'.
I was dumbstruck
Believe me when I tell you there were at least seven hundred mourners both inside and outside the church.
And his wife wanted a 'short 'mass?

And yet the final insult, to my Mother, was to come.
Patricks Wife would not give his Ashes to my Mother for over six months. And when she finally did, she sent a note:
'Seeing that they mean so much to you, you can have your precious Sons ashes' (note: 'your sons' not Patricks).

From this, she never recovered and the following year in May 1998, she joined them both.

She died of pleurisy and quite possibly Lung Cancer as well, aged seventy years.
I feel that losing her Father, her youngest Brother, her husband and now her firstborn took more of a toll on her mental health from which she was already, shall we say unstable.
And with that you can add she died of a totally broken heart.

With the passing of my Father in 1991, then six years later on, my only sibling, and then the following year, in 1998 my Mother joining them both, I was in effect, 'on my own'.
It had such a profound effect on me, and one, that I seriously thought I would not see in the new Millennium. (due to my smoking?).
It also affected my dancing. I was not able to create any new dances or even perform. And for almost twenty-four months I became a shell, going through the motions of staying alive.
I wasn't depressive, it just played on my mind.

CHAPTER 11
THE MILLENNIUM YEARS

Millennium, what Millennium? I was in bed for 23.00 with my earplugs in.

In the May of the new Millennium, I finally awoke. I started to push myself. I fought with myself to become more positive, and also decided to stop smoking.

First, I tried those 'fake' cigarettes, didn't work. Then I went for the nicotine patches, again these didn't work and proved to be quite costly. So I tried to cut down using will-power. By the start of the following year 2001, I was still smoking about fifteen a day – which was down from the twenty to thirty a day, which was a pretty good reduction, but I wanted to stop totally.

Then in the March I decided to go the Doctors as I had heard about a new tablet called Zyban.

I told him what I had tried and failed. He then prescribed a two-week course of Zyban. That was the maximum and he could only offer it the once as it was full strength and there were side effects.

Within four days in March 2001 I had completely stopped smoking.

I continued with the fourteen-day course to be absolutely sure.

It was also the tenth anniversary year of my Father's death from cancer.

[I still get the odd 'sniff' but after twenty years I have no intention or desire of starting again. Besides, it's far too expensive now anyway].

Though I had taken short solo holidays over the past few years, mostly going to France they were only once a year and for no longer than ten days. These holidays were more than just that. Claire was still finding disapproval with almost everything I do. And especially dancing.

2008 was going to be my 'breakout' year. I am going back out there. Working holidays, connected with my dancing, performing 'workshops' and classes, and the occasional adjudicating.

For the next ten years these 'holidays' were to take me to several countries around the world, mainly to Europe, the Far East and Australia.
Whereas Claire's holidays were always to Spain or Gibraltar, and always with friends.

Quite different. And as different as we were becoming.

Also, whereas Claire's breaks were a couple of weeks two or three times a year with friends, mine tended to last six or seven weeks each time, except Europe, which lasted from a few days to around ten.

At the start, I used to ask Claire to join me for a couple of weeks in either the Far East or Australia, but she refused point-blank.
It was quite apparent that she did not gel with non-English White speaking people. She didn't trust them? but I can categorically say she is not a racist.
I felt it was more of a lack of confidence in getting to know other people and their culture, it can be daunting most times. And though quite different to my outlook, I accepted her feelings on such.

When Claire went away, she just 'went', sometimes with only a week's notice. And was invariably, quite happy on her return. And with no qualms from me.
But when I went away, the aggravation started up to six weeks before I even packed.

Claire would become extra argumentative. Being very snappy and always demanded that a room in the house 'needed redecorating' before I went. This particularly annoyed me as sometimes it was less than a week before I flew. But I got on with it for the sake of 'peace' in the household... and my life.
Even though she was working and earning a decent income, I ensured all the bills were paid upfront and gave her money for essentials before I left. This was never reciprocated.

Though I thought unfair at the time, I just accepted it.

And when I returned, there was never a 'welcome' as such.
I had been away, on a five to seven week working holiday, a holiday that I regularly telephoned home every two or three days, but all I was ever welcomed with, were the robotic statements
of *'everything ok, then'* and maybe a *'do you want a cup of tea'* that was it.
A bland non-emotional 'welcome home'. A bit of a 'downer' you may say.

Whilst away, I always washed/cleaned my clothes in the launderette or used the Hotels cleaning service and so had very little to put in the washing machine on my return, but even that was sometimes met with disdain. I just got on with it.
Derisory and sarcastic comments, almost bitterness, about my holiday always followed for the next two or three weeks.

I say *holiday,* but they were working ones for a lot of the time, something Claire and many others have not been involved in on their holidays.
You get free time, but you have to work around it and be mindful of your schedule, a schedule where you have to present
yourself as Professional and certainly, socially approachable.
It was/is of little sacrifice because you get to see, to breathe, to be a small part of the community and history of that country.
And of course, it also helped pay for the airfares and sometimes a little extra which was always good with the bank balance.

As for the general bitterness shown to me on my return, I later put that down to jealousy. Claire was quite possibly envious of my independence, the fact I could look after myself quite well on my own.
For example, any mention of where I had been, what jobs I did, who I saw, where I visited all I got was,
   *'I'm not interested where you go to or what you and your many photos of your so-called dance friends and what you get up to.
I don't know them, I have never met them and I don't want to'.*

So much for trying to create a conversation, any conversation.
And yet, when Claire came back off her holiday, it was quite different. The opposite in fact.

I listened to her stories and looked at her photo's, if she wanted to tell or show me, which she invariably did. And I did so out of genuine interest.

And yet, it transpired each time, she rarely had a 'good time' wherever she went, as the conversation was interjected phrases like '*that was horrible*' or' *it was boring*'.

Claire found the cultural background of any country and place of interest she has visited as boring, she simply was just not interested.

And yet, as they went to the same places two or three times a year, there must have been some attraction. The mind wonders.

So, you may ask, '*why did she go there in the first place?*'

A good and fair question… and one that I cannot answer.

One would could think '*was it because I was not there with her?*'

Or was I her 'comfort blanket', that she felt 'safe' with, whilst I was with her?

The reason I say this is because during the 1980s and the start of the 90s prior to separate holidays, we went to the South Coast most years, sometimes twice, and she thoroughly enjoyed being there as much as I did, going to different places, talking with total strangers. Every-time we came back home, she was happy. And yet a few years later… such a change. Maybe it was indeed the cultural change?

[Looking back, I could not help comparing back to how my Mother treated my Father then, when the reality of him dying struck home, she basically 'fell to pieces'. He was her 'comfort blanket' i.e., I wasn't with her on *her* holiday, but I was her safety net, and also her punch bag].

Hell, I'm not a psychologist, especially where a woman is concerned, and so I just accepted it without argument.

Though it did make me unhappy, and a further feeling of non-worth of not being wanted either individually or as part of the family when the solo holidays started.

I learnt to accept a reality that what Claire now preferred was a more permanent arrangement, and not just for the holidays whenever the mood (regularly) took her,

.

CHAPTER 12
THE PHOENIX and WILL-O'-THE-WISP

PLEASE NOTE: It is from this Chapter and up to an including Chapter 37 that this part of the book (Book One) has to be read in conjunction with Book Two *'My Seven Year Itch with Cancer'*
I will only use edited and *Italic* **block printed** segments with asterisks, if they coincide with time-line events that are in Book Two.

**In mid-July 2013 I self-diagnosed Prostate cancer.
I had no symptoms at all. I just had this terrible, numbing gut feeling, which was later confirmed only after tests
August 2013: The Cancer treatment started and continued until February 2014.
February end, stomach cancer/lesions are found.
** August 2014, I noticed a large lump in my left breast.
I was not in a good place. I truly thought I may not see the year out**

Whilst the cancer was of primary concern, I was doing my best to focus my mind on other things by using Facebook and joined some of the Groups who posted on there.
One such group was *'Growing Up In Woodhouse Green'*.

At the start of December 2014, I saw the name Sophia Lawrence appear on the Group page, and whilst the name was completely unknown to me, and there was nothing within her few comments whilst answering other members, that would suggest I may know her. For some inexplicable reason, my thoughts, straight away and with no hesitation, went back to the girl on the bus.

It had to be the same girl.

Nothing could stray me from that thought.
I will swear on any, and every 'Holy book that there was nothing in her chat, in her actions, her recent(?) photo that would remotely suggest she could be, nay, **is** the same girl.

[But how? I racked my brains, and so many times since, and I cannot come up with a single explanation as to what made me *know* it was the same girl. Her profile photo was a grainy black and white modern day one with her (?) eating an apple? (or something), nothing I could relate to at all.]

The only way to find out for certain was to ask her some questions. Questions that only THAT girl, that woman would know, hopefully, the answers to.
It was weirdly strange, but something inside me told me that she would indeed have the correct answers, even though it had been over forty odd years ago.

So, with my confidence level suddenly on the up, I posed a couple of questions to her. If I remember, she took time in answering them. Was she being cautious? I suspected so.
But as the answers did unfold, this particular Sophia appeared to get the number 75 bus from town and get off the stop ***before*** Minister Parade. And she was indeed Brunette.
Although she could not recall me at all, this HAD to be the same girl, there was absolutely no doubt in my mind.
What are the odds of meeting like that? and forty-six years later.
And seriously, what a time in my life for this to happen.

Having found some old school friends previously on Facebook that I hadn't seen or heard from in a long time, and also a Lady from 1970, Lynn Cohen whom I mentioned briefly in Chapter 4. And now to cap it all, there is this Sophia, whom I met and talked to only once, forty-six years ago and 'found' again on Facebook in quite the strangest of circumstances, uncanny, almost spooky.
It's like someone was constantly pressing the 'restart' button.

I digress, I know... but what a time to think about rekindling old friendships. Seriously?
The 'reunion' with Sophia was to be short-lived anyway. As towards the middle of February, she was nowhere to be found, certainly not on Facebook (or so it seemed).

In February 2015, my male breast cancer had not transpired, a false alarm, but it did raise questions over missed procedures during my previous treatment. I was still under observation for my Prostate and Stomach cancers

Then suddenly, on April 10th 2015, I saw Sophia commenting on another group that I had joined in early February 2015.
It seemed she had been a member of this group since Winter, late 2014.
She made mention in passing later, that she lost her passwords to the other groups. Strange? I never used a 'password', unless she meant she had changed her 'email'. No matter.
And Sophia had even remembered our conversation in the previous group. She also remembered my 'nickname', which I haven't used in this group at all, wow.

We replied almost automatically, to each other's comments. And the 'bouncing off each other' like when we were back on the bus, started up almost immediately. It was incredible.

By late April 2015, I felt like that school kid again. I was excited, and yet so perfectly relaxed when talking to her on-line.
And what a coincidence that I found whilst making a comment on one of the Facebook groups about a certain road near where I lived, that Sophia made a comment that her husband had lived close by, before they got married. And then she mentioned the street.

OMG... that was less than a ten-minute walk from the house Claire and I are living in still. The one we moved into a couple of years after we too were married. That would mean we were even closer to each other than when we were kids and then teens.

And that rather strange confidence, that had recently started to build itself inside of me, made me also want to pursue this new friendship even more. Who would have thought.
I say 'strange' because I could not find the origin of where or how it started, but the bursts of confidence, it was a bit like a *'Gift'* given. Could this girl, this Sophia, be connected to it somehow,

but how could she be? There was certainly nothing tangible there I could see.

I started to privately message Sophia on Facebook, though we were still not FB friends at the time, with general chat.
And, as the days went on, I got the very distinct impression Sophia not only enjoyed our chats online, but it seemed as if she was actually looking forward to having them. And I will not tell a lie, so was I.
This new confidence seems to make itself more known when talking to Sophia; it was so unusual. I cannot put my finger on it.
I found that I was becoming more open, more relaxed, as if I was talking to someone I had known for a very long time. Sounds a little silly considering just how and when we first met half a lifetime ago, but it was a strong 'connecting' feeling all the same.
So strange.

Our conversations were fun, and from the very start, the same gelling together of tangent questions, answers, repartee, and retorts came to the fore, as it did all those years ago.
It was if those years in-between did not exist.
The quick-fire answers to make you think, came fast and furious, it was a game we were both enjoying.
But it suddenly ended abruptly in the middle of June 2015.
Once again, for no reason, Sophia disappeared and yet again no one knew (or were not saying) where she had gone.

As well as missing the banter, I found I was missing 'her' as a person. This was crazy. I don't even know her.
But from that day in March, I can honestly say there has been not a single day I had not thought about her.
I'm a romantic by nature, yes, but this was quite 'different'. I suspect it was because she made such an impression on me all those years ago when we first met. That must be it.
In mid-summer 2015, late July I think it was, I read a post on the chat group I had joined in February, about a chap, Eric Lawrence, who had recently passed away.
I thought at the time, that's a coincidence, same family name as Sophia's, a relation, even a Brother perhaps.
A day or so later, Sophia commented on the post. It *was* her.

So that was the reason Sophia had disappeared, Eric had been her husband. I felt truly saddened, so sorry for Sophia, but why?
Like before, I didn't know the woman, she was a stranger. I'm getting light heartedly annoyed because I cannot figure out the bloody answer. Why is she bugging me like this?

Time moved on, I spent some time in France with the French side of my Family, and Sophia was still nowhere to be seen, heard of, or even mentioned by name by anyone. And no longer in the group I joined in the February.
As time went on, my concern for her welfare and her whereabouts were becoming more fluid.
Yes, life had to carry on, but she was still there, in the back of my mind, I was still concerned enough to keep her 'activated'. A strange phrase I know, but it seems appropriate.

Then, at either the end of November or the very start of December 2015, everything changed yet again
I cannot recall if I saw a comment from her, appeared on a Facebook Group, or whether she contacted me directly.

But everything seemed to happen so fast.
I found myself feeling so elated that she had 'come back' that everything became a confusion of events.
I so missed this person, this woman, but Heaven knows why.
I don't know her.
I have no connection with her, other than a bloody thirty-minute bus ride some forty-odd years before.
I certainly do not hold any affection for her, other than being a friend of sorts, so what the bloody hell is it.
Oh God, I hope I don't find out she is a relation of some sort, a cousin or a secret Sister, ha-ha.
I have to smile at the total improbability of that ever being the case.

This is so oh, mentally 'school boyish' and I'm actually loving every minute of it.

CHAPTER 13
KITTEN AND THE TRUTH DRUG

For whatever reason, she had removed herself from the group we first met up again on, the '*Growing Up In Woodhouse Green*' group.
She wanted to re-join but needed someone to 'second' her. A friend who was already a member of the Group.
Strange? But I said I could do it, though I told her I would have to become her 'friend' on Facebook to do so. She seemed to welcome that reply, and within 48 hours, at the start of December, we became … Facebook friends.

I recall in mid-December 2015, whilst we were chatting, Sophia playfully 'growled' at me, the usual '*Grrrr*'. I clearly remember 'correcting' her directly after…
   "*Now, Now, Kitten.*"

..and *that* was the first time I used, and with what was to become, my affectionate 'nickname' for her. And one she became very fond of.

From December 2015 to August 2016, and even through our separate holidays in Los Angeles and Asia, we kept in contact, sometimes chatting for three or four hours non-stop.
During that time, we found so many different subjects to talk about. It was quite refreshing, as well as enlightening.
Cautiously, we were both finding out more about each other each day.
She told me of her late husband, and how he suffered and eventually died from Cancer.
She also told me how, for ten years previously he suffered from severe depression, became neurotic, and later from psychosis. He thought everyone was talking about him, even on the tv news.
It was an awful time, and it made her life a living nightmare.
There was the one time he was so psychotic, she had to have him sectioned for three months. I wonder if that was The Priory?
The Priory being where my Mother went, and both my brother and I were told she was 'convalescing' fifty years ago.

I wondered at the time, just how much of all this affected Sophia mentally, and if she had taken prescribed, or other, 'medication' herself to cope with the pressure. They can become addictive, extremely so in far too many cases. Déjà vu (with my Mother) had entered my mind – and what my Father must have gone through. Bless you, Sophia.

I also felt it prudent at this time not to mention my Cancer, even though I was put into remission with the Prostate in March, as she may have, quite possibly, thought at the time…;
'Oh yeah, is he trying to soften me up, bring out some sort of mothering instinct, make a connection'?

Nonetheless, it did help me during our conversations, to become more aware of her feelings towards her husband. And to also have more than just a casual idea as to what he and she may have been going through with the depression, and later, the cancer, due to my own and my Mothers experiences. Her continued love for him appeared very real.

Heaven knows why because I certainly didn't, but I felt I needed to keep talking to this woman as if it was imperative that I do so.;
(A) *"Lawrence's Kid … MIA."* (MIA=Missing In Action)
(S) *"Having rough time Alex. Lying low X."*
(A) *"ahhh... emotionally?"*
(S) *"Yep!"*
(A) *"It comes on.. and thumps you right in the chest, head full of mixed emotions and memories."*
(S) *"I'll be ok. Just can't stop crying at moment. Thanks for caring though. Going now. X."*
(A) *"As long as you are 'ok'... if not, I will keep pestering you. But on a serious note... even if you just want to shout... xxxx xxx xxxx (landline number) ta-ta Kitten."*
(S) *"Thanks Alex. Just feeling sorry for myself. It will pass. Thanks for your message. X."*
(A) *"Nope... you ain't feeling sorry for yourself. You feel vulnerable in yourself. You still get feelings of turmoil, they just come on for the slightest reason, or even no reason at all. You Tigers can bottle it away, then when alone all the emotion comes out. Is it right, is it wrong to act in this way... both yes and no.*

Yes, it will pass... make no mistake, the feelings will not go away entirely and in a lot of ways you don't want them to... you feel secure in the knowledge the aura is still there. You now have to do a juggling act - but it will get a lot easier. And you will become more relaxed, more controlled, more trusting."
(S) *"Thanks Alex. I hope so X. PS on 4th Merlot!"*
(A) *"FULL glasses I hope.... But always remember... You can't look after others if you cannot look after yourself."*

And another time....
(S) *"Morning my 2016 Lucky Charm! Lot better this morning thanks Alex'. Onwards not upwards 'eh. What about you? Having a good morning?"*
(A) *"Hiya Kitten... except for sliding down a muddy hill at 6 am. fine. The dog loves giving me 'extra treats' when taking me for walkies...so we both dived into the shower... Ladies first of ourse. Ha-ha."*
[I then put up a youtube video link of a dance partner]
(A) *"The joy to watch Leila dance. I have been helping her cope and get through her cancer treatment. Lovely lady."*
(S) *"Ah, I wondered what your connection was."*
[Sophia then put up a photo of herself and Eric]
(A) *"Always think of Eric in that way."*
(S) *"Thanks Alex, but at the moment it just makes me feel more alone. Sorry I'm a drag at the moment X."*
(A) *"This is where your inner strength and you do have a lot of that - you're a Tiger for Christ sake - will be needed'. Friends can be supportive, but it's you alone who will make the difference between going on the downward slope of self-pity and morbidness or slapping yourself a few times (sometimes more than a few) and face your bright and beautiful future with all the reality and enthusiasm you can and will muster'. Your constant memory of Eric will not fade away overnight, it will take a long time. So spend that time not dwelling on things lost but the gains you will make."*
(S) *"Thanks Alex. You're a star! I needed that Xxxx."*

I have absolutely no intention of forming any sort of relationship, other than trying to help her in some small way.

And that is all I was wanting to do. Was it my nature, or was it her? It was as if I needed, I was compelled, to help her.
And in the May, I mentioned this to Kitten.
We were just talking and I openly mentioned to her, that at the time I felt that there was, must have been, a special reason why this connection needed to continue.
I was looking for the word, but Kitten said it first – ***Kismet'**.

Also, at this time I had no idea of any Family connections she may have had, other than her Niece, Jenny and a friend called Angela, that is.

The openness within our conversations continued. As funny as it sounded, it felt as if she had injected me with some sort of 'truth drug'. I felt a strange confidence growing within myself and this allowed me to talk openly to her, without any inner 'fear'.
With Sophia, I found I couldn't or didn't want to lie or even 'fib' (half-truth) to her; she asked me a question, I just gave her the answer. Many times, diplomacy 'went out of the window' for the sake of truth.
Was I choosing to 'let my guard down' completely? Becoming vulnerable with her? It was almost like the feeling I had when on that bus journey. I have to say I am confused by it all. It is a little scary – but strangely, not in any bad way. And all this wasn't like me at all. But why the hell am I so relaxed about it.

She asked about my Wife and Family, and I just told her the truth, how it had become entirely 'loveless' and just basically going through the motions (or lack of) since 1994. There was no ulterior motive in telling her this. Wow, just what IS that truth drug… ha-ha
She didn't ask for any detail's, and I didn't provide any.
I did tell her however, that divorce was out of the question because there were no real grounds. I told her I could leave, but that would throw up some major financial issues.

During these 'truth sessions,' I noticed that Sophia quite often avoided my questions of her. In this, she was quite 'skilful'.

It was as if she wasn't sure enough about me for her to trust me, or she did not want me to get to know too much (?) about her life, her background. She was private, and it seemed very much so.

Some topics were never discussed; simply because they were irrelevant. Issues such as our financial situations, our social life or even what jobs we were doing, we just never asked.
We certainly never talked about 'meeting up', even for a coffee, and there was absolutely nothing in our conversations that could be construed as anything remotely 'romantic'.

And all the time, during this period, as our friendship appeared to be thriving, she still insisted she could not recall our first meeting at all. Maybe she did, but didn't want me to know that. Such are the ways of a woman, which are always confusing to men, ask any man and they would openly testify to it. But all the same, there was something surreal in how we just seemed to 'get along' with each other.

CHAPTER 14
COINCIDENCES OR KISMET, NO SECRETS

It was during one of our long conversations and short group chats online, that an incredulous revelation came to the fore.

I found out that other than a possible twelve-month break (1973 to 1974) from 1974 through to June 2016 (a total of forty-three years), we lived within four miles of each other.

I had learnt previously in the April, that at one point, we were separated by LESS than HALF A MILE, an eight-minute walk.

The number of times I must have walked or driven within twenty yards or less, (driven past the street of Eric's parent's house) whilst visiting my Wife's Niece, who lived in the next street to theirs.

It was astounding. Even to this day, I still cannot take that in. Because, even when we first met in 1968, we lived less than one and a half miles from each other. And that was about eleven miles from where Sophia and I lived four or five years later in the early 1970s, with thousands of houses in between.

Good Lord, she may have even seen the Foxglove (*not Pink*) coloured Ford Cortina mark 2 and thought;

*'What sort of pratt owns **THAT**'.*

People may say that they have been living in the neighbourhood or even had the same next-door neighbour for as long. But this, ***this*** is something quite different.

A very small World that is now producing a lot of quite remarkable coincidences it seems.

Sophia said that she and Eric first started dating in 1969, but wasn't until 1976 they got married.

And in the meantime, for a short while prior, I surmised they may have lived together at his parent's house whilst they started their Lingerie business, selling at the local markets, etc.

When they married, they rented a house a little further away, whilst Eric renovated over the next couple of years, a much larger house in Allington.

[One they were to stay in for the rest of their married lives].
I thought at the time, it must have been the 'thing to do' back then. Buy a home, then start 'making a total mess' in renovating it whilst living in it, having been there three times (in three different houses) myself.

Something 'strange' started to happen during our online chats.
As the days turned into weeks, they were becoming more 'probing' but in a most pleasant way, and not one sided either.
The repartee and retorts were becoming more... intimate? Not in a sordid obvious way, more double-edged, we were still both 'teasing each other'. It was playful, but was there a deeper reason for it?
To see if we would 'fit together' more closely? Yes, it would be so good to maybe get together, socially for a coffee or even a meal, but truth be known I am a little afraid. But of what, I do not know.
Online teasing is one thing, but in real life? that's so different.

During this time, I have never pushed or even created a suggestion to arrange a meeting. I felt I would be cheating on Claire, though our marriage was less than fragile, basically finished, we were still married.
As much as I would have liked to, and as much as my new-found confidence was growing I could not bring myself to blurt out...
'Would you like to go for a drink, a meal, with me, maybe'.

Though from what she spoke of regarding her multiple holidays, it appeared I may not be in her league anyway... but all the same.

In early summer of 2016, ****I had received the news that I was now in remission from my Stomach Cancer. As very few people knew of my illness in the first place, I saw no reason (as before) to 'broadcast' the good news****

Not even tell Sophia. But I unintentionally let it 'slip out' mid-stream, in a conversation about food of all things that started at 7am in the morning.
(S) *"Morning Alex. Hope you slept well. Off to make myself a cup of Vanilla and liquorice tea. How good am I being on my diet!"*

(A) *"G'morning to you Kitten... Hmmm... different flavour...BUT what are you eating with it... truth!"*

A few minutes silence

(S) *"I'm back now. Not eating it with anything. Started no carb diet 2 weeks ago and have lost the few pounds I gained on holiday. Few more to go to be in bikini shape. Have you walked your dog this morning?"*

(A) *"Yes.. 5.15am.. dog took me for a walk on the fields"*

(S) *"Just having bit of cheese. Hardboiled egg and sliced tomato for lunch and meat and salad for tea maybe. Can't give up the Merlot though. A step too far!"*

(A) *"Since October I have lost 10kg.. for the last 5-6 weeks I have been steady at 82kg.. need less, not my ideal weight... tummy loss 50mm"*

(S) *"Why? Were you a bit chubby".*

(A) *"You want the full report now or the quickie version?"*

(S) *"Yes please. Didn't like to ask.*

(A) *"You SHOULD ask... be kaypoh... it's the only way to learn... you have confidence - use it".*

(S) *"Thought it maybe personal"*

(A) *"You should still ask.. certainly, if talking to me"*

(S) *"Ok ok mr bossy. I'm asking"*

(A) *"For the last three years (since July 2013) I have undergone continuous treatment for two separate life-threatening Cancers – Prostate and Stomach. Though my PSA count has started to slowly go back up, my Consultant has declared me 'fit for community'.. in other words, I am now in remission – but still under observation. There was also the Breast cancer scare".*

(S) *"Bloody hell Alex. What a shock. Does your diet play a part in your recovery?"*

(A) *"Nope... but gets me back to my leaner meaner lovin' machine self.... lol Treatment has been in the form of HR treatment, Chemo Therapy, Radiotherapy, plus the usual full body and pelvic scans, Injections, Scans ..etc etc*

(S) *"So all this time you've been helping me and you've been through very rough times yourself. That's so nice. Thank you. Going to be confident now and exercise kaypoh. Is everything in working order? Lol"*

(A) *"It's well documented that If I had not pushed and threatened my Doctor the chances of me being able to help anyone would have been slim to impossible. I had no symptoms, just a gut feeling something was 'not right'".*
(S) *"Wow. And do you feel perfectly well now!"*
(A) *"Yes. everything is in working order. The only difference is that I now have an inbuilt contraceptive system in place... lololol so yes... I feel fine... thank you"*
(S) *"Well I'm bloody starving. Off to make another cuppa and nibble on my cheese. See ya later X."*
(A) *"Ok... off ya go... take care Kitten...*

Afterwards A cold shiver went through me. My timing was wrong, so bloody wrong.

I didn't want Sophia to think I was trying some sort of 'sympathy' trick to gain her attention more. In truth I did not want her to know, because of what she had recently gone through.

But at the same time, I was glad I did, because I knew deep down inside I could not, should not, keep it a secret from her. I felt Sophia had a right to know - how weird is ***that***?

A week or so later I had made plans to go to the Ironworks in Hamilton for the August Bank Holiday 60s Charity dance music day.

I'm not sure if Sophia was aware of me going, she certainly hadn't made any mention of it in our chats.

I should really have taken that opportunity to ask her for a 'date' (*woohoo*), but simply, I never did. But was there a fear of rejection, in there somewhere? Sophia gave no indication of what she was doing for that day anyway.

And so, with having no idea if she was going or not, I didn't think about it anymore. I did not dwell on it.

Anyway, the chances of us meeting would be astronomical as they were expecting a huge number of peoplc to attend, and hopefully even more than the previous year – in the thousands easily. Something about a 'needle in a haystack' comes to mind. I missed a golden opportunity, but hey, as the song went 'That's Life', it certainly is... and my story with it… ha-ha.

CHAPTER 15
THE IRONWORKS, THE GIRL, and A GAMBLE.

The Ironworks had been an iron foundry for over 150 years and then lay empty for many years after that.
Investors moved in and turned it into a hub for eateries, wine bars, and late-night dancing. A lot of money was spent in the conversion.

The previous August festival, attracted over 3000 people and made a lot of money for the named charity. And it looked as if there were going to be even more people attending this year.
All the units run off one main wide 'corridor', with a stage erected for the artists.
Virtually all the bars went along with the theme for the day, '60s dance music', and all proceeds from tickets went to the same named charity as it did in the previous year.

I had been there for about thirty minutes and started to video a group of musicians I personally knew, on the main stage.
I videoed them as they started to sing the Solomon Burke classic 'Cry To Me' and continued until the end. My intention was to do some more video's later on that afternoon.
(More about this particular video, later).

I started to walk toward the back of the stage, but was stopped by a Lady who knew me. We chatted for a minute or two, and I then continued on my way.
On reaching the open space to the back and right-hand side of the stage, our paths crossed at that very moment.

I side-glanced to the left, saw Angela, then my eyes quickly shifted and I saw Sophia (I inwardly gasped) and at that very same moment, she looked at me, and asked.
"Alex? are you Alex Milnz?"

That was the second introduction and another question. The first, being on the bus, and that started with a question as well. Weird.

I drew in a quick breath, and for a split-second, I was speechless. She was no longer a girl, she was a beautiful woman. Then the auto-pilot devilment in me, took over.
With a dead-pan face, I quickly replied
   "Sorry...you have me mistaken for someone else."

   "Oh, sorry." came the reply from Sophia.

Now this is odd, because I instantly got the distinct impression that she wasn't expecting *that* answer. It was as if she already knew who I was. How?
Did she already have a photograph of me on her phone?
Why?
I then took a step back and at the same time turned toward Angela,
   "Excuse me ... Angela?'. 'Can you tell Sophia she was right, she found me, I'm Alex"

A half-smile came on Sophia's face, and an even bigger one, with a verbal exclamation came from Angela

WOW… what a coincidence...!! Or was it ?

For whatever reason, Angela appeared to be more thrilled at the sudden meeting than Sophia was... but then, Sophia could hide her emotions well.
Now some may laugh, but I believe that to be a birth trait. Sophia, like me, is a Scorpio and a White/Metal Tiger; in fact, only 28 days separate our births.
My nickname for Sophia was quite correct. Kitten was indeed purrrrfect. What a corny cliché... but oh so very spot on.

   We spoke for less than five minutes; It was like '*this isn't happening, is it*? I was in a daze, numbed though alert.
But I managed to take a couple of photographs, typically staged yes, but maybe the only photographs I'm likely to get of them.... of Sophia.
They said they were going somewhere to eat and have a drink.
We said our goodbyes, and then Sophia was gone.

But I was elated.
I felt like a school kid. We had met again, after forty-eight bloody years, would you ever believe that?
And NO, I didn't wet myself.
But someone did it for me.

A few minutes later, an over-exuberant dancer spilt a drink all over the front of my suit jacket. I had to go home to change.

Whilst back home getting changed, I found that I needed to see if Kitten was online. She was.
As it was a glorious sunny day she was having a drink and a bite to eat at one of the outside eateries. I couldn't type fast enough.
And so we arranged to meet at the back of the stage area, where we had met initially, at 4.15pm.
I dashed back into Hamilton, arrived just before 4pm, went straight to the stage area, and waited until about 4.30pm.
Sophia did not show up. I was annoyed and felt a tad deflated.

I knew my Daughter was going into Hamilton for a meal with her husband and for which I previously was given an open invitation, so I phoned her, and less than twenty minutes later joined them both for a meal at Enrique's on Little Paul Street.
Needless to say, I felt a bit rejected when I joined them, but still managed to give up a welcoming smile.
.
About ten minutes after ordering something to eat, and it arriving in front of me, I found I desperately needed to speak to Sophia again.
Sophia, the 'no-show' woman. This was ludicrous.
Once again, I found myself acting like a bloody school kid. It was so annoying. And so, halfway through the meal, I took a gamble. I asked to use my Daughter's phone and I messaged Kitten on Facebook.

It took me (or so it seemed) simply ages to type it out on the phone, I'm bloody hopeless. My meal was getting cold. Sophia answered back almost straight away. She insisted she WAS there and mentioned a group that was on stage.

She was right. That group had just started up when I decided to leave at around 4.30ish. So she must have shown up a few moments after I left. Damn 'n bugger!

It also later transpired that Kitten had pm'd (private messaged) me at 4.20 pm to say she 'was just finishing a drink'. Double damn 'n bugger!

Kitten had assumed I had a 'smartphone' and also, have it with me 24/7. I don't possess a smartphone, but if I had, and read the message I would certainly have hung on a little longer.

[But as it turned out, if I had, the night might not have ended as it did].

I texted back to ask as to where they both were.
 "Tosca's Queen Anne Street." came the reply

WOW, that was about a two-minute walk from where I was actually eating, incredible. Yet another unbelievable coincidence.
I messaged back,
 "Be there within thirty minutes."

Strange that this girl was having this effect on me.

Like a long-lost pal, I needed to catch up with. Ha-ha and that would be some catching up after all those years.

Because of that first meeting, that bus journey, I have mentioned the event many, many times over the years. And yes, on the very rare occasions I have wondered what she was doing at that moment. But that's it. No thought of trying to reconnect. Even when she came back on the scene eighteen months ago and I was talking to her on-line, the thought of meeting up with her never crossed my mind, except of course for the one time mentioned in the previous chapter.

If it were to ever happen, then it would – and it did. It's happening right now

And it feels so good.

It must have shown on my face as I came out of FB, handed my daughters phone back to her, she stared at me curiously for a few seconds. Then carried on with her meal.

I too continued with my meal and told her that I was going to meet a friend around the corner at Tosca's – which was true.

After I finished, I then thanked them both for my meal, said my goodbyes and casually walked out and true to my word, I joined Kitten and Angela' within the thirty minutes.

I don't know, but all this seems to be getting stranger, but actually more wonderful, by the minute. It's almost surreal, like I was in a dream of sorts.
And I am seriously beginning to wonder, if this Kismet and my subconscious were not intertwined in some mysterious way.
I'm sure I could have read somewhere, possibly by Sigmund Freud that they were indeed connected, and I would not be surprised if I found my Cousin Marie, who is a psychology Professor in France, agreed as well. And I trust her implicitly.
What would be her professional and personal take on all of this be?
I will have to have a chat with Marie soon, I think.

I'm a cat (Tiger) after all, always curious. And in my case, always looking for answers. Though we all know the old saying about curiosity and the cat, don't we? Ha-ha.

CHAPTER 16
TOSCA'S and the STATION OF DREAMS

As I approached Tosca's I could see them both through the large front windows.
There they were, two drop-dead gorgeous Ladies sat at a window table, and I was about to join them.
Both Sophia and Angela were quite chatty. Not surprised really as I assume they had been drinking for a good part of the afternoon, and then the later supplement of a bottle of Prosecco which I purchased was going down quite fluidly.
Strange that I did not join them with the drink, did I want to keep a clear head? – but for what reason? Not thirsty…? ha-ha.

Our conversation became very 'open', and as people who know me, know that I have very few Taboos, my answers to their questions may have taken them back a little.
Especially so when Angela asked,
"Do you have a Girlfriend in Asia?"

My instant reply was,
"No, but I have several friends who are Ladies".

This then led to Angela asking the very direct,
"Do you have sex with them?"

Wow. She was out to startle me and then gauge my reaction.

But she hadn't reckoned on this as a reply from me though,
"I have pleasured them, and they have pleasured me but I have never had intercourse with them."

Angela genuinely almost gagged on her drink.
She blurted...
"I don't believe you... no man could do that."

Then came my killer line, the stunner was …
"It's quite easy because I have not had intercourse in almost twenty-five years."

Angela was quite visibly shocked; all she could say and kept repeating was…
"No, No I'm not having that... impossible."

I just sat there with a blank look on my face. Gotcha !!

I leaned forward at some point, and Kitten 'sniffed' the aftershave I was wearing.
She smiled, she liked it. And before she could ask (was she going to? maybe she had already recognised the fragrance).
I informed her it was a perfume by Molton Brown called *'Singosari'*.

I then remembered I had three vaporiser sprays in a small inside pocket of the shoulder bag I was carrying. I still had them there from my last trip to Asia and had not cleared the bag (scruffy bugger).
The sprays contained, Singosari, Londinium (both Molton Brown) and L'eau Bleu by Issey Miyake. Time for a little vanity?

I thought to 'shock' Angela once again, and she was. I don't know what she was thinking, but her face was a picture when I placed all three sprays on the table.
"OMG... what are you doing with those... are you a perv or something... put them away."

The sprays were bull nose shaped, like a small personal 'vibrator', so I was not surprised at her reaction. I still smile at her facial expression.

They both sampled the perfumes, the Issey was 'ok', they could not make their mind up about the 'musky' Londinium, but they both liked the Singosari, though Angela did mention, it was a little too 'flowery' (or sweet) for her taste.
Job done, back in the bag.

After a short while and during the general conversation, Kitten gave me some discreet, but positive body language messages.
Her crossed knee kept resting on mine and not by accident.
She made no move to 'straighten' herself. I was quite flattered.

(Kitten later informed me '*I did not realise I was doing that*'..., but she did)
I felt she needed to gauge my reaction for some reason. I suspected the drink was making her 'devilish'.
If I moved my leg away, then she would have known there was no interest. But no way was I going to move my leg.
The interest was there. It may have always been there.

When Angela left the table to go to the Ladies Room (was it planned, I wonder? a little flick of the head to Angela maybe). Kitten leaned across, and quickly kissed me on the lips... then pulled away... two more times she leaned forward, kissed me and pulled away.
But on that third time, she abruptly stopped, as I leaned forward, to kiss her.

With that full-on kiss, no single word can describe the feeling.
I melted. It was so, so good... so gentle, her lips were full and warm, it was surreal and yet (this is weird) felt natural, almost familiar. It seemed to last forever. And I wished it could.

Angela returned, and we carried on chatting as if nothing had happened, even Angela seemed casual as if unaware of what had taken place. So, maybe they did not plan it, and it really was a spontaneous act from Kitten.

All too soon, the girls had to leave. They needed to get the last train home.
As we stepped out of Tosca's, I automatically held Kitten's hand. Then a few seconds later, I held out my left hand to Angela, and she took it as we strolled off to the Railway Station.

All the way to the Railway station, we three held hands. I felt like I was a King Bee with two Honey bees... WOW.
We walked into the station, and Angela was starving, she needed food desperately. And so a rather large Baguette was the perfect order (as photographs proved). As well as inside the Ironworks I intended to take more permanent memories of the time spent with Sophia, as it may have been the *only* time spent.

Time to make their way to the platform where their train was waiting and ready to depart from.
We walked side by side, hand in hand to the platform. We both suddenly stopped. Kitten turned to face me. This was like something out of an old romantic movie, because we both knew what was coming.

We held each other in our arms and kissed, not caring who saw us.
Kitten placed her lips against mine and opened her mouth slightly, then a little more. more still and like a faithful servant, I followed.
Then, we were both like Goldfish, 'eating' each other alive (metaphorically speaking of course).

Even Angela let out an exclamation, "*Oh my God."* ...whilst turning her head to see what was happening.
I turned my gaze toward her whilst still giving mouth to mouth resuscitation to Kitten and saw bits of Baguette spraying out of her mouth, into the air and onto the floor. It was so funny to see, like something out of a comedy film I almost burst out laughing, but I did manage a little 'wobble, ha-ha'.
I then 'cupped' Kitten's face, and gently kissed her lips for what seemed an eternity. It was the most Heavenly thing I have done.
I had never done that to any woman, and to my possible shame, not even my Wife.
We both then resumed with kissing like cannibalistic Goldfish, whilst looking into each-other's eyes. Kitten looked at me and said,
   "You're a good snogger." [kisser].

And my very obvious, and truly meant, reply:
   "And you're pretty damn good yourself."
....and sealed it with yet another long kiss.

What a totally unexpected, beautiful end to the day, A day that started off with no expectations, no hopes, no nothing, and yet here I was, in the arms of and kissing the mouth of a most beautiful woman. A woman I had only met and talked to for thirty minutes, forty-eight years previously and quite possibly to the month.

But, too brief the moment, the final call for the train came over the tannoy.
Did I hear Kitten give a sigh? because I certainly gave one.
Kitten and Angela went through the gate and down the platform, to where they both were to board the waiting train.
I did not see Kitten turn her head to look back, but such were the events of the evening I am more than sure she would have taken a 'sneak sideways peek' before disappearing into the carriage.

I turned and started to walk out of the station, not knowing what future lay before me, or maybe even possibly, before us?
I was in a daze, as if I wasn't sure where I was. I walked out of the station and walked (almost like 'on air') to the centre of town, and onward to home.

To this day, I still get that 'special', warm feeling each time I think about that first kiss and those few moments at the station.
And if I could relive a moment in time over and over again, that would be the 'moment.
I wouldn't tire because each time would be as fresh, and as exciting as the first.

Despite their often strong and seemingly cavalier exteriors, Tigers, especially the males, can be very sentimental and emotional, sometimes possibly too emotional, which others may see as a weakness.
But, with what just took place, I did not care in the least.

[Now if I had not been both desperate and curious to contact with Kitten that night, we would never have been sat there and been part of the series of events that actually transpired that evening, which profoundly changed my life. Sophia said it first, a short while back, *Kismet*.]

And I have jumped the gun yet again – apologies, back to the time-line.

CHAPTER 17
IMMEASURABLE

The following day I asked myself just HOW we managed to cross paths at that exact time, and even more so, SHE recognised ME... instantly.
We are all 'a bit slow' on the uptake sometimes, but, then it dawned on me, that she must have had a photo of me, on her phone.
There were plenty of recent ones on Facebook that she could seek out, which it seems to have been her obvious intent – but why?
Even though I did not tell her I was going, I did tell a few other people. So Sophia could have played 'Sherlock Holmes', because it was her intention to 'snare me'. To see me, 'in the flesh'?

Well, she certainly did that.

And as I have an old-style mobile phone (text and calls only) I could not put a photo of her on it, and I did not take it with me anyway. I only had her face as a memory to recognise her – which I did.

A couple of days later, on the evening of the 30th, I spoke to Marie and Albert on the phone and told them about all the coincidences that happened in connection with Kitten, up to the August Bank Holiday, at the Ironworks, and what followed.

Albert, being a Professor of Applied Mathematics, said he would out of curiosity, work out the percentages. Marie and I chatted for about twenty minutes more. She wanted to know so much more about Kitten, maybe because I could not stop talking about her.. ha-ha.
Then Albert was back. He said he could not believe the result, so he did the calculations twice again. And again, the same result.
He was totally amazed and said,
 "*So hard to believe, but they are 'off-scale. Thrice the programme gave the answer as ... 'immeasurable'"*.

Marie sounded knowingly casual, when she simply answered.
"I am not surprised in the least"
And came up with her own understanding for it,
"Something deeply spiritual was happening, and for whatever the reason, it was inextricably binding the two of you together'. 'It's Kismet, but so much more. You two were destined to meet up again from all those years ago, make no mistake about that. 'Someone' has something really big planned for the both of you."

Now Marie, a Professor of Psychology can get spooky at times, and this actually spooked me.
It certainly was a 'stunned silence' from me, time.

[From that day in late 2014 to this day in July 2017, and with my hand firmly placed on my heart, there has been, almost certainly not one single day that I have not thought about her and smiled)

On my 'name card' that I have used for over thirty years, are the words:
'I cannot see you.
nor can I hear you.
...but I feel your presence.'

[I now realise that to be the absolute truth. Could it be she was also in my subconscious thoughts even then? I wonder]

****

This *was* to be to end of my own personal memoirs to look back on.
But as fate, or call it Kismet, would have it, thirty months later I was to find, be it through outside encouragement from the writing of *'My Seven Year Itch.. with Cancer'* or my own personal quest for answers, I needed to continue with the book. Little realising what was to come, in real time, beyond the memories].

BOOK ONE

The Girl On The Bus - part two

[REMOVED SPOILER 'A']

THE STORY CONTINUES...

CHAPTER 18
BEYOND THE STATION

As I saw Kitten and Angela board the train, I had this totally unbelievable romantic fairy-tale urge to go rushing through the gate and jump on the train.
I so wanted to kiss her once again.

Kitten later told me that two 'young boys' (?) got on the train and went beetroot when they saw her, but mentioned that they had seen her 'kissing' that man.
I wonder if they were really that genteel with their expression.
I could not help smiling when Sophia told me of this.

Ahhh, the innocence of youth?
'Tis indeed a rare sight, seeing two seniors, 'mouth wrestling'.

As I walked away from the station to catch the bus home (how romantic an end to the day is THAT. ha-ha), I was quite literally in a daze.
I could not believe what had happened, from being at the Ironworks with no expectations, to meeting up after forty-eight years, the kiss in Tosca's and finally the railway station.
An unbelievable, mind whirling, beautiful twelve hours.

And, for the life of me, I NEVER EVER expected anything like that to happen. Sophia was well and truly in my system.
I could not get home fast enough to contact her again.

I arrived home just before midnight, went straight on to the computer, and Kitten was there already.
Was she waiting for me?
I doubt it. More than likely she was/had been chatting to Angela.
I remember my opening line,
"What an incredible, deliciously wonderful evening. Rarely do words fail me."

With that, we talked away for maybe thirty minutes or more.
But our chat was different, warmer, almost intimate (but not in the biblical sense).

Our strange little game of 'killer line' repartee/retort/answer back (something that started almost fifty years ago) as to who could get in the last killer retort, that even the other player knew was coming and couldn't do anything about it, thus stealing the game'.
We have also, for the fast few conversations added a little 'side-bet' of a 'fiver', though who actually 'won' sometimes went a little array.
And even the tone of those conversations started to take a different turn, almost teasing.
It was late, and Kitten was tired…
(S) *"I'm turning over."*
(A) *"Nice back."*
(S) *"Cheeky."*
(A) *"No, I can't see those."*
(S) *"Fivvvver."*
(A) *"I knew it as soon as I said it, big fail."*
(S) *"Too late was the cry."*
(A) *"I'll knock it off your bill …so that's £25 you owe me now."*
Note: 'Fiver' is £5

Sounds silly and childish? maybe…
But, we could bounce off each other's words like nobody's business. It was so weird, but felt so natural at the same time.
It was a game of honesty. It was refreshing, keeping alert and having fun. But what was uncanny was that we could quite literally talk about anything and still 'bounce off each other'.
Were we like 'Soul Mates'?
A nice thought, but no, and only time would tell otherwise.

For the next couple of days, we chatted as and when we were 'online'.
We both had our other social activities and just got on with them. There was no movement on Sophia's or my part to try and get another meeting, though I DID say at one point that,
   "I would love to see you again."

Nothing would have given me a greater thrill for her to have said... *'ok'*.

CHAPTER 19
THE REQUEST

It was about this time that I looked at the video I took at the Ironworks. It was good. I was happy with it.

**[But it was not until eight months later, when I decided to upload the video onto 'YouTube' that something caught my eye. I was totally gobsmacked, it was a TOTAL WOW.
The story behind this will follow the books time-line as it had a big impact on me and as you too will realise when you continue reading this book.]**

**On the morning of the last day in August I had my monthly PSA test, this time including a full renal profile.
This was a decision I made in the April, not the Doctors or the Hospital's. I informed my doctor, that because of previous 'hesitations', I would be happier within myself in having the blood tests once a month for a short period. He accepted my point**

On the same day I decided to 'open out' to an online 'Request' thrown down by a dear friend.
'The Request' was for friends to openly talk about their cancer recovery, how they coped.

I didn't have to think about it when I opened up, because I had gained so much in my confidence over the last twelve months or so.
It was a positive thing to do. A profound change from previously, when I was drained of all my confidence and exhausted hope.

I posted a very brief outline of my Cancer, and I did so whilst thinking of my lovely Princess, Leila, who kept her Cancer quiet until the very late stages.
I strongly believed that I owed it to her to speak out about my illness.

As through her final weeks, she confided in me. I felt helpless; all I could do was talk to her, talk about her Cancer in the most casual of ways, but most of all, talk about our love of dancing, both together and solo and food.
We both loved to experiment with food (cooking and baking) recipes.
I was trying to take her mind off the Cancer, and the pain.
If only she had opened up and spoken to her Doctor sooner.

Within the hour, Kitten saw the post and commented on the post, basically reiterating what she said to me, personally, in the July.

"All the time you were comforting me over Eric, you were going through the same with your Cancer. I'm truly humbled."

I had not realised that my comment in another Facebook group could be seen by my friends as well.
But at the same time, I was happy (and relieved) to post what I did. And equally pleased to see Sophia's comment. A comment that allowed her feelings and gratitude to be publicly shown. She is amazing.

It was now 'out there', no longer a secret that only three or four members of my family, and two very close friends in Asia knew about. I owed that much, to my dear friend Leila.

I felt relieved, that I was released from an unnecessary, self-inflicted burden.

CHAPTER 20
MO'DAKA, SINGOSARI, and REISS

During an on-line chat on the 1st of the month, Sophia said something to me that was very sweet and at the same time, intrigued me;

"You have obviously been through a lot and yet you picked me up during my bad times and made sure I was ok. That means a lot to me. We have history and you are lovely. What else can I say ...."

'We have history'. What did she mean by that?
That I told her we had met before? on the bus.
A meeting she could not remember.
And she said it as a third party.
Other than that, our 'history' for what it is only extended to December 2014, a mere eighteen months.
Or was there something she does not want to share with me?
If there was 'something else', then she will tell me in her own time, when she is ready and not before.

Then on the 3rd of September, Kitten messaged me

"We're going into Hamilton and might end up in the Heartland Quarter... do you fancy coming along?"

[Me thinking: *'Whaaaaaa...'* and something about *'Wild horses*!!']

I remember that when she was getting ready, she said she was going for a shower, and that she had put a photo of herself from 1969 (?) onto a 60s Group on Facebook.
The quick-fire repartee and retorts' came in...
(A) *"That's really weird, as I have just sent you a photo of myself from 1968 as well."*
[slight pause, as she checked?]
(S) *"You look dishy."*
[Sophia then takes and sends a photo she thinks of herself]
(A) *"Is that a dressing Gown?"*
(S) *"Oh, sorry, it's my bedroom door."*
(A) *"This is getting intimate, sorry interesting."*

(S) *"Freudian slip?"*
(A) *"No, deliberate."*
(S) *"FIVVVER!"*

Gawd…. We were so good at this, gelling together. I just smile.

Kitten messaged me later, about 9.30pm to say both she and Angela were in the Mo'Daka on Hardy Street.
Wooooosh… I was there, within twenty minutes.

Kitten and Angela were sat near the doorway as I walked in.
I kissed Angela on the lips (I don't think she was expecting that) and I seriously don't know what made me do it.
Seemed 'OK' at the time to 'just do it'.
Honestly, this new-found confidence seems to be having a bit of a strange effect on me, and I like it.
And then I looked at Kitten, and I'm not sure who kissed who first. Who bloody cares, we kissed.
At the same time, the Singosari perfume I was wearing made her twitch her nose (again) whilst having an almost nonchalant sniff.
   "You were wearing that the other Sunday, I like that."

How lovely. She remembered the fragrance. It is a nice one for sure.

We sat chatting for only thirty minutes or so, but during which time I presented Angela with a Zodiac 'Dragon' and Kitten with the white Zodiac Tiger (The Teegra), their Chinese Zodiac Birth Animals.
(wow, gift giving... on only the second meeting…. ha-ha)

Time was running out, they had to catch the last train… again.

We walked through Paulden Square, a now popular area and just passing the public house where I took my (future) wife on our first date some forty-four years earlier.
Then, totally out of the blue, a young girl from a group of people walking passed us, suddenly stopped, turned to me and asked,
'Excuse me, what's that aftershave you have on, because it is the same as one of my lecturers' wears, and I adore it."

After explaining to her it wasn't really an aftershave, I told her the name of the perfume and the brand.
She thanked me and started to turn away when I tapped her on the shoulder saying,

"I can do better than that, do you want to spray some on yourself?"

She looked a little confused, but before she could answer, I handed her the vaporiser spray to use
"Is this the perfume? Oh God, yes please" came her reply.

She duly sprayed some on her wrist, then her neck before handing it back to me. She thanked me, then walked away with her friends.
She was obviously a very happy young lady at that moment.
It actually made me feel really good as well, but I wondered what Kitten thought of it all. She had just followed the event and never said a word. She just gave that lovely half-smile of hers, and that was enough for me.

We continued our 'threesome walk to the station and whilst doing so Kitten suggested to Angela,
"Let's forget the train, shall we get a hotel for the night instead?"

(Wow, did I just hear that right?)

Angela instantly boohooed the idea.
Sophia just replied, *"Ok, the train it is"*.

I wondered then, and later, what would have happened if Angela said, *'fine, let's do it?'*.
I had the strangest feeling Kitten 'had a plan' and that plan included me.
To be absolutely honest, I don't personally know what I would have done if Angela had said *'yes, let's get a room'* and Kitten invited me to the room.
It was far too soon for anything like **'that'**, I wasn't ready, and I was more than a tad apprehensive.
I would have been entering a strange world. One where my emotions could have got the better of me.

I honestly feel I would have made my excuses, and left. Seriously.
As soon as we arrived at the station, their train was in, so it was a quick kiss, or two or three, and Kitten was running for the train.

Just past midnight (I think), I messaged Kitten and thanked her and Angela for a lovely night, and I finished by saying;
"..and I wish it could have lasted longer."

Sophia replied,
"I wanted the same, but sadly your circumstances have made it very difficult."

I thought to myself: *'so the 'let's spend the night in a Hotel' did include Moi?'*
She then said,
"It's late, let's sleep on it."

That sounded ominous.
I would have been very disappointed if that was as far as it went, but I would have understood.
It may have seemed 'unfair' because I was in a loveless, and quite honestly, an almost, at times soul destroying marriage, but I was married, and that was that.
But deep down inside, I knew I wasn't going to leave it at that, no way was I going to settle for not seeing Sophia again.

For the next few days, we did our own thing, and when we met up online, we chatted away continually... how can two people have so much to talk about. It was incredible.
Our repartee and retort games were in full flow, we gelled, and both really enjoyed that.
A couple of days later during a on-line chat, Sophia said,
"Dashing to get train into Hamilton to take my great nephew and great niece for lunch before school tomorrow".

"I'm going into Hamilton myself. I was going to join you, but you will still be with the Family", I replied

Sophia quickly replied, '
"That might prove difficult."

Oh dear, a refusal to meet?
I suspect she did not want to be put in an awkward position of having to explain to her family members just who I was or what I was (if anything) to her, especially when Eric had passed only fourteen or fifteen months before.
It would have been too soon.
But I got that, and respected her for it.

I continued;
"I understand. I would have liked to have thought we had a relationship, well maybe not 'that' because 'Relationship' is quite ambiguous. Enjoy your lunch"

Her reply surprised me;
"Yes of course we have a relationship. Miss you!"

I still went into Hamilton centre though and then onto Reiss, as they had a sale on. Even though their (male) styles and cut are more for the 25-40 age range, I found over the past four or five years that
the number of items I had bought from there looked good on me, and fitted extremely well. I 'felt good' wearing them.
A little vanity is ok.. but sometimes men are worse than what women are notoriously (and admiringly) known for.
Yes, I like 'looking good' (without breaking the bank) and smelling good as well. And why not. It also helps with self-confidence.

I also sometimes managed to get a discount, even on sale items, which helps with the cash flow. But, alas I was out of luck this time. They had sold out of a limited design shirt I liked the look of, a couple of days before.
They looked really smart, and at a quarter of their normal selling price, they would have looked' even better. But, no such luck.
I'm no 'dedicated follower of fashion', 'catwalk collector' or such, my wallet and my common sense wouldn't allow me to purchase over inflated first season prices anyway, so if I really liked something I would wait a couple of seasons for them to come on sale, and even better when if it's a members only online sale.

As there was nothing else of interest at Reiss. Off I went to Primark looking for Blue and Beige belts. What a comedown, some may say but Primark is a great place to get essentials, but again, no luck this time. Sheesh.

And I didn't run into Kitten, and family, either.
I would have avoided them if they had of come into view. I wouldn't have wanted to embarrass Kitten.

I messaged part of this useless bit of information about Reiss to Sophia later that day.
She was must have been busy and didn't answer me until the next morning.

CHAPTER 21
INTO THE KITTENS LAIR

I received the results of the PSA and Liver tests. Liver fine but the PSA showed a jump of two full points. Await this month's

Early in September, with my inner confidence growing daily and working wonders (is Sophia the cause of this?), I told myself that I wanted to get to know Sophia more and hopefully get to see her again soon.

That's when I brought up the subject in a chat with Sophia, about wanting to make a visit to Rosemount and to look around the place as it had been many years since I was last there.
To see what changes (if any) had been made over the years.
I will say now that I have always had a 'feel' for the place. It felt homely, local and inviting.
I remember it, from being a kid passing through Rosemount many times on a bicycle admiring the shops and the houses.
And as we lived near each other as children, and she knew Rosemount was only about five miles, or a thirty-minute bike ride away, she knew I was genuine and not trying to wheedle
myself into her life by conning her with familiarity and false interest.
And also around 1970, both I and an old school friend, Jon (who also became a disc jockey) used to visit Rosemount on a regular basis as we were both dating girls who lived there
So this led to me adding to my last online message from the day before,
　"What's life and Rosemount like now where you live?"

Kitten eventually replied
　"Well a very good morning to you. Just opened my eyes and checked messages. Thought you'd forgotten all about me. Last convo you said talk later. Rosemount is just great. Had dinner at Angela's again last night with her Mum and twin Sister. Thought I would have got a little note from you when I got back but you were obviously too busy! Another coincidence. Reiss is my favourite shop. The one shoulder dress I'm wearing in my

profile pic is from there! Our paths cross again."

And yes indeed, that dress was something else, it was stunning and looked as if it was made especially for her. And Reiss as well. Wow.

And reading her message again, she certainly is giving me the impression, that *I'm* making an impression – on her.
Then Kitten came right out and asked,
   "Do you want to come down, and I'll show you around?"

I screamed inwardly to myself *'Oh, you betcha !!'*
She asked, (and once again, the quick-fire repartee and retorts came in so automatically, we were bouncing again…)
(S) *"Are you tied to a time?"*
(A) *"No, I'm not into Bondage."*
(S) *"Damm."*
(A) *"Fivvvver."*

I think Kitten then came out with the 'royal' *'Bugger and shit'* when she realised she had been 'gotcha'd.

I have mentioned this before. This repartee game and retorts and anticipating what the others answer was going to be may seem childish to many, but it's all quick-fire, keeps the person alert to the other person, good fun, and helped us be at ease with each other.
Try it yourself with someone, but theres the rub. That other someone may be very hard to find. With Sophia it just 'happened' and for that day I will be forever blessed.
The song *'Oh, I've Been Bless'd'* by Bobby Taylor instantly came to mind when I used the phrase. *(oh stop it, Milnzy.. ha-ha).*

Kitten wanted to know how I would get there, I told her, by car, and she replied,
   "That's fine, park it behind mine because it's a restricted parking zone where I live, but I have enough space for two"

She then proceeded to give me her address.
Wow, it was in the village itself.

I was looking forward to this and yet a little afraid...
Apprehension? Adrenaline?
I had no preconceived ideas or plans about how *'I'* wanted the afternoon to go.
I certainly did not have thoughts of 'trying my luck'.
This girl, this woman, was becoming quite special, and I wanted to treat her accordingly, and with respect.

I jokingly asked her something whilst still chatting online, which for a split second after, I thought... *'bloody idiot'*, I was a little scared, tongue-tied, lost for something to say, call it what you will.
I instantly regretted putting fingers to keyboard.
I informed Kitten that,
　"You could make the first move if you wanted to... I would not think any less of you for it."

She replied,
"I am old school, and that if a man was interested, he would show it."

Remembering Tosca's. I was little confused, but surely this is called small talk... maybe even foreplay? We were both probing....
I answered, with the very obvious, yet still probing,
　"He would look a right fool if the girl wasn't interested..."

Then Kitten gave it the 'all clear' in a way I have never come across before (or since), and it was obviously aimed square at me...
　"Well, that's the 64,000-dollar question isn't it. Does he have the confidence or not, especially when he has a complicated life himself."

With that answer, Sophia knew damn well as to what I was trying to say and her answer was also directly aimed at me.
Well, my confidence is improving daily it seems. So that sealed it.
We would both go along with it and see what happens.

But no way could I ever have envisaged as to what was to unfold.

That afternoon in early September, I parked behind Kitten's car. I stood slightly back and looked at the house and immediately I got that same warm, snugly, secure feeling that I had when I first saw my Cottage all those years ago.

It was a very strange sensation, especially because I thought I would never get that feeling again. But here I was, stood in front of a house and I was 'glowing'. I felt really good. So hard to express really.

I knocked on the door, Kitten answered... I went inside and was immediately greeted with a warm, soft kiss, then another and another. What a way to greet each other.

As I was not expecting it, it took me by completely by surprise, for a microsecond that is. Ha-ha. Wow, what a 'moment'.

Yet again, she appears to be making the first move. The same as she did at Tosca's.

Was this a natural trait for her, to lead or was it that she was just eager to enjoy the moment.

This woman who was supposed to be 'old school'.

Or did I have a, unbeknown to me, sign over my head that said *'I'm Yours'*?

I doubt very much that such an experience like that would ever be forgotten. It felt so good and so beautifully 'right'.

This may sound a little odd, but it felt natural, as if I or we have done this so many times before – which is obviously impossible I know, but still.

After we composed ourselves, Kitten delightedly showed me around the house. She was quite rightly proud of her home. Everything seemed to be nicely laid out, nothing out of place.

The latest magazines on the coffee table in the centre of the room, for herself or guests to read.

It was more like a 'show house' than a 'home'.

I cannot, and will not, fault her for that, it is what she has become accustomed to I feel. Her way of living. And I accepted that.

I'm not the opposite, but I do like somewhere in a house where I can be 'untidy', or just place something down. I smiled whilst thinking about this.

A vision of me being relegated to the shed at the bottom of the garden.
Oh lord, she didn't have one did she. ha-ha.

But, I had to ask myself, what made me have a vision like that?

But seriously, the house did feel like what a home should feel like (to me anyway).
A place where you feel secure, happy, a place where you can sometimes take refuge from the realities and bitterness of life that surrounds you. You can shut yourself off basically.

I wasn't sure if these are any of the reasons why Kitten is living here, but I'm sure she too 'may' have got a 'tingle' when she saw it, be a beautiful coincidence if she did.
But dare I say it, we are both Tigers, conceived and born in the same year, so we have the same, or very similar, traits. There is a lot to be said of a Tiger/Tiger relationship, both good and bad – mostly good actually from what I can remember reading a long time ago..

Time to have a walk around the village. And with your very own, totally gorgeous tour guide. I am one hell of a lucky fellah.

As we left the house, I looked back, and with my usual lack of tact, a trait I have had for many years, I made a knowledgeable and artistic suggestion to Kitten,

"You may want to thin out the ivy on the walls as it is not good for the wall structure and also try and put some small lights in the ivy. That would show off the beauty of the place and look 'picturesque' and inviting, on any night of the year."

"Hmmm, maybe' came Kitten's reply,

She was probably thinking;
'Cheeky bugger, only been in the house five minutes and already he's telling me what's good for it'.

CHAPTER 22
JOINING HANDS and EVERYTHING ELSE

As soon as we stepped out onto the pavement, we automatically went to hold each other's hand.
It had that *'it's always been this way'* feeling. It was beautifully spooky and *felt so right*.
I know I have used that expression before, it's for when something happens that feels so unbelievably natural.

It's strange and so very true, that my Wife so disliked 'holding hands' immensely, even when we were dating, she would never allow me to even try. She would pull her hand away, maybe she was embarrassed by the action?
But Kitten, Kitten seemed to welcome it, to relish it in fact and I was so pleased. And I am enjoying the fact that I am able to please Kitten with the simplest of actions, and in return she covers me with this warm disarming effect that feels so extraordinarily comfortable. I'm truly beginning to enjoy being in this Woman's company, immensely so.

As Kitten showed me around the village', nothing structurally appears to have changed in all those years. Not a 'time stood still thing', but nicely inviting, a warm familiarity.
After a short walk, it was decided we needed to have a coffee or maybe a (alcoholic?) drink somewhere, and a chat.
The D'Jango, where Kitten 'wanted' to go, was shut when we got there, so across the road, we walked, and Kitten took me to a little bistro called Ayia.

We had a couple of red and white wines each. Kitten looked seductively casual, dark loose top, black needle-cord Jeans that showed her lines beautifully.
She **'knew'** I was looking at her.
I couldn't help it. I would have been blind not to admire the way she looked.
About an hour later, we were making our way back to her house, still holding hands.

And as we entered through the door, that secure feeling came straight over me again. It felt so really good.
As I closed the front door behind me, we kissed, and both nearly fell over one of the two-seater sofas. Embarrassingly funny.
And Kitten took full advantage of the moment.
She was on 'home territory', her 'lair'.

She quickly walked around the sofa, and 'flopped' down with her legs stretched out forward and together.
I quickly followed her around, and just stood there, looking down at her, admiring her.
She was looking at me with those soft, alert eyes.
She then seductively, raised her knees upward, to her chest.

'Christ !!' I thought.
Even **I** could see what she was implying by her actions. She was inviting me to take her, to make love to her, there and then.

'Bloody Hell !!'.

With an almost soft urgency in her voice, she asked me,
   "Welllll, what are you waiting for? You know what we both want."

I will be honest; my mind was a whirlwind.
Is this happening?
I leaned forward and as I did, she parted her legs for me to snuggle down on top of her.

And whilst our bodies, though fully clothed, were pressed together in copulation mode, I was thinking,
'For Christ's sake, what if I can't 'perform', it's been years', I'm going to have to 'spend a little time' working on it [foreplay?] with Kitten to see if that helps'.

Did Kitten read my mind? because in the next moment, she pushes me away, stands up, takes my hand, and starts to lead me through the house, and up the stairs.
Following her, up the narrow stairs, my eyes were transfixed on her bottom. I couldn't look anywhere else. Ha-ha

We entered her bedroom at the front of the house.
Whilst kissing, gently 'biting', stroking and caressing each other, I was slowly undressing her.
She allowed me to remove every piece of clothing she had on, whilst admiring the whole of her beautiful form, her gentle curves, the softness of her skin.
Here was a woman who was giving herself to a man, a man who for so long had remembered her as that *girl on the bus*, but now as a man who has now grown to appreciate and respect her as a woman.

This 'undressing', as pleasurable as it was, also allowed me time to get 'aroused' - as best that I could.
And I do truly enjoy being able to pleasure a woman, and I get pleasure from seeing the joy it can give, even without the full act of intercourse taking place. It just seems to come naturally for me.

Kitten then started to disrobe me, whilst kissing and caressing my body. Two minds thinking and acting as one, how fantastic that is.
She suddenly stopped, stood back and just looked at me whilst I removed the last item of my clothing… and it wasn't my socks.

She just looked at me, expressionless, seeing me like a new born and totally hair free. Had she seen all this before?

I have shaved off all my pubic hair for a number of years, having felt more comfortable, you could say almost cleaner, this way.
And whilst it may have held a form of uniqueness to me, I'm sure many other men have done and felt the same.
Besides, for the guys out there who know, it's bloody painful getting your pubic hair caught in a zipper. Ouch, BIG time!!
Now, what she did next may seem *odd* to some readers.

She took a couple of steps toward me, turned around, and moved in front of me so we were in a 'queue'.
I lovingly, put my right arm around her waist and my left arm across her breasts, slightly covering them.
She then, in return, 'snuggled' into me and put her arms across my left one. Then she turned her head to the left. And I also turned my head to follow her direction and gaze.

And I instinctively knew what she was doing.
Kitten had full length mirrored wardrobes, and she was looking at us both, almost voyeuristically, and I was doing the same thing and not in the least embarrassed.
Was she looking to see if we looked good together? Maybe.
She had that beautiful half-smile on her face again.
If there were anything else she was thinking of, she never spoke about it, but I had an idea of which I thought of whilst looking at us both in the mirror, and it made sense.

It may have been in the 'here and now' for me, as easily as it may have been from a past memory for her with someone else, and I accepted that completely, and honestly, it looked and felt so beautiful.

Kitten then turned around to face me, gave me a quick kiss on the lips and flung herself backwards, across the bed.
She had had enough of that (foreplay?), she wanted to make love.

For the first ten minutes or so, I wasn't *'quite there'*, **[a more detailed explanation of why, is in Chapter 30]**, in fact, for most of the three hours or so that followed, I never quite achieved a full solid erection, I will be honest and say about 80%?
But I seriously thought it was getting stronger as time went on.

Considering my cancer treatment and being told my libido would be affected, with only a small possibility of any sort of erection, let alone a sustained one. I was thinking to myself.. *'Yesssssss, thank you God'*.
Nothing stopped us for the rest of the afternoon, from making love and exploring each other's bodies.
As I lay next to her, the softness and sweet smell of her body wrapped itself all over me. The smell was 'pure', akin to a new-born.

[I close my eyes, and to this day, I can still smell her, see her]
.

It was so soothing, so relaxing, and so very much disarming.
I couldn't help a wishful thought, as to what would it be like to wake up next to her, every single morning and smell that.

Yeah, wishful thoughts, and only in your dreams, Milnzy... in your dreams.

Whilst we were having a coffee before I left, Kitten said,

"*'Sometimes a woman just wants to be taken, there and then... no seduction, no foreplay".*

It was said in such a matter of fact, general conversational way, which I thought was good, relaxing.

And I immediately thought to myself;

'Was she saying that's what she wanted me to do, to happen as soon as we walked into the house. On and off the sofa, in the living room... with the window blind up?'

If I had realised, that could have been our 'starting point'.

As I left, we said our goodbyes at the partially open front door, with Kitten 'hidden from view' (because she was in an open dressing gown, and we gave each other a number of short kisses, there is no way I wanted to leave, but....

Driving all the way home, I was thinking, '*Did I do enough to make her smile, to make her feel wanted, dare I say, loved, metaphorically*'.

It wasn't a Macho thing because I would not have been asking myself those questions if it was. It was a 'caring' thought. And I'm finding that I seem to be caring for her a lot, quite a lot in fact.

As my confidence levels have been on the up and up recently, I just wanted to feel that '*the boy did good*' and that I had pleased Kitten.

She did smile, quite a lot, in fact.

I hope it was me. But if it wasn't, then that was her 'comfort blanket', and I could not take offence because of it.

When I got home around 8.30pm, the dog took me for my exercise, and then I was back to chatting to Kitten again.

I need not have been 'worried' whilst driving home.

Almost immediately from the start of our talking to each other, and me asking her if she had any visitors (ie Angela) after I left.

What Kitten's comments expressed to me, was that she was (quite possibly) more than pleased.

Then came a long pause as she was sending me a message.

*"I had no visitors after you left, Darling. Felt a little worn out after my shower. No sniggering. Think I'll sleep well tonight.
I haven't made love AT ALL for I don't know, fifteen years? A new experience for me, but so lovely. They say it's like riding a bike. I'd add to that. It's like riding a bike with stabilisers. Angela wants a blow by blow account which indeed I do expect from her after her encounters. I, on the other hand, am a Tiger. Like to keep things close to my chest!"*

I thought that was so funny, so honest and beautiful
For the next three hours or so, our conversation, like always, was varied, very stimulating and never once dull.
It was then that I broached the idea of taking a shower together,

*"The next time... hopefully, there will be one... I would enjoy taking a shower with you. If you never did that with Eric, you both missed a great new realm to 'intimacy'. It is your choice
what you share with Angela. I would not be embarrassed in the least."*

Kitten quickly replied,
"That is a little too personal, and between me and Eric. As for Angela. I know you wouldn't. She is after all, your perfect match! Lol Bring your massage oil next time for our post-shower. Oh I am a terrible woman but you're a long time dead. No problems from Claire when you got home?"

"No, none", I replied and continued with, *"Ideally, a half massage, make love, shower, half/full massage"*
I realised my mentioning Eric was not wise, well not in 'that' way. I can indeed be undiplomatic at the most sensitive of times.

Kitten actually sounded excited to hear this,
"Sounds good. Did you have a nice time today?"

What a lovely unguarded question. I replied,
"More than a nice time. I am wondering just what the next unexpected gift you are going to 'shower' me with.... yes I did have a nice time... and by the smile and wicked look on your face, you did as well."

Then came, immediately and out of the blue yet again, our repartee and retort game:
As a carry on from my previous reply to her unguarded question;
(S) *"Absolutely, hitting our hay now. Don't dare wake me at 7 am Well you couldn't wake me at 7 am. Lol."*
[I never realised until five years later, her reference to the 'Hay'.. it wasn't 'the', it wasn't 'my'… it was 'our']
(A) *"I'll sneak into your place at 6 am and give you an unexpected alarm."*
(S) *"Don't wake the horses, Squire."*
What a 'Goodnight' that was, so comical...
(A) *"Sweet dreams Kitten, Sleep well and wake refreshed... well awake at any rate..."*
But it didn't quite end there
After a few funny picture (gifs) messages from each of us,
(S) *"Enough. Get to bed! X"*
(A) *"Not even midnight... sod off, unless it's with you..."*
(S) *"Awe. Huddles and cuddles X. Ready for round two minus the extra glass! So cheeky!"*
(A) *"Correct... something I have jotted down... lol"*
(S) *"I don't know whether you believe me but I hope you do when I tell you I have had very little experience and none whatsoever for the past twelve to fifteen years. Yes ready for bed now. Night X"*
(A) *"I have no reason to doubt you.. it just makes me want to hold you even more. Nighty night"*
(S) *"Nighty night X, PS. I want you to teach me to dance"*
(A) *'hmmm.. horizontal.. or vertical?"*
(S) *"Both. Feeling very randy right now"*
(A) *"Keep that thought and feeling... nighty night."*

I understood immediately what she meant by *'minus the extra glass'*
And it had nothing to do with the wine, Kitten was going 'solo'.
I only wished I could have been there to witness the beauty of it.
And two things came to mind immediately during our chat.
Her; *'I haven't had any experience for the last twelve to fifteen years'*.
This, I suspect, would have coincided with her late husband's long illness

And to be honest, I could not have thought badly of her even if she had not told what she did.
Because every woman has needs, has desires.
It's not, as many men seem to think of, as their own 'private luxury club. That is sheer arrogance and lunacy and I have never been of that mind.

From a purely personal view, I would not have been shocked if she said or that I was to find out later, that she had frequent affairs with different men either in the distant or the recent past, or even with women, even both and at the same time.
It would have surprised me, yes, but 'shocked', no.
Though it would make me wonder as to; what 'I' was to her.

We can frown upon something we dislike for sure, but we should only become judgemental if it directly affects us in some way. And maybe that would be true if I were to be directly affected with it. By that I mean having deeper feelings for Kitten, and if I were to fall in love with her. Now 'that' would bring up a host of new emotions, and I would suspect, complications.
An interesting situation indeed, and one that I could not give in all honesty, a black and white answer to. Is there really one?
 Just because 'we' don't like something, that it offends our personal sense of morality or lifestyle, it does not mean that everyone should be of the same mind and follow suit.

We are individuals.
I could not demand her to stop such activities. I could only ask her to consider my feelings and try to come to a compromise, whilst not removing any pleasure she gets from it, even just innocent flirting. Then again, is there such a thing as 'innocent' flirting? with no secret, lustful thinking?
I would not think so, we are all guilty of such at some point in our lives, but some people do make it a **very** regular thing.

And in doing so, I may find that by allowing myself to openly acknowledge that whatever Kitten has done in the past or will do in the future, I accept that she has done or will do so, is for a reason she feels comfortable with or I at least, hope so.

And that would have to be good enough for me. I may not like it, I may not like it at all, and there may be repercussions, but it will be her choice, and with it, her honesty.
And if she ever wished to share with me the reasons for those choices, then that would be more than a bonus.
It would also help me to understand and appreciate her as a person even more. And to reiterate, even if it were not to my liking, I would do my uppermost best to understand and if needed, give my support. That is my promise and a commitment to honour.

If I were to think about it, seriously, I would like to believe that I would consider, honesty and something I cannot explain fully, my faith and trust in her, but yes the biggest I feel, would have to be the emotional side.

The faith and trust is a bit of a strange one, and may seem odd to some, it does to me, yet I feel strangely comforted by it.
Is it, removing any self-doubt she may have about herself (this particular consideration may seem a little odd and strange to others, but it's just a deep feeling I have about Sophia), that she will find her true pathway? one where she will find true happiness and contentment?
Heck knows, maybe a mixture of everything good.

All I do know is, that my faith and trust in her is based on nothing but th hope and goodness that she will take on her path, based on 'the right thing to do'. Not based on *'at the time'*, but for a *'lifetime'*. I can hear myself saying (and smiling slightly) '*Now **that** is deep Alex, really deep, and all very confusing* '.

And secondly;
She wanted me, to teach her to dance

.

From the sedate, dream like Waltz to possibly the more intimate Rumba, it would, honestly, be a total pleasure.
As kitsch as it may sound, It would be like a 'dream come true'.
And I personally feel that it would help serve another and more important purpose, for Sophia.

For her to feel safe, with me, and to build her confidence in achieving something she wants to do. And that would be very much the same for me.
That, as well as simply as enjoying the moment.

We have so much to learn about each other, and feeling safe in each other's company is the correct and only place to start.

Though only having known her a very short while (but is that really correct?) I truly am enjoying my time with Kitten, and I hope she is enjoying that time as well.

Saying that, I have to admit I sometimes become a little worried. Is that the correct word? Intrigued possibly. But whatever the correct word or phrase is I am concerned as to just why I 'need' to be close to her.

Now this may sound silly and I maybe I am not expressing it right, but I sometimes feel 'someone' (not me) is pushing me, nudging me, to remain in her company for as long as possible? Is that crazy?
Maybe I should force myself to 'step back' a bit, ha-ha?
Told you it may sound silly. Maybe it's just because she IS, the girl from the bus, and I have found her again. And I want to be **alive** with every minute that I can get, to spend with her.
And yet, I truly cannot say that this is love. It is far too early to have that strong connection with someone. I care for her yes, but love... no.

So, WHAT the hell is pushing me?

CHAPTER 23
A SENSITIVE RELATIONSHIP

During our many online chats, I recall this one ... it's one that I should have read, understood, and acted upon... and once again, looking back, it's the only time Sophia came close to mentioning what she wanted from the relationship.
Maybe if she had communicated with me more often, I would have been more receptive.

Two days after our first lovemaking.
Sophia started by saying,
"You are a sensitive person, you picked up on my insecurity."

I thought to myself, *'Picked up on her insecurity?*
Had I? What was it? If I did, I never realised it.

She continued with,
"I'm scared where the relationship is going, the 'intensity',
I don't want to go into a full-on relationship. Can we carry on in a more relaxed way?"

I remember that on hearing this, it did take me back a bit.
Is she saying this after only one lovemaking session? Or is she 'letting me down easy', being diplomatic?
Or was Sophia scared of any type of 'emotional' relationship, which I wasn't 'pushing' for anyway, maybe in the future if there was to be one, but not yet.
Was it because she couldn't cope with it? Was she picking up a vibe from me, one that even I am not aware of? Or was it simply, she wants casual sex as and when she wanted it? And her idea of casual sex was more in the way of *'Wham-Bam-Thank you, Ma'am'*. A sort of *'friends with benefits'*, a new buzz phrase going around and in reality, a friendship created for one thing only, and that is not a friendship in any form. It's just a cheap, ugly phrase.
But yes, I have had a (failed) 'quickie' in the past, and yes, it felt good at the time, but surely, something like that can never compare with a full-on session with intermissions.

And since, I have never been or would like to be deemed, what the famous Mae West called one of her lovers, *'a two-pump chump'*.

Still a little confused about this turn of events I replied,

"Please do not feel ashamed of what happened the other day. I certainly am not, but I have to abide by your words".

I continued.

"So the massage is off then, lol. I will be totally honest, I have never treated 'sex' in a casual way. There is nothing 'primitive cave man' about me. Both people need to enjoy the experience of being together."

I couldn't make love to a woman, then 'pass it off' the next minute, like 'recreational sex'. Maybe if I had more indiscretions or flirtations in the years gone by, I would not be thinking like this, but there hasn't, and so here I am, as I am.

Kitten replied, possibly nervously due to my reply

"Ha-ha. For the time being. Lol."

I continued,

"I enjoy your company, just being with you. full stop."

"'I don't feel ashamed Alex," replied Kitten reiterating, . *'I just need to slow down. I hope this is ok with you?"*

So it was Kitten who needed to slow down, it was she, who felt was becoming too involved?

We desperately need to talk about this, but for the moment I could do nothing but agree, and told her:

"I abide by what you say... and whilst you are honest with me I will totally respect you for that."

Kitten sent a smiling 'gif' (Graphics Interchange Format) picture

I replied

"'So... is it a case of... Hello Ms Lawrence... Hello Mr Milnz, fancy meeting you here... lol."

Her reply went something like,
"*That's the other extreme, definitely no.*"

I quipped in again. As I was becoming a little miffed and puzzled at these half-answers, answers with 'no substance', but at the same time, wanted to make light of it.
"*Bit of a quandary now, a real game-changer.' 'You want the man to make the first move, yet he will not be allowed to.' 'He wants to take you to dinner (just dinner) or a meal, but he will have no way of knowing if you would take that the wrong way, and you still want the man to make the first move if he is interested because you are 'an old-fashioned girl. I give up.*"

[silence]... Kitten went quiet - totally

Oh well, here goes nothing I thought to myself, and said...
"*Oh bollocks, do you fancy going out for dinner one night?*"

Sophia replied (but saying nothing),
"*That would be nice, Alexander. Can I let you know?*"

Wow, she just called me by my Sunday name.
This is the first time she has done this.
It didn't seem in an affectionate way either, more of a cautious deep-thinking way?
Whichever way, I should take it as a 'see the hand' moment?
I told her that she was "*in the chair.*"

It seems to me that she may be petrified of becoming too involved? Because I was a married man? I could understand that, but it didn't do me any favours all the same. I care for her, yes. But that's it.

In Kitten's company, I found that she made me so relaxed and secure I could completely open up to her, totally let my guard down (and it's always been like that when I am with her, it's almost perplexing) but sadly, it was never reciprocated (not even close).

[Maybe that led to the later misunderstandings].

I did wonder however, when she was married to Eric, if she became the 'dutiful, subservient Wife' and all that entails.
I could not see it personally, I have to say. And that idea would be totally abhorrent to me anyway.

I recall one of the comments Sophia made the following day. She 'sounded' irritated.
She informed me, yet again,
   "You are very intense in your attitude toward our relationship."

I thought to myself. *'Oh no, here we go again'*
My reply was short, but to the point.
   "Intense, quite possible, because I take a concerned interest. Taking an interest is like an Alien life form today; shallow I am not.' 'Far too many people today are too shallow to bother about other people's feelings. Being concerned to them is, like integrity, totally not done, an Alien life-form."

Sophia never replied to that. It's often confusing when she does that as I'm not a mind reader. But she was thinking – deeply.

The following day, there was 'some issue' regarding our FB (Facebook) friendship. It was off and on, continuous.

One minute we were 'friends', then the next, we were not.

This went on for most of the day.
I made light of it when I finally managed to talk to her when our friendship was *'on'*, but I wondered if Sophia was becoming a little worried that our time together, our relationship, is becoming more than she can cope with? What she bargained for... either too quickly or too much.
Then, in the early evening, Sophia sent me an almost bittersweet message, but I needed to go with it. Take it in.
She said,
   "I very much want us to be together again, Alexander, just take it more slowly."

There was that 'Alexander' once again.

I really should have taken more notice the first time. But, was there seemed something else behind that message, something deeper.
Perplexing.
Was it a cry for help, she wanted time to come to terms as to what was happening?

What had happened was undoubtedly more than 'one-sided'. And that's maybe why the friendship became 'off and on'. She may possibly be battling with herself as to which way to go forward.
And I, seriously, should have listened more intently.
And that little voice in my head telling me to keep her close, what the Hell was that about?

[We all know of the old phrase about hindsight, well, that would have been so very helpful at this moment. But that's always the case, isn't it just?]

CHAPTER 24
PIZZA, COFFEE, and A 'HAIR DAY'

A couple of days later, and everything was back to 'normal'.
I messaged Kitten around 9.30 am
   "Kitten... Please remember... a drink...Lunch... Dinner... Supper... even breakfast as a 'date'.. can mean just that.' ' No 'lust in the dust', just good company and the joy of being with someone you simply enjoy being with... and if you have only just opened your eyes (to view this)... you are missing a beautiful morning".

An hour later she replied,
   "Yes, you are psychic. Just opened my eyes. In the middle of speaking to you when Angela phoned..... !!!!!'
   'Yes, it is a lovely day. Hope you had a nice sleep. Do you fancy a glass of wine again at Ayia. You could come here again about 1pm if that suits you?"

That is nice, to be asked if I fancied a drink, she had listened to me. It's to be a date. We are finding our feet, so to speak. I like it.
I replied, though trying to control myself,
   "1-1.15pm? Ayia... fine".
[But really I was thinking *'oh for Christ's sake,...Yesss!!'*.]

Sophia just replied,
   "Lovely.".

I told her that I was,
   "Driving to Carlton then straight down to Ayia".

Sophia then said something like,
   "No, come to my house, park behind me. We'll walk across."

I replied with something really daft,
   "OK...wear a pink carnation and high heels so I will recognise you."
She replied... *"It's a date."*

Yes it was… a real date, and one I was going to enjoy as such.

I parked up behind Sophia's car, and it was, again, a glorious day, and with the house lit up in sunshine, felt as inviting as ever.

Sophia answered the door. And as I entered, and with the door only just starting to close behind me, she gave me the warmest, softest, most inviting, passionate kiss ever.

As the Lord is my witness, I just melted. I cannot describe it in any other way. It was that very first, meaningful kiss at Tosca's all over again.

My God, this was supposed to be a date.

How could this woman ever say she wanted to go 'slowly' when she greets a guy with a kiss like that.

Almost immediately, well, after a couple of extended false starts…ha-ha, we were ready to venture into the outside world.

We walked outside into the warmth and brightness of the sunshine...

And once again, 'hand in hand'. If this sounds 'mushy', I don't care, but I would take this girl's, this woman's, hand anytime, anywhere and never, ever feel embarrassed. Why should I be?

We walked around to Ayia, only to find it closed. It was being renovated and to be re-opened in a few weeks, with a new name – The Jailhouse.

And so we walked across the road to the D'Jango.

I suspected Sophia may have been here before as she was extolling its virtues as we were walking up to it.

We made our way to the dining area. It has an almost rustic feel to it, and it also had a retractable roof for when the good weather allowed, giving it a whole new atmosphere.

I took an instant liking to the place.

We checked out the menu and ordered a simple Pizza for the both of us and some wine (I think) from the bar, quick and simple.

Simple? No way was that Pizza 'simple', it was fantastic... a total WOW - really. I'm a 'foodie' and I love good food.

And the woman sat facing me? well, she just made being there totally complete. She really did.

After we had finished, Sophia suggested going back to her place for a coffee.

We sat in the back garden in glorious sunshine, drinking coffee and chatting. Idyllic. All this and the beautiful company, what more could a person ask for. This is what a real date should be like.

Sophia was asking all the questions, and again, she wanted to know '*how we first met*', because, as she said, she still couldn't remember.

Was she just passing pleasantries or did she really want to remember. Or, possibly, was she 'testing' me, to see if this telling of the story was the same as the previous time. It was. How could it not be?

She asked me about what work I did before retiring, and before that. Not many questions, but questions someone asks to make their guest feel more relaxed. Something I felt she was quite used to doing when she was married, and helping her late husband with his business or socially.

Once again, was she genuinely interested? Were those words just pleasantries? or was she just cautious? More to the point, am I being too inquisitive? Defensive even, needing to know her reasoning behind any question she puts to me.

Even though Sophia disarms me whilst in her presence, apprehension is not far behind. I cannot remember the last time when someone took an interest in 'me'. I feel need to lower my shield, my inner shield even more, maybe even completely – it didn't do any harm last time, though that was almost fifty years ago, people change.

And even though I'm still trying to get to know her, I truly am, she appears reluctant to talk about herself.

But I'm so pleased, especially on this occasion, she does seem to be becoming more relaxed in my company and that is so wonderful to see and feel. And maybe because of this she opened up a little more and I did learn that she had a sister who died at an early age. Her mother used to sing in the local venues in Carstairs and Dunston, I may have even seen her (seriously).

She only mentioned her father, fleetingly.

Also, she or rather Eric, had a dog, a Retriever or Labrador. But (she never gave a reason, though I have an idea) she took the dog to an animal home/sanctuary somewhere north of Hamilton after Eric passed away. She said she had not been to see it since.

A short while later, I don't know just how it came about, but as I washed the coffee cups, I turned around, and Kitten was just stood there, looking at me, with that same half-smile I am getting so used to, on her face.
She then grabbed my hand and led me, once again, up the stairs.
And for the next three hours we made love, explored each other's bodies, kissed, sweet-talked and (not really a surprise as the pleasures were recalled from less than a week ago) I was now fully erect all the time, *'additives not included'*. I was relieved that I was able to make up for anything found wanting the first time we made love.
Time overtook us again, and I had to make my way home, leaving Sophia to 'sort out a Chinese meal for late dinner.'

But that dinner was sadly, and very abruptly 'put on hold' as Angela's Mum, Niamh, was rushed to hospital with a coronary issue that night, and causing more than a fright.
Thankfully, Niamh (whom like a number of Kittens family or friends I have never had the pleasure of meeting) within a short while made a full recovery, Bless her.

But once again, I find myself perplexed with Sophia.
One minute she was serious about taking it slowly, which I was prepared to go along and calm the 'male urge'. And then we end up, for three hours, like the World was coming to an end.
Hmmmmm.. I feel a *'could'* coming on;

Could this be what she is afraid of? That every time we see each other, even glance at each other, we need to 'smother each other' in kisses and constantly make love.

Could it possibly be that she has an almost insatiable appetite for sex? for making love? She wanted to feel loved, to feel wanted, but just for that period when she was making love?
Could THIS have been the 'insecurity' she was trying to refer to after our first lovemaking session. Did looking after her late husband affect her more than what she has told me.

I just don't know what to think. If only she would communicate and open up to me more.

Our repartee and online retort game was in full flow again early the following evening, I recall. Sophia had been running around all day due to Niamh being in the hospital.

(S) *"I'm shattered, in PJ's hair tied back. Lay on the bed, watching the tv. Need to rest."*

(A) *"Do you fancy cheese on toast? I'll be around in 15."*

(S) *"Don't think I'll get much rest, though."*

(A) *"Promise I'll be a good boy."*

(S) *"Can't say the same about me."*

(A) *"What's on TV?"*

(S) *"The news and current affairs."*

(A) *"Oh, so we are on the news then."*

(S) *"HA HA HA FIVVVER yes, yes, yes."*

(A) *"Worth it."*

(A) *"Question.."*

(S) *"Well?"*

(A) *"When I mentioned the Diggles Youth Club yesterday when we were sat outside.. your response was.... ???"*

(S) *"I went there. Down stairs at side of church. And ..?"*

(A) *"Correct... and that, my dear lovely Kitten.. was THE club mentioned when we first met.. on the bus you asked me if I was a DJ at Diggles."*

(S) *"You're memory is so much better than mine!!!"*

(A) *"As soon as you mentioned it yesterday afternoon, no one could ever be unsure or deny that YOU were the same girl. Just the year now.. either 1968 or 1969.. "*

(S) *"Well I'll have to bow to your better memory on that.
I had in mind earlier, 67 or 68 but you could be right."*

Well, Sophia remembers just **when** she went to Diggles. Though I too went there, socially in 1967, as it wasn't until sometime, possibly early in 1968 that I started to DJ there, and then later by the September of the same year, became the joint 'leader' and helped run the place two nights a week, though the first of the two nights was for setting up of the place, tables, stock etc. for the following night's disco.

Is 'that' all she remembers, the dates? Going off that, I must not have made any lasting impression on her.. ha-ha.

But through her initial question on the bus, she DID remember seeing me at least. And that's a plus or starting point I suppose.

But I seriously now, have to take her word that she really cannot remember anything else. Oh well.

And something else 'popped' up during our online chat.

Another extraordinary coincidence or just proving this is indeed a very small World. And believe me, there were so many 'little things' cropping up. It was unbelievable, maybe a little spooky.

I'm not sure if it was through a photo Sophia put up or something she mentioned, but it appeared that her hairdresser was called Tony Abbott..., and Tony knew (Professionally or other) a person I had known maybe ten years, Anton Lawrence, another hairdresser, and also a make-up professional.

The remarkable thing about this is, Anton, who is Indonesian, lived in Perth, not Perth Scotland, but Perth Australia. Add that, to the growing list of coincidences.

I seriously enjoy being in Sophia's company. And as corny as it may sound, It was like being on the bus again. But more so.

There is 'something' about her I just cannot put my finger on though.

It's more than just enjoying her company …or the intimacy.

How can I explain it? I can but try.

I'm not in love with her, but it's as if I have known her, and loved her all my life. I'm being serious. Impossible yes, but it feels so real.

It's as if I know her, but at the same time, know absolutely nothing about her at all. I told you that it was impossible to explain.

It's crazy I know. It's also a little unnerving... but I find I am compelled to carry on, accepting this strange situation and feeling. Possibly and hopefully by doing so, allow the mystery to unravel itself over time, given that we will have .. time.
But I find I am asking myself, just *why* is it so important that I need to know?

But in the meantime, I am going to enjoy every blessed minute I have with Kitten, however long that may or may not be.
Getting to know her better, to try and make her feel more comfortable and safer when I am with her, as she is doing so with me. And if that means taking it slower, backing off, though I would in truth be afraid of losing her in doing so, then so be it.

As I have mentioned before, I have a faith and trust in her, and I cannot fully understand just what it is. Is it the removal of any of the self-doubt or the other thoughts mentioned previously? whatever it is it's a very strange feeling, but, whether the answer reveals itself or not during this time, then I will face the challenge, if there is one to face that is..

The following day I received this month's PSA results – no change, that's good. I didn't like that jump last month though. It unnerved me more than just a little

CHAPTER 25
CHINESE TIGERS

It was around this time that Kitten asked me about this whole Asian Birth sign thing, which I had talked about lightly, and in passing. And if I followed it closely, did I truly believe in it.

There are indeed many aspects of Chinese Astrology (Sheng Xiao or Shu Xiang) which perplexed Western people. They couldn't follow it. Westerners wanted something less complicated to read and follow. And so, came about the much-sanitised Western horoscopes.

I am by no means an authority, just an interested onlooker. I have gone through a very basic version of mine, with Kitten, as the full version contains many other aspects, including the actual hour of birth, each of which will 'tweak' the life chart.
To be done correctly, the life chart should be completed just after the birth of the child. Their 'road is then mapped out in full.
I can honestly say the one I had done (much later in life) is, indeed closer, a lot closer to the real me, in both the good and the bad, than any Western Star Sign Horoscope.

But, let it be known that even though we are guided, a Tiger (or any other sign) can always refuse to go down the path mapped out for them, they can choose their own path in life, for they are Master of their destiny. They will, however, know if they have chosen a different and not so 'honourable' path through deep inner feelings, but for many selfish reasons, they will carry on that path.

My answer to Kitten was relatively short compared to my existing knowledge (which is by no means complete).
The grouping, our grouping, would be at times, competitive; there would be flashes of irritation simply because we would be so much alike.
These hostilities are non-violent, often very short-lived, and usually borne out because they are so much alike and not through malice. Though, saying that, they can be very cutting when they

feel the need. But, it is often regretted almost immediately after the occasion.
They can often be too quiet or too talkative. It requires work to make this relationship work, but if both partners are willing, the relationship would become the most formidable within the whole of the Chinese Astrological Zodiac. That, and any other.

I did not want to bore her with a more detailed monologue as laid out below.

When two Scorpio-Tigers meet, they very often make intense lovers, wanting emotional involvement more than anything from a relationship. They certainly get it from each other, but Scorpio, perhaps more than most Western signs, needs a partner to complement, and with enough differences to keep things interesting. If they take time to appreciate each other, there is considerable mutual respect and common goals in this relationship.

A Scorpio-Tiger man is a passionate person with a very clever and inspective mind. This holds true in everything he does, especially in love. And even more so when he finds his true love and he opens out in the most extraordinary way.
He can handle pretty much any situation on his own and is tolerable of most.
He is a strong individual, full of mystery, who is constantly looking for a power to share and is quite loyal to his loved ones. He is very good at hiding the true emotions he holds so deep.
He is intense, suspicious and quite a jealous creature in any relationship. But at the same time he is the best man a woman can ever have with humble words, tender touch and burning passion.

A Scorpio-Tiger woman is alluring, mysterious and magnetically beautiful. A subtle stare, fascinating smile or gesture tells a lot about her mystery. Her seduction precedes her and surfaces if one knows what to look for. She is proud and stands tall in what she believes in. A Scorpio-Tiger woman does not show an abundance of emotions, especially in public. But like her counterpart, when she finds her true love she opens out and shows her innermost

feelings. What she portrays herself to be, does not always hold true to what she actually feels deep down.
The female allows dominance in her lover if it is present, at least in the beginning of the relationship, and knows how to manipulate things to go her way.

The loyalty, honesty and passion they both share for many things, including each other, far outweigh the hostilities sometimes shown. Even though they can share the most profound understanding known to the entire zodiac, they can also get too dark together and slowly sink into their pool of unresolved emotions. Their emotional understanding is worth cherishing only if they are both open to their feelings and accept their own inner needs.

It is a known fact that true Tigers can be highly spiced up (sexually charged), and their lovemaking can be long and vigorous affairs.
Also, by their very nature, Tigers are protective of their loved ones, but they can also be the most flirtatious and promiscuous. It is a known fact that the female is well experienced in this 'art', but she often only does this to experiment, gain experience, enjoy the 'hunting', to feel free, and sometimes to tease her existing mate.

But, they can also tire of a 'tedious' married life, and to show a strange kind of 'command', they love the extra attention they often seek and receive from one or sometimes, more than one new male or even female acquaintances.

This attention can take many forms, and are sometimes of a sexual nature. This is where her existing mate has to show a deep understand and allow her the flirtations, for that's what they are, flirtations. Her mate can show his understanding by even joining in or showing a visual appreciation. And she will show her appreciation to him in such a way, he knows he is truly the one she loves and he is hers until the end of time.

To create a balance, in the 'Human World', the male Tigers are not that coy when it comes to doing the same, but because the

Female Tiger can be and often is, the 'stronger' of the two, he is often more cautious in any flirtations he may have.
Though this may be something the female Tiger may wish to contribute to, by joining in. Creating another, different type of pleasure
    It's a formidable relationship that requires a lot of understanding and a willingness to bend like the willow. It can and does work through true acceptance of each other.
They often need to lead separate lives and give each other enough room to allow them to breathe.

Because of the uniqueness, which is based on trust and a deep understanding, the relationship should never be treated disrespectfully by either partner.
This is the one thing that can hinder such a beautiful relationship; in fact, ruin it all, if some serious compromise and forgiveness is not exercised on both sides of the spectrum. However, anything that causes an argument between them has to be appeased, quickly and sufficiently or severe damage could be done and this would really be a shame given the beauty that can be had with a relationship such as this.

    Also, because of their uniqueness, they are acutely aware of their surroundings and try to create calmness, in which they often become quiet for long periods.
They are deep thinkers of all matters.
Even in public, where they often come across to others as quiet and un-assuming, can and will, if they have found their true love, openly show their love in subtle, but obvious ways, a sudden kiss on the lips, sometimes short, sometimes a little longer but always full of warmth and passion, a quick kiss on the neck, the clasp like holding of hands, looking deep into each other's eyes whilst not saying anything, even in company.
Yes, when they have met their true love they can and often do 'wear their hearts on their sleeves'. But let anyone be 'inquisitive', and they put up their shields and display their armour for this is 'their' love and it is very, very personal.

It is a fact known to many of the Academics and Sage's (who wrote the above), that this pairing not only is the most formidable of any groupings within either the Chinese or Western Zodiac, it is also the most respected, most admired - and yet, most private.

The detail mentioned above is not to be taken as literal for every Scorpio-Tiger dual relationship. But does any of the above mirror what Kitten and I feel, and interact with other? We would need a great deal more time in each other's company to form any statement of that honesty. Given time, I would like to believe we will be able to compare and maybe even add to the above. I know already as to my make-up, as does Kitten know hers, but together, as a team? I am looking forward to learning even more, but also remembering that there is no guarantee as to how long we will be together, or even see each other come to that.

As most couples know and accept, any true, meaningful relationship, as I have mentioned previously, has to be 'worked on' – together. It cannot be rushed. Both parties must learn patience, and the knowledge and wisdom of such will be of great asset to both and lead to a greater fulfilment.

There are a number of even more detailed books on the Scorpio, Tiger and Scorpio-Tiger dual relationships to be found in bookshops and online. If you are not of a Scorpio, or Tiger, again you will also find books for your education and possibly intimate knowledge, more suited to your birth sign. Read carefully and wisely.

CHAPTER 26
LA DOLCE VITA, BREAKFAST AND A&E

Our next outing was to La Dolce Vita on the 17th, less than ten minutes' walk away.

I had passed this place before and it had the same externals (and name) as a restaurant I had been to in Shellfield on the coast, a couple of years before with some friends.

Hopefully, it was the same company group. The service was so-so, but the food, now that was delicious.

This time, the company will make it even better, and of that, I seriously have no doubts.

And this was to be very special occasion for the both of us.

Kitten has asked me to stay with her, at her house, that night.
I have never been in a situation like this before. Because I am married (and there is no getting away from that).
What is Sophia saying or trying to say to me?
I hope I don't mess up and say something I can't really uphold. I truly like her, I really do.
I want to get to know her even more but I cannot give her any false hopes. But who am I kidding, maybe she just feels it's a simple natural progression to actually sleep together, because it's *'what you do, isn't it'* – no deep emotional thing. Maybe that's it.

Kitten mentioned the day previous that she had invited Angela *'for the first bit only'* (I chuckled when she said that) as she was feeling down, possibly due to her Mum's accident and her own disappointing love life.

I certainly had no objection. How could I? She was Kitten's best friend and, no doubt, 'confidante', and besides, I would enjoy both seeing and talking to her again.

Angela always appeared confident (though like us all, it is sometimes a mask), giving the appearance of being a little 'pushy' at times.

But she seems to be single-minded, has her own thoughts, and she likes to try and 'wind me up', and no doubt gets (inwardly) annoyed when she realises she has maybe, met her match.
And smiles (inwardly again) when she feels she has 'got me'.
Yes, I do enjoy her company.

I arrived at Kittens, along with a change of clothes, toiletries, and some massaging oil, as requested by the 'wicked lady of the house'
It was 'decided' by both of us, that we needed to freshen up – in the shower. And so, we removed our clothes in the bedroom, made our way to the shower on the other side of the house totally naked, without a care in the world... and why not I ask.

We showered together (saves water and heating, so I'm told ha-ha), washed and refreshed each other's bodies.
The fragrant 'Evelyn Rose' I brought with me, washed over our skin with nothing left untouched.
If you have never experienced showering together, you have missed out on one of the most glorious, intimate events in the whole World... beautifully natural.

And when it came to drying each other, I asked her to play a game of soft, gentle drying only... no kissing, no caressing, and no touching of skin to skin. Just drying each other's body.
This would indeed take a LOT of self-control... I hope we fail... ha-ha.
I dried every part of Sophia's body... and I proved to be a good 'boy scout', and then the 'girl guide' went for the challenge, as she proceeded to dry me.
She was 'behaving' until it came to below the waistline. And temptation got the better of her. She gently kissed the tip of my man-hood, just the once. But it was so sensual and so loving.
I just looked down and said, straight-faced,
   "You have just blown a fiver"

I stifled a chuckle. And Kitten just looked up at me and smiled.
We walked back to the bedroom actually holding hands, and proceeded to get ready for the evening and Angela's arrival.
She had dressed, and starting to brush her hair when I took a photograph of her and then kissed her gently on the lips. And that half smile came back again.

When Angela arrived, she 'beamed' at us both, knowingly – have I missed something?
Whilst Sophia was in either the kitchen or the dining room, Angela and I were chatting in the front room.
I said, "*I love those two houses across the road*" (pointing to them)

To which Angela replied,
"*I know the couple that live there. He comes home only at weekends and she is in a relationship with another woman. And he knows.*"

Now, was Angela once again gauging my reaction?
I instantly replied,
"*'That's good. Each knows where they stand through compromise and they accept it.*"

"*They may even do a threesome*" chirped in Angela (again was she gauging my response, was she probing?).

"*Possibly, that's totally up to them.*" I replied, somewhat confused as to how or why the subject ever came up.

Kitten then came back into the room, and all three of us walked across the road to La Dolce Vita. This time, only Kitten and I, were holding hands.

I gathered both Angela and Kitten have been here before, as they said '*Hi*' to a small number of people already there, including the Concierge and the Manager.
We had a couple of drinks at the bar, then time for food.
I asked Kitten to sit next to Angela rather than me, as again, I did not like the idea of Angela playing 'Gooseberry'. Besides, I had no idea what Kitten, or I, for that matter, would have got up to 'under the table'.

Because the general rump steak fayre had run out, only the slightly more expensive Aberdeen Angus Rump steak was left (and as luck would have it, only three portions remained).

Angela tackled the Manager for a 'deal', who in turn suggested Angela tackle the Head Chef for the last steaks available.

A deal was struck on the last three steaks... Good lord, Angela is a person after my own heart, because it's certainly something I would have done or cheekily tried... and more so if I were a regular.

The Aberdeen rump steak, with each cut being individually cooked to perfection. And along with the side and trimmings, the meal was excellent,
Once finished, and after chatting, both Kitten and I were each 'fighting over who will 'card' the bill.
But Angela 'put her foot down' and said the bill would be split three-ways equally.
WOW, going Dutch big style. Both Kitten and I looked at each other and knew we wouldn't win, so we agreed.

I had managed to take a photograph at Kittens and so I took a few more at the La Dolca Vita to add to the collection. I later passed them on to both Kitten and Angela,

Angela appeared a little 'giddy' as we stepped out into the fresh air but insisted
"I can take myself home, thank you".

Angela seemed to stumble, and I became concerned, but she insisted,
"I'm 'perfectly fine".

Kitten squeezed my hand as if to say *'thank you for being concerned over Angela'*.

We parted company and made our way back to Kittens.
As soon as Kitten opened the front door, all concern for Angela went 'out of the window'.
As the door shut behind us, Kitten kissed me and at the same time was kicking off her shoes and having done so, took my hand and was leading me up the stairs.

Once again, Kitten's soft body smell wafted over me as we made love for the next four hours, being almost 3 am when we finally got to sleep.
And 'the dream' continued, for another two hours when we fully awoke, about 8 am.
And then, a very special moment happened.

Kitten became lovingly intimate. I lifted my head from the pillow and witnessed a most beautiful scene.

I stroked her hair, kissed her lips, and we made love again.
This beautiful woman, whether she realised it or not, was 'pressing all the right buttons' and I found myself in a position of wanting to be near her, be with her, more and more.
And it wasn't solely down to the sex.
Kitten said previously she needed to slow down, maybe I do as well.

We washed, and whilst I was getting dressed, Kitten, in her dressing gown, went downstairs and started to make a breakfast of Baby Tomatoes on the vine, bacon, avocado and toast.

Now this will sound positively 'Mills and Boon'ish and maybe even embarrassing to some.
But as the Lord is my witness, I had a lump in my throat when I saw what she had made and not forgetting that she had told me she is 'not a kitchen person'.
I sat at the table and just blurted out
"It's been so long since a woman made breakfast - just for me."

I must have sounded 'unstable' or a wimp at the very least. Kitten just stood there – emotionless. Was she embarrassed by what I said?

I have thought about this. Was it the house? Was it Sophia? Was it the lovemaking that made every minute of every hour spent with Sophia so calming?

Whether I am right or wrong to do so, whether it may seem to some that I am somehow cheapening or making light of our relationship I don't know, but to create a list has its own reward and allows me to appreciate my time with Kitten even more.
If the shoe was on the other foot, Sophia's answers or list may be completely different, so here goes;

    Kitten, because she is so disarming and the only person I have indeed opened up to without caution or fear. It's as if I had known her all my life

    On equal par, The house, ever since I saw it and walked across the threshold, I had the identical feeling of security, contentment I had with the cottage I had bought in Hawksmere.

    Finally, Lovemaking. It appears we both enjoy our lovemaking immensely, and yet I feel we may be almost as content, just knowing that we are there, by each other's side, even metaphorically.

Now ***that*** would be something so very special on its own.
Would.. could, that ever happen? on a regular basis? I would like to think so.
Something to discuss maybe, possibly in a few months' time?

My thoughts: I am content in the knowledge of being able to make love to Kitten, because I feel it's something that we both want to enjoy as it seems to bring us closer together.
There is no way on Gods Earth I ever want her to feel 'obligated' in that she has to make love because it is what is expected of her.
I hope she would be honest with me when she feels she does not want to make love, to tell me. Allow me to be understanding.
When I make love to her I want to show her what she means to me, that I want to try and make her happy, to feel wanted for who she is, to feel and be loved.
I hope I do most of those when I am with her, and not just whilst making love. I certainly try.
But knowing that being together too often, can either bond us together or it can drive us apart. The line can be very fine indeed.
I drove home, relaxed... and contented.

A few hours later – CALAMITIES, Angela was in A&E.
What is it with this family and Hospitals?
First the mother, now the daughter.

When Kitten contacted me and told me, I was both annoyed and concerned.
Annoyed because I could have prevented it.
Last night, when she got home and whilst 'dancing in the kitchen', she slipped and badly twisted her knee.
I mentioned to Kitten,
"If only we had walked Angela home last night".

Kitten replied that Angela
"Would still have been dancing."

But I replied,
"Maybe, but the timing would have been different and the accident may not have happened."

"'Obviously', Kitten replied, *'That's real life."*

When Angela was discharged, Kitten totally surprised me, maybe because I did not know her well enough, I don't know... but it was indeed something I did not quite expect.
Kitten became an 'instant nurse'. And under instruction from Angela (Kitten, by her admission, is a non-kitchen person), she created some lunch and dinner the following day.
Now to some people, that would seem an almost 'non-event', maybe I am too sensitive, but I saw and indeed felt something quite different.

I am not putting her on a pedestal or even putting her up for a 'Super Person of the Year' award, but I'm proud of her.
Proud, because she tackled something she laid claim to being *'no good at'*... and even more proud (if there can be such a thing, certainly 'pleased'), because she succeeded.
She was willing to try something new, a new adventure for her.
And then I wonder if I am also a 'new adventure'? I hope so and more.

It did cross my mind as to when she was caring for her late husband, that would obviously include his feeding would it not?

Because I have no knowledge as to just how incapable he was, I wonder how that was managed, as she is not a kitchen person? Maybe they went out a lot or he was the cook, and a capable one.

One thing is for certain, though some may sarcastically say it was for materialistic reasons, I would say that to stay and look after her Husband like she did must have taken a special kind of love, one that had matured over the years that they were married.
And it will take a long time for that love to fade, and so for her to be true and honest with any future partner about the love she has for them. And, let's be honest that could very well would include me.

And I can do nothing but accept that, and lean with it, if ever such a time came. For *that* would be Kismet.

And of course, if she would ever allow me that time.

CHAPTER 27
A FEW DEEP THOUGHTS

One thing (of many) has happened since I first came into contact with Kitten again. I have remarked on it in passing before

For many years prior, my confidence in myself had steadily declined to the point of almost being destroyed, leaving me feeling worthless.
This is mainly, but not entirely due, to the actions of my Wife and my family in general.
This has taken many forms, and many times I have said to myself,
'Why me, have I got that particular look whereas people can abuse me, ridicule my actions, my interests, almost at will, and make me feel totally and absolutely worthless?'.

When this has happened, I have had to, from somewhere, seek a light, something to grasp at or on to, to give me enough strength to be able to get back up and carry on as before, but also knowing that the next 'kicking', the next 'put down' can come at any time.
I fought back all the same, gaining a little more confidence within myself, but still a long way to go to get back to my prior self.

But of recent, for quite a few months actually, I have felt a deeper, more profound type of confidence growing very, very slowly within me, mentally, it's been like a *'Gift' given.*
And recently, what new confidence I have gained, seems to have been boosted even more with the seeing of Kitten again.
There is no doubting she has increased my self-worth, and I bless her so much for that.
But as I said, this more profound confidence is different. I truly cannot explain it in words. Nor can I give its origin.

But what, if anything, is the connection with Sophia?
Or am I missing something completely?
It can't be that I am physically close to her because my confidence was growing a long time before we even met. It's truly perplexing.

I do enjoy being with her, yes, even though it's frustrating sometimes, trying to get a conversation out of her, to tell me about herself.
I'm not a Joseph Dunninger or something out of 'Star Wars', I am not a mind reader
She has her reasons I suppose, but it's so hard for me to make out where she is coming from and what she truly wants, her desires, her quirk's, her dislikes. I know it take time but it would be so much easier with the joy and beauty of conversation.

Kitten has a quite remarkable presence, one that would make her stand out in a room full of other women. She has an Aura surrounding her. A glow that attracts you to her, like a Moth to bright light. And it's far more than her actual physical beauty. Something deeper, more intense. An inner beauty?
Maybe it's that what I saw all those years ago, on the bus.

And as for her physical beauty, I am fully aware she has had some 'cosmetic work' done on herself, her face and maybe other areas, but it's certainly not been overdone. She doesn't appear to wear a great deal of creams and make-up and I may be lucky one day, to see her without any on at all. Seriously, I would look forward to that day.
If the truth is known, I wouldn't mind having some 'work' done on myself. But that is her choice, and she has her reasons for doing so.
Her eyes are my main focus. It is true what they say about eyes telling a story.
But there are the attributes, the ones that can never be surgically changed. And those seem to shine through like a blinding light.

The lower portion of both her legs are heavily marked, which she says was from her regular sunbathing sessions and walking around wearing non-full-length attire when going on holiday three or four times a year.
Angrily, I know there are far too many men who would be put off wanting even a short-term relationship or even a one-night party date because of such, and if she didn't wear trousers or a long dress.

Men can be as vain as anyone and would not want others to think that the woman on their arm is *'not perfect'*, for this would cramp their image and lessen their personal, present or future street credibility.

I will be completely honest. When I first saw her legs, I thought to myself, *'Christ, those must be painful at times and maybe sometimes embarrassing for her as well, but if she fine with them, then it's certainly fine with me'*. And I never gave them a second thought.

Though I did talk to her about them, in truth to show her I am not repulsed in any way, and I did so in a general way. Whether she believed me, I do not know, but it was the truth.

Given the opportunity, I would have asked if she ever needed to bathe them and soothe them, I would have no qualms in doing so, and lovingly.

I had even kissed and caressed them during our most intimate moments together, moments not even for this book. And I didn't need to think twice about doing so. I was doing what came naturally, kissing and caressing her legs.

In dancing as in life ... I have often used the following phrase,

'Any imperfections are perfection in disguise.'

And this is how I feel about any physical aspect of Kitten. I know of the imperfections, and yet, what I only ever really see is... Kitten, as a whole person. Yes, she is special and in so many ways..

All this, and 'not' be in love with Kitten? Simply... yes.

It's not because I am married, as marriage does not stop extramarital feelings entirely.

Feelings of love are sometimes, sadly, one-sided affairs and often risk-creating an end to a promising friendship or relationship, which can be crushed quite easily, if one's love is declared too soon or even not at all.

This affection I have for her, seems quite different.

And then, I sometimes feel I could not afford to live in her World, and by that, I don't fully mean financially. Let me try to explain.

Yes, there would be times I could not afford to do certain things because of financial restraints, but I would not, in all honesty, stop Sophia from doing what she may be already accustomed to, because of it. She would have to make those decisions herself.
I'm also talking…. emotionally.
Because I have no doubt there would be times when Kitten may be away for a few days away with friends, or even at a more formal event. She may meet a person who is carefree, no financial restraints, and obviously 'demanding' of her attention. They flatter her, she possibly becomes overwhelmed and one thing leads to another, and she has a relationship, an affair with them. And I found out.
Of course, this does not happen to all women, or men come to that, if the roles were reversed.
And this is where total trust comes into play. It's hard, very hard. And everyone is an individual.
And because of that, it is the emotional side that I may find it hard to deal with. But to keep the one I love, I would have to come to terms with it, and accept it as a part of life. Many understanding men would feel the same way I am sure.
In such cases, flirtations or indiscretions do happen, and the relationship would indeed be tested for honesty and love.

For one to hold out an open hand, for them to come back and hold on to, would be the greatest proof of faith and silent forgiveness a person could ever offer.
In all honesty, I would want to be able to do that, and I feel that I could, should a time ever arise. But my partner would have to be as completely honest with me as I would be with them.
I ask and tell myself this, because I AM confused, where do 'I' want this relationship to go.

I cannot commit myself to her, yet I feel drawn to her in some inextricable way, and have an almost desperate need not to lose her again. It's not a clingy thing, nor is it loneliness.
But something keeps telling me to keep hold of her, that I need her - but WHY? It's not love, so what am I not seeing.

I will admit, I am nervous, and I say all this because….

I had found out only two days before, by an off-chance remark made by someone, that Kitten was financially 'well covered' (their words) due to her late husband's business and property.
I felt depleted, almost inadequate, 'out of my depth' even.
But my protective caring instincts kicked in.
And in her front room, at the unopened front door and on my way home, we kissed and I told her.

"Look, I have just found out that your late husband has left you secure, financially, not just secure, but very secure.' 'I'm telling you now, and it certainly won't be me, but in the future, there will be Wolves knocking at your door promising you many things.' 'Please, for your own sake and safety, don't be fooled by them, they will use every smarmy trick, and I do mean 'every' trick in the book to get your money. Even if they already have money, they will want more."

Her reply was short,
"I'm a big girl, and I'm aware."

I cautiously acknowledged her reply.

So yes, and even after this, love is still not 'on the table'.

I cannot make any 24/7 commitment to Kitten for the simple reason that I AM married. And I'm sure she wouldn't want that anyway, certainly not at this time.
But that does not stop me from wanting to get to know her more.
To try and become a true friend as well as dare I say it, maybe even a deeper, more lasting affection.
That is the only 'commitment' I could offer her.

And if love were ever to develop between us, then that would be over time, and truly be the 'cherry on the cake'.
That part may never happen of course, but I would still, hopefully be her friend, and a 'real' friend at that.

CHAPTER 28
DINNER WITH (UNEXPECTED) DESSERT

Three days later, Kitten asked me if I would like a *"homemade light dinner?"*

Angela has given her instructions on 'what to do and how to do it'. So how could I refuse? Once again, this woman is trying something 'new'... first breakfast and now this.
This may sound ridiculous, but I am so (quietly) proud of her, it gave me a little lump in the throat.
I like what this Lady is doing, doing not only for me but also for herself.
For all the public displays that may say otherwise, I can be quite emotional where matters like this are concerned.

Though 'another' lump in my throat is also giving me a little gyp, something I have had for a long time, now with a tickly cough. I need to go back to the Doctors as the anti-biotics don't seem to be working.

And so, Kitten prepared a light Dinner of Salmon, with the salmon, topped with pesto, breadcrumbs, parmesan cheese baked in the oven, and served with new baby potatoes.
And for dessert, Devon Ice cream. All created by Kitten, and I had the photographs to prove it.
Kitten with absolutely no makeup, a white, stained cutaway top, black jeans, and she looked bloody fabulous. I got my wish.
Was this relaxed attire and seriously, no makeup, for my attention? Was she waiting for my reaction?
I hope she was pleased, because even if she had just come in from the garden, covered in dirt and no make-up I would still have kissed and hugged her.

[When I (later) gave Kitten a full set of the photographs, she said she really liked the one I took of her looking at me through the kitchen display cabinet door, as she was getting some dinner plates.
And it's that photo that I still carry with me to this day].

We ate at the dining table, and after, as I sat down on the two-seater bamboo conservatory sofa in the dining area, Kitten asked me if I wanted a glass of wine. I said ok, and she drew a bottle from the rack.
And then walked over to me, straddled me, pushing her pelvis into mine, kissed me full on the mouth, sucking on my tongue hard, leaned back and said,
"We are drinking this upstairs... you bring the glasses...I'll be there before you."

Once in the bedroom, I spotted Teegra on the headboard of the king-size bed, and on the left-hand side. I knowingly mentioned,
"That's not the side you sleep on."

Kitten replied,
"That's your side... Alex's side."

"No', I replied, smiling and pointing at Teegra, *"That's 'Kitten', that is your Birth sign and my present to you."*

Kitten just beamed and replied.
"'I love you calling me that [Kitten], *and when you are old and grey, I still want to hear you call me that."*

The cheeky, lovable swine.

But THAT was so special of her to do.
I have no doubt it is something two lovers, in every sense of the word would do so naturally for each other, to make the night 'theirs alone'.
And 'our night' turned out to be a very special night indeed.
For me, it was to become an everlasting, forever, memory.

Looking back, was this to be a 'moment' time for Kitten, was this her *'make your mind up'* time'?

Did we make love? Oh yes, and it just gets better and better, not only my words, but Kitten's as well.

We are finding out more about each other with each occasion.

Then after about an hour or so, something, so beautiful, so totally unexpected, happened.

As she surfaced from under the sheet, with legs half beneath her, she sat upright, looking down at me. The sheet loosely draped over her, partially covering her head and little else, the look in her eyes, the half-smile. It was like modern day Renaissance painting. That is the 'picture' that will stay with me for my lifetime.
It was a look of contentment, of longing, wanting, of inner beauty.

I asked her with a smile, and maybe a little conceitedly of me,
　"What's with THAT look?"

She knew exactly what I was referring to, and her answer,
　"I don't want a part of you... I want all of you, always."

As the Lord is my witness, I did not expect THAT.

Did she really say those words? She certainly did.
Is there any doubt, by anyone on this planet, that what she was referring to was my whole body and my soul, all of me?
Oh Lord, somebody pinch me.
And those words that she spoke, will stay with me forever.

Did she genuinely mean she didn't want to share me with anyone, even Claire? That she wanted me there, by her side, always?
If so, then that said to me that this relationship had gone up to a whole new level.
I never dared to think, to hope she would say something like that.
It totally threw me, but in the most beautiful way you could ever imagine.

Was this something like a commitment?

And don't forget, this is from the Woman who insisted that she wanted to *'take things slower'*

Did I reply, did a word pass my lips? I cannot truly remember.
Most probably not.

I just looked into her eyes and gave her a most loving, and knowing smile.
Did she want me to reply?
To say the same to her.
I couldn't and not because I did not want to.
And that, even then, was ripping into to me.

This was so very real, it was really happening, and I never wanted to be with anyone so much, as at that moment.
And I am not meaning the sexual enjoyment side of things.
As the Lord is my witness, I cannot express the feeling into words. It's so bloody annoying.

And yet, I was being torn apart.
I cannot commit anything to her.
Not even loving her. Yes, both may come in time, but at that moment, I wanted so much to say something to her and not a *'you said something nice and so I will say something nice to you in return'* reciprocal.
But something she may have really wanted to hear, and just as importantly, something I wanted to say, I needed to hear those words from myself.
But nothing came forth, I was struck dumb and I couldn't utter a word.
Was I scared to commit myself to a Woman I had deep, caring feelings for? I could not tell her I loved her because that could be a lie.

I could not even tell her that I too, *'didn't want a part of her, I wanted all of her, always'*.
And yet that part, was so very true.

Surely if I loved her I would want to make a commitment, but I am so unsure.
Everyone wants a soft place to fall when things go wrong, but there is often a price to pay. I don't want to have it both ways.

Oh for the love of Christ I wish I was single, it would be so much simpler, wouldn't it?

It's a well-known fact that Scorpio's and especially Scorpio-Tigers do not wear their hearts on their sleeves, but they are willing to sacrifice that, when they have found 'the one'.
And will show it at the unlikeliest of times through word or deed.
I am indeed in a form of turmoil.

Though I cannot say, for absolute certain, that she *is* the one, but as God is my witness, if this were ever to be the case, I could never be happier.
Surely, I cannot be in love with her, can I?

Almost midnight driving home, and it kept going through my head, those words she spoke. They must have been genuine.
Surely no woman would say those words and not mean them.
Again, was she making, in her own way, a commitment to me?
A promise to the future?
For us to be together, in a more constant way?

This is something I am not in a position to make a commitment on, unless I was prepared to leave Claire.
And, if that were to happen, it would not be for another three years, as the Law stands at present, under 'separation', for a divorce to be granted.
I ask myself, would Kitten be satisfied with that outcome?
She would still be having an affair, a relationship with a married man during that time.
And of course, she knows that because of financial restraint, I could not move out of the marital home.
Or for me to move out and ask to share her home? I doubt that would happen, and even so, not without a very serious discussion.

The strain on both Kitten and myself could be great.
Would we both be up to that?
To have that much understanding and patience with each other – and so quickly?

And of course, if Claire were to ever find out about Kitten somehow, I have no doubt that she would have great delight in citing her as 'the other woman' in a divorce court.

Though I suspect that proof and names would have to be given. I'm not sure how that works.

But that is something I could never allow to happen.
Kitten does not deserve such embarrassment, a humiliating position to find herself in.

[REMOVED SPOILER ' B']

CHAPTER 29
BOOBS, MY BODY OR ME, A PHONE CALL

The following day, whilst we talked online. Sophia brought up the subject of her Hysterectomy of fifteen years prior and her continued use of HRT. I think she knew I would be concerned for her health regarding the taking of the HRT at her age. And I was.

Sophia explained her reasons for taking it and was very mindful of the risks. I remember what she said earlier, about it being *'twelve to fifteen years she had full-on lovemaking'* (or any sex?). I was always under the impression that HRT actually heightened a woman's desire for sex, and yet she is saying she has had no sex in all the time she has been taking it.

Maybe it was a case of the HRT helping to reduce whatever psychological (and physical) issues the Hysterectomy had created. I have a PhD, but not in a medical field, but I do know that there are three types of Hysterectomy and each can be, and often are, very traumatic. As to which one Kitten had, I do not know. The information was not forthcoming.

But she said she feels good taking it. She tends not to listen to experts (WOW... another coincidence, Is Sophia the Twin we each were never told about...). She explained,
   "To them, it's the fountain of youth one moment, and the next, it's the Devil's spawn."

She is an intelligent woman and looked deep into it and also checked her family history for breast cancer. I accepted her decision and left it at that.

It must have been a traumatic and more than trying time for her, for that was the period when her late husband, Eric started to become seriously ill and having 'episodes'. And having the Hysterectomy caused her sex life to plummet along with all the anguish it would have caused.
And having to start caring for her husband at the same time.

I really and honestly, felt for her.
Maybe because of what happened with my Mother.
It is talks like this. I feel, helps to bond people together, to make them feel that they are a part of that other person's life, acceptance.

A little later, I said to her,
   "I am honestly concerned about your health and wondered (jokingly) *if it was me or my body you wanted."*

She replied,
   "That was lovely, but I feel I'm in pretty good shape for a woman of my age... and the answer is, I KNEW you a long time before I knew your body."

It may seem odd to some people, but that to me, was a beautiful acknowledgement.
But 'a long time...'?
Does Sophia, or others consider less than two years to be a long time?
Now, if she was talking as if from the bus trip, then yes... that is a bloody long time... ha-ha.

   There was something else that was talked about that day. It sounded comical, but I wondered then if Sophia was possibly showing some insecurity. It was whilst we talking about her boobs, she was jokingly complaining they were getting bigger, and it was my fault.
(A) *"MOI... [meaning me] and how is Angela doing, by the way."*
[All quiet for about four or five minutes, Sophia then asked,]
(S) *"How do you know Angela was phoning?"*
(A) *"I didn't."*
(S) *"Very odd.'*
(A) *"It's cosmic, man"*
[as used in the English cult tv comedy series 'The Young Ones']
(S) *"That doesn't explain how you guessed Angela had just phoned me."*
(A) *"I didn't guess because I didn't know."*
(S) *"You're spooky."*

(A) *"It was a coincidence,"* I insisted.
Sophia retorted
(S) *"There seems to be an awful lot of that happening recently"*,

Now what the Hell was that all about?
I haven't the faintest idea, and I still haven't because she came across as being quite serious about that final statement.

It was forgotten in a blink of an eye because she then said,
 "Angela is doing fine and getting better each day. And that she was (her words) *'straining at the leash'. SO BE AFRAID."*

I distinctly remember the capitols being used to emphasise…
What a bizarre thing to say, but I could not help smiling.
Kitten also mentioned that she was:
 "Going into The Lincoln next week for a colonoscopy."

Now, I knew where The Lincoln was and what it was... I also knew first-hand about the pre-meds AND the Colonoscopy... not pleasant.
It seems Kitten has to go there every twelve months for a routine check-up. My Sister-in-law also has to go there every twelve months for the same procedure, and to have any polyps removed if present.
I take her there on the odd occasion, wait and then take her home.
If Kitten wants to talk about it, that's perfectly fine with me, and I hope she does. Even though she appears to find it hard for most
of the time to do so, I believe, I hope, in the days, the weeks ahead, she will allow herself to have enough faith and confidence within herself to allow me, to slowly come into her life.

****The next day (23rd), I had my x-ray appointment for my throat, and I was feeling a tad apprehensive****

And Kitten raided the local Pizza Parlour with Angela and Angela's mum. Must be a good Pizza place as it serves alcoholic drinks, I smile, that figures.
Obviously, it seems Angela's mum is partial to a drink as well as a photograph that Kitten sent to me, proved… and why not.

A thought, which is still at the back of my mind.
I mentioned earlier regarding 'someone' pushing or nudging me all the time to become closer to Kitten.
I assumed originally it was because she was *the* girl from the bus and that I had found her again.
Now, I cannot help thinking, is there something more to it?

I have no doubt the obvious answer from many, would be that *'you are either in love or you are falling in love with her'*.
Sorry, but I will stand by what I said earlier and that hasn't changed, I am not in love with her.
But I do care for her, her well-being and all what that entails.
I would never want to hurt her physically or mentally or allow anyone to do so. Though, emotionally, that is something that cannot always be helped even with the best of intentions. But certainly, and without a shadow of doubt, I feel that there is a connection, and a very strong one at that. I apologise if all this appears to be the continuation of Chapter 27.

Yes, it certainly helps that I am very attracted to her and it's not just in a physical way. And that I also care for her. And maybe, in time, my feelings for her may grow deeper as I have mentioned before that I may actually find a lasting love and to find her feelings for me are the same.
That's for a possible future, but right now there IS something quite special about her and again I will say, I feel that she is someone that I need to keep hold of.

There is no 'fixation', but at the same time I feel I need her continued presence, and not necessarily twenty-four/seven.
But again, as I have mentioned before, I need to know just WHY she means this much to me.
Maybe, Kitten can see, can feel this, and maybe from that first intimacy, hence her wanting to take it more slowly and being concerned as to just where this relationship was going.

And, possibly to find the answer, I just may have to do what I said before, to ease off seeing her.

I don't want to be the cause of any upset or be the reason for any anxiety if I do or I don't, to either Kitten or myself, it's perplexing for sure.

I know if I did ease off, it will hard for me to do so, but it would need to be done.

I would dearly love Kitten to open up a little, to communicate with me, to give me some sort of direction, guidance in helping resolve (or ease) this issue. And so, I'm at a loss and yet I welcome being with her. She both calms and frustrates me in the same breath.

What is going on with me, this really is all so new to me. I have never had this strange feeling, this connection before.

But hey, could I not be 'over-thinking' all of this

Ha, yes, this too, has even crossed my mind and maybe, seriously I should stop being curious. Just let things happen, take their own course. Any answers will come in their own time – if ever.

In the whole I am happy, happy being as I am, happy being with Kitten. My hope is that kitten is happy also, being with me.

Que sera sera.

CHAPTER 30
A DIFFERENT WAY TO SERVE SOUP.

The day after, Kitten left me a message that she wanted to see me that evening,

"I feel slightly poorly. Very tired and bit of a sore throat. Your welcome to come over but I might not be great company. PJ's and TV. Let me know"

I messaged her back saying I would bring her a selection of *'oh so good'* soups with me.
Cream of Wild Mushroom, Goan Spiced Chicken, Thai with Lemongrass and East Indian Mulligatawny – there is nothing like a variety.
She replied and started off another round of the game:
(S) *"OK. Hope you like X Factor. Lol"*
(A) *"Oh yes I arbore X Factor"*
[I was being humorously sarcastic, but I think Sophia thought I meant 'adore']
(S) *"Perfect.. Perfick"*
(A) *"FIVERRRRRRRRRRRRRRRRRRRRRRRRRRRR*
I knew you would follow up with something funny"
(S) *"Twat"*
(A) *"I could clam another fiver... but..."*
(S) *"Don't believe you!!!"*
(A) *"Your choice...I thought you were gonna say 'bastard'"*
(S) *"Gonna get in shower and see if it brings me round but I will be in in my PJ'S".*
(A) *"Ok.. need to get dressed.. sat here naked.. can I wear my sarong.....not while driving.... lol"*
(S) *"WARNING!!!!! Kitten will be bare faced. Turn back now!!!"*
(A) *"I HAVE seen you naked... and I like what I see"*
(S) *"Ok if you're sure. Leaping in shower. See you soon".*
(A) *"If I'm sure..?? daft question"*

When I arrived, and Kitten answered the door, she did look a little 'under the weather', but she showered me with kisses as soon as I came into the house and closed the door behind me.

What fellah could resist such affection like that? And I was happy not to. I feel so blessed, I truly do. Here comes that Bobby Taylor song again... ha-ha
.

Once again, Kitten wanted to make love, poorly or not; she wanted her 'fix'. And I so enjoyed making love with her. We could not refuse each other... what a beautiful 'sickness'.

      Now to some, the following will sound positively bizarre, but I can say most honestly, we did so without any thought of impropriety. We were so relaxed in each other's company.
So much so, I have to occasionally 'pinch myself'.
And this time it was... so natural.

Question to myself:
Why am I using the word 'natural' so often when talking about Sophia?
It's as if we done something or I have witnessed something so often, it's become an 'everyday occurrence', which is crazy.
Or is it simply that I, we both feel so comfortable in the presence of each other. Like two peas from the same pod?

Halfway through our lovemaking, we both decided we were hungry. (I smile at this, thinking I was watching a film, because it only happens in films, right? – so wrong)
So, we both went downstairs, naked... I suggested trying some of the soup I had brought with me, as it was quick.

We both sat at the dining table, totally naked, enjoying Mushroom soup from large rice bowls and using spoons that I brought with me, to compliment the chopsticks I had gifted her previously.
What next... Kimono's? ha-ha... hmmmm would look good though.

What a relationship and understanding we have got. Even married couples may be shocked at the idea, but it was totally spontaneous and perfectly natural to both of us. You should try it, honestly.

After the soup, we grabbed a bottle of red wine, a couple of glasses and headed back upstairs.

We watched a little TV and then made love again... Now come on, how beautiful is THAT.

I had previously mentioned our first lovemaking session. It was a case of 'practice makes perfect', and all the 'practice' **(and since),** has been with Sophia.
Because of my Cancer treatments in 2013 and 2014, I had issues with my Libido, an all too common side-effect.
Both the Consultant and Doctor stated that I should not build my hopes up (no pun intended) regarding getting any form of erection, as erectile dysfunction effects seven out of ten men.
But I was blessed that after a year, and the amount of Chemotherapy and Radiotherapy treatments undertaken, I could produce an 'acceptable' erection, but I had serious doubts I could count on it, at the required moment.
And so, by the time of the second lovemaking session, things had improved quite a bit.

Sophia also understood why I could no longer produce semen.
Even though she said
 "I would have liked to have tasted it" she accepted it.

How extraordinarily wonderful is that, to actually say those words.

At first I was so surprised, then I accepted it for what it was, a beautiful intimate compliment.
And adding that to the other personal words, are from someone whose possible love? certainly affection, for me, appears to becoming more and more evident by the day.

There was also an extraordinary 'flip side' to all of this.
I found not been able to produce semen, it gave me longer 'staying power', (I cannot think of another phrase that is more suitable) and I was able to continuously pleasure Kitten for even longer... three and four hours longer (and possibly more?). No wonder she sometimes said she was sore.
Though in consideration, I always 'slowed down' when she mentioned this.

And I took no 'additives', do they actually work anyway?
For whatever reason, some woman may find it hard to allow themselves the joy to express, verbally or even visually the pleasure received, to fully enjoy the moment and allow their inhibitions to flutter away.
This is often the reason why a lot of caring men feel they have 'failed' in their endeavours to please the women they love.

And if Kitten was ever disappointed with our lovemaking sessions, she has never hinted, even visually.
This woman is so diplomatic.

Basically, we enjoyed having sex, making love, (call it what you will) and that's how it should always be.
Never one-sided, because it's there for both to enjoy.
And each to give pleasure to their partner.
And if it doesn't, then talk about - together.

Yes, there **are** times when a man may not be able to facilitate full sexual intercourse, but there are so many other ways he can pleasure the woman.
A man can often only produce one, or possibly a second climax in quick succession, whereas as a woman can have many orgasms.
It's a biological fact and must never be treated as a failure by the man on his part if he cannot respond.

But, as mentioned previously, there are many ways to pleasure a woman and the same applies to a woman when she wants to continue, to pleasure and arouse her partner.
Just allow yourself to be fully confortable with your partner and they will be with you, and then cast aside any inhibitions you both may have.

Clair however, had a different view on lovemaking.
I truly feel she was brought up to believe sex was only for making babies, and not really for enjoyment. A chore almost?
Yes, she did 'seem' to enjoy the foreplay, and the act of actually making love, but I could never really tell for certain.

She never contributed, reciprocated, visually or verbally. And only on the very odd occasion, did she ever join in with very basic foreplay.
It was all one sided. And sadly, over time it became wearisome for me. What was the point, I thought? It takes two to Tango, so true.
I became celibate, and just accepted my fate as such.
And like my Father before me, it wasn't really my choice.

I had learnt a few (intercourse) 'positions' from when I was with Patricia, and previously from visualising pages from books such as, 'The Perfumed Garden' from the age of thirteen.
So, other than with Patricia, I was never in a position (no pun intended) to put any (bar one) to the test fully since.
Until now that is.
Kitten and I have fun. We have each tried different positions and as I have always said, sex/lovemaking is always best when enjoyed by both parties. And we do.

I like to think, deep inside, that Kitten was beginning to feel more confident in my company. And I in hers, though in that, I may have a slight advantage.
Because from day one she has had the key to unlock my shield and totally disarm me, and I in return allowed it to happen – actually I had no say in it, I was on auto-pilot. Still can't get over that
My general confidence, when I was with her improved and it came to the fore. Such was her effect on me.
But again, there was also another confidence, far deeper and one I truly cannot explain.

Our repartee and retorts games are always in full flow.
Some being so wild and hilarious, and some… well, some were causing Kitten to use (mockshockhorror)… swear words and exclamations, which in themselves were rockin' funny – I ain't no prude.
Life was good, and getting better in Kittens company

And Angela's knee is getting better too, day by day; I was pleased to hear.

Well, it must be the case if she had such a great night with her love interest last night. Good for her.

I do like Angela. She has a lovely disposition of sometime being quite quirky in her reactions, a lovely smile and laugh.
She can be very deep, and then a moment later, disarmingly open.
The night at Tosca's is a good example.
She deserves her happiness and why not.
Everyone deserves such.
You go for it girl.

CHAPTER 31
NO SEX? – NO CHANCE!
THE BEGINNING OF THE END

I clearly remember there was something about Sophia's side of our chat the next day (25th); It was 'different'. More open. More relaxed

(S) *"Angela had a fab night which I'm so pleased about. Jenny and Marcus had a great night at The Lodge. We had a lovely night drinking wine watching tv and making love. Something I want to do with you forever. All is well in the world. LOL*
(A) *"Pleased Angela had a good time as well... I hope Jenny and Marcus made good use of the fireside rug...."*
(S) *"Me too!!!!!"*
(A) *"As we too... I think that really goes without saying... and I could have stayed all night.. Nobody was at home"*
(S) *"Bloody hell. I had bacon eggs toms and avocado in the fridge".*
(A) *"Tell you what Kitten.. last night.. when we were sat at the table.. it was so natural. even with no clothes. it was beautiful, Thank you"*
(S) *"Yes the whole night was very natural".*

What a way to acknowledge a new day.
I asked Kitten,
   "Are you doing anything this afternoon?"

She replied,
   "No, nothing planned, why?"

I remembered a while back that she had gone to the 'Rambling Man' restaurant with a long-time friend. I 'think' her name was Julie-Ann.
I knew where this place was... I passed it every time I went to Kittens.
I continued,
   "Do you fancy a late Sunday lunch? 'maybe a coffee back at your place, but no sex."

I was honestly trying to be diplomatic; I really thought it might be too soon for Kitten; well I mean, it was less than twenty-four hours since our previous lovemaking session.
She replied in a way I'm getting used to,
   "Ok, but only if you let me pay, it's my turn AND WHAT DO YOU MEAN NO SEX... LOL"

Nothing like being straight to the point... and yes, the use of the capitols was as Kitten typed the reply.
I replied,
   "Ha-ha-ha.... I'll fight you for the bill, and I play dirty. You are now fully booked"

I arrived at her house at about 2.30pm, and after a little chat and a short, but very passionate bout of kissing, we left at 3pm.

Not a great deal to choose from with the menu, so we both went for the 'Sunday Lunch'. The food was 'fair', nothing outstanding, but enjoyable, sadly, only 'warm'.
We then drove back to Kittens, and to making love.
Not being crude, but we have been like a pair of bloody Rabbits for the last month and today confirmed it.
Where the Hell do we find the energy?
We seem to feed off each other.
Seriously, every time we make love, it's as beautiful as the time before. We appear to be insatiable.
And after nearly four hours, it was time to go. I left about 9pm with Kitten watching 'Victoria' on TV.

On the way driving home, the same thought crossed my mind as it had done once before.
Am I quite happily making love to Kitten because it's what I feel she wants me to do? she wants from me? or, is it because it's what I want to do? to make her happy? to feel cherished and wanted?
But each time and like the time before, I end up feeling surely it's what we ***both*** want. And I'm content.

The following day, it was chat time again, we actually talked about our physical weights. Also, Kitten told me that she had to remember to take her pre-op 'relaxant' that night and in the morning. Like, how 'normal' a chat is THAT.
I do enjoy conversations with Sophia when they happen. It can be rewarding in so many ways. Love it.

Even though she was going to The Lincoln tomorrow, our banter never faltered. I also wanted to be there to hold her hand, if not in 'real form', but spiritually.
Christ, what's up with me?

Kitten mentioned during out usual chat
"Just had a bowl of cream of mushroom soup. Followed by......ANOTHER BOWL OF MUSHROOM SOUP!!! Deeee Lish. Perfect for my pre-op light diet. Your timing spot-on again !!!! X"

Kitten drove up to Jenny's and then on to The Lincoln in the afternoon.
A delay in the procedure, but she was back at Jenny's by about 9.30pm. So pleased, everything went fine.

The next day, I received an appointment to see Dr. Murray at the Smedley, for the 30th. Short notice indeed, I have a bad feeling about this

And Sophia's pain kicked in. I know the feeling all too well. We had a laugh online, and a quick 'snap' each other.
"I'm popping over to see you" I told her

She did not want me to see her as she was.
Then she relented, and asked;
"This is so unromantic, but can you bring me some 'Wind-Eze?"

I just replied,
"I have seen you when you are fine, and so I'll see you when you are poorly – that's how it goes."

I had become used to the 'feeling' I get when driving to Kittens. Every time, it was filled with a crazy mixture of apprehension and adrenaline. And this evening was certainly no different.

I knocked on the door, no answer. I took a side view look through the window, and there she was, in her PJ's switching on the television.

She opened the door and greeted me with a warm kiss, and I, in return, gave her the Wind-Eze... what a nice romantic exchange.

I could hear the television upstairs but it did not seem to be on the same channel as the one she switched on, and was now curled up on the two-seater sofa, watching (how strange).

I sat down on the other Sofa, and we chatted for about twenty minutes.

I could see she was uncomfortable, quite possibly due to the pain. Or was I spoiling her television watch?

Ok, time to leave her in peace.

I have no idea what made me say what I did as I stood up, but I did. I told her,

"Claire knows about you. Not about our relationship, but about the girl I met on the bus all those years ago. And that she was quicker than me on the repartee and such."

What the Hell did I mention that for?

I had already mentioned this to Kitten a while back.

Claire knew of 'the girl' as others did, when they asked years ago.

But then I followed it up with something that didn't make sense.

Yet every single word, will be etched in my memory for ever.

"I love you, but I'm not 'in love' with you. The love I have for you is a caring love, but maybe in time that could change."

I was trying to say that, because of what she said on the 21st, I could not return those feelings.

I couldn't in all honesty provide that commitment, not at this time.

But I felt I so wanted to, I truly did.

I was getting all tongue-tied, and it was a garbled mess.

Then I saw Sophia roll her eyes to the right. I instantly realised..

*'Oh God, I'm saying things she did **not** want to hear.'*

I apologised, and told her I would talk online later.
She got up, we kissed at the door, and I was gone.
I was kicking and cursing myself on the drive home.
She was poorly, and I came out with all that shite.
I kept mumbling to myself through gritted teeth.
'Milnzy, you're a fucking idiot'.

Later online that night, to 'cheer her up', I mentioned that
   "I have already bought you a Birthday present that you will like."

It was the last production of Singosari by Molton Brown.
She responded by saying
   "You don't need to buy me presents but it's nice you've thought about my birthday already"

I quickly answered jokingly,
   "Too bloody late now, you should have told me the other day.

   "Oh well you'll just have to give it me now - unless you can get a refund!!!! She replied.

That started a quick-fire five minutes repartee and retort session.
I hope it took her mind off the pain, be it for a short spell, and possibly even made her smile.
It sounded as if she had put what happened in her house only a couple of hours ago, behind her and everything seemed good again.

But (to me) something didn't seem right – I let it pass.
So why was it still bugging me for the rest of the night?

Maybe I really do need to pull back.

CHAPTER 32
THE END OF THE LINE

The following day (29th), Sophia said her tummy felt a lot better.
And I, in turn, have come to an awakening, a possible realisation, with the conclusion being that I'm really smothering Kitten.
I seriously need to give her more space, more time on her own.
For both our sakes. And the sooner the better I feel.

**The 30th came around along with the appointment with Dr. Murray. During which he gave me an examination, after looking at the x-ray for a while
He said he is going to take a sample biopsy for the Labs.
A flashback to the first time I had a biopsy – and the result, maybe this time I won't be so 'lucky'. BUT, I was ready for any outcome with a positive vibe, but I cannot tell Kitten yet, it's still too early and in truth, I was scared of her very possible negative reaction.**

Some light conversation with Sophia online. Later that night, on the 30th, Sophia messaged me to say Angela had called for a drink and that they had a 'heart to heart'.
So, the Prosecco I bought flowed freely, it seems… ha-ha.
But why did I have an uneasy feeling, terrible butterflies in my stomach that something dreadful was about to happen?

Because I was right, and I didn't have long to wait either

On October 1st, I asked Kitten
   "Can I see you tonight, there is something that I feel needs to be explained"

I wanted to explain what I was 'trying' to say on the 28th, just so there no 'misunderstanding'.
I also told her I was going down to Staunton on the following day (Sunday) and asked if she would like to join me, but only if she felt up to it. I needed to tell her, that I feel I should give her space.

She replied,
"I have already promised to be Angela's 'assistant', so doing the prep for a friends party in Woringly, tonight, so be busy, sorry"

This seemed to be very sudden.
The 'heart to heart', I'm sensing 'something isn't quite right' here.
I asked jokingly,
"Can you pencil me in for Staunton on Sunday?"

Sophia did not answer.
She just sent me a GIF of someone turning over to sleep.
I answered by saying,
"You want to go back to sleep for another hour? Or until I go away?'

Her reply said it all,
"'Yes, that's it."

I knew then, in a micro-second, something has happened, the 'heart to heart'. Our time together was over, but why.

Worse was to come.
The following day, the final deep cut was made.
And I remember her message to me so clearly.
*"I had a good time last night, and I'm glad I went as an old friend had been in touch and took my mind off things. Paul was my first serious boyfriend, and he is in the final stages of his divorce. And although he is a lot older than me hearing his voice again, I realised I still had very strong feelings for him. I cannot continue to see you with Paul now back in my life. I would like us to stay friends, but that is all.
You were a wonderful support for me after Eric's death. We had some good times. But I must go where my heart tells me."*

The words hammered into my chest. I was gasping for breath.
I could not believe what I was hearing (reading), what she was telling me.
It was out of the blue. It was surreal.
Questions filled my head. Questions that I needed answers to.

I think she may have expected me to say, '*Oh, ok then, see ya*'.
But I couldn't answer her. I was in shock.

Then after a short while, I replied to Sophia,
   "*Please tell me the truth about this 'Paul', just when did he come back into your life, when was the last time you talked to him.*"

She replied,
   "*Paul came back into my life about a month before I met you. I had been in contact with him right up until the 28th*"

The 28th? That was the August Bank Holiday! The Ironworks!

The obvious crossed my mind. '*Did she say the same to this Paul, that she had met someone else etc. etc.? A monthly change in Men. NO, that's stupid to think that, but something is not adding up here*'.

I asked many other questions; my mind was in a whirl.
My head was a total mess.
Something didn't feel right; it didn't make sense.
It was all too 'clean-cut' as if it had been planned.
If nothing else, and for my saving grace was that I have never called her any disgusting names, even in my thoughts.
No matter what she did or said, she would not warrant such abuse.

I told her that I was in Staunton and,
   "*Now that you have told me, your conscience is clear and that I will still be your friend in the short term.*"
I added,
   "*If you should ever need someone to talk to or if you was in trouble, talk to a stranger and talk to me. I will never, ever refuse your call.*"

And I meant it, as I still do.
I thought about what I said and then messaged her again...
   "*I just lied to you. I'll be here for you for the duration. I'm not losing you again, no matter what the circumstances are.*"

She didn't reply.
After the conversation I left the pub in Staunton, leaving my orange there and almost forgetting my laptop, and drove home. I cannot even remember driving home for God's sake. I felt numb. I must have driven the sixty miles home on auto-pilot.

I think I sent Sophia two lengthy messages, shortly after, trying to explain everything, but realising the damage, whatever it was, whatever caused it, was already done. It was permanent.
The last message I sent I recall vividly was full of angst. I wrote that I felt I was being treated like a toy, to be played with until the next new toy arrived and then discarded.
I was indeed wearing my heart on my sleeve. Was I being childish or venting my true feelings.
Sophia replied, saying that,
"You were never a toy, that was never, ever the case."

But once again, she never elaborated.

I was hurting so much inside. My head was a total mess.
This, and a possible Cancer in the throat. I was so confused.
I felt 'used' and yet at the same time, wanting to get back to her, be with her.
Was this purely physical or something deeper. But, whatever it was, to lose something so beautiful, so quickly, without explanation?

I was still thinking about all of Sophia's claims of '*telling the truth*' (about Paul). It seemed too 'nicely tied up with a bow'.

Sophia always said to me,
'*Don't read into things that are not there*',
But how would they convince people they were not 'there', if the seeds had already been planted.

I have found over the years that people who say this, usually fear that some truth may be found out, that they are hiding something or sometimes, as does happen, they genuinely do not want any fall-out.

One minute I felt that I was just the one guy. The next minute to find I was only at the head of a queue, only to be pushed aside to the end of the line when the next suitable candidate came along,
Surely, that can't be right because right up until that night, everything seemed so perfect or at the very least, looking really good.
What DID I say to upset her so much?

Was it that I wasn't in love with her, that my love for her was a caring love? Did she expect more, less or she just didn't want to hear the word 'Love' mentioned at all.
If so, I can't take it back.
I can't turn back the clock.
But if it was THAT which created the end of our relationship, I feel she had treated me unfairly, but if she misconstrued what I had said, I can now easily understand how.
But the following day, she never mentioned it. It was if nothing had been said. We chatted as normal.

I was going to tell her, I was going to give her more space.
But she most definitely beat me to it, and more permanently.

I find now that I have two paths to choose from, one of which I had to go down.
I can only hope is that the choice I make is the right choice is the right one, and not just for my sake.

CHAPTER 33
ANY PATH TAKEN CAN BE THE WRONG ONE

Going back a couple of weeks to the 21st and Kitten saying,
"I don't want part of you, I want all of you, always".

That had nothing to do with making love; it WAS about love.
She seemed to be implying she had fallen in love with me (or at the least... had intense feelings for me).
She didn't want to 'share' me with anyone; she wanted me ALL of the time?
She cannot ever turn around and say... *'Oh, I didn't mean it **that** way, you must have misunderstood me'*

The Teegra on the headboard,
"I love you calling me that (Kitten) *and when you are old and grey, I still want to hear you call me that"*

No dissection needed with that, surely.
What is there to misconstrue about that?

And going back only the other week, she confirmed by saying our lovemaking is
"Something I want to do with you forever".

'Wanted to do forever?'. Usually, when said in the heat of the moment, it would be, 'it could have gone on forever' or 'wanted it to go on forever'.

Was she afraid of the feelings she was having for me?
Did she feel 'I want this Man, but I want independence', freedom to be myself again, to be a 'single woman again'?
Not realising she could have had both, just needed communication.
She wanted the break, and I served up the perfect 'excuse'.

And the other path...

When on that last night, I mentioned Claire, and about my (caring) love, she panicked and thought that this was getting too deep or, in her words, *'too heavy'*.

She couldn't cope with the emotional stress she thought it could lead to. She did not want to be tied to any commitment. She wanted out.
Or that I may already be in love with her, and (obviously) I didn't realise it, but she could 'sense it'.

Then again, and let us have it right. It's the modern World we live in.
She just wanted me for the sex and attention?
I can't help thinking, that that, could be a very strong possibility.
She was still on HRT and a Tigress. She didn't want a relationship, she wanted an 'arrangement', a sort of 'Pretty Woman' – sex, but no kissing, and it's too personal.
And she wanted this arrangement to last as long as she felt the need, or a change of male concubine.

I rang alarm bells and altered the arrangement by mentioning the dreaded word – ***'love'***.

Whatever the case, whatever path I take, in truth; she wanted 'rid of me.'
So rather than discuss it, because she didn't want a 'confrontation', she, and more than likely Angela, concocted a story about 'Paul' suddenly contacting her again at the 'heart to heart'. A 'clean break.'

The last thing she expected was what followed.
It was also the last thing I expected or ever wanted to do.

My path has to be that she has strong feelings for me or maybe falling in love with me, and the verbal 'evidence' appeared to confirm this.
But it was too soon after Eric? She couldn't cope with it?
I felt she was possibly fragile and unsure of herself.

And then, there is my possible cancer, how would she take to that?
How would I?
After all what she went through with her late husband, if she still had any feelings for me I could not let her be hurt like that again,

I have said for many years that Scorpio's and Scorpio-Tigers are masters of this form of 'illusion', that of giving out a different vibe to people other than what is really going on with them.
This also gives people the impression that they are 'cold', when, in fact, the complete opposite is the case.
It can take a long time for them to 'come out of hiding' I know; I have been there many times.
There is of course a third path, just to walk away.
But if she did have feelings for me, that could hurt her even more than I could allow.
And because of that, it's a path I will never go down, under any circumstances.

I cannot turn around and ask anyone for advice. I am on my own.
I may be totally wrong in all this, but I HAVE to choose, and quickly.

CHAPTER 34
CLINICAL CHATS and SPATS

*****For the next few days thinking about Kitten took my mind off the Biopsy. I was getting concerned with each passing day***

Thankfully this boost I have been getting with my confidence doesn't allow me to become overly morbid.
I wish I could find the source, bottle it and sell it... make a bloody fortune.

But all the while, in the very back of my mind, was the possibility that those events might overshadow anything I wanted to do, to reconcile with Kitten.
And if there was a chance of getting back together, how long would it last if I had to tell her.
But that was for a possible future, this is the here and now.

I was trying to be gentle with Kitten, not wanting to upset her any more than I thought she may already be. I was walking on eggshells because I did not want her to misconstrue what I was talking about.
I wanted to talk to her, honestly, so much, but I could not push it.
So pleasantries were passed back and forth, VERY light banter.

There was none of the usual repartee and retorts; the conversations were almost clinical... sanitised.
To be honest – *dead*.

After the first week in October, I decided I needed a face to face meeting with Sophia.
Rightly or wrongly, I needed to talk to her about the possibility of cancer in the throat and my fears. Not for any sympathy or an agenda to try and get her to come back to me.
I needed that meeting for her to understand why I wanted to draw a line underneath all of this. It has to be done.
Because, if Sophia did have any feelings left for me I desperately needed a true clean break with no chats, no telephone calls, no

communication, nothing whatsoever. That would truly hurt me, I know... but....
I did not want her to feel any sadness, remorse or guilt later on.

And maybe, it was not such a bad thing anyway, because I would always be a 'second-in-line' to her now, I could never be a front runner again.
But I had to try for the meeting, if not for her, then for me.
Being honest, I wanted to feel the sadness in my own way. Out of sight from anyone and everyone.

There was no way I wanted to tell her 'online'. That would have been so cold, completely heartless. But as always, in hindsight, it may have been the 'only' way.
I asked her for a meet-up of her choosing, nothing (in her mind) 'heavy', just a chat.
Her reply was sharp and to the point,
"Nice try, no cigar... ha-ha."

That hurt; it really did
[and she was never to know just how much].
But we carried on chatting as if that last remark didn't happen.

Then came a 'cliff hanger' moment. I fully admit I was feeling quite emotional and rejected, because I wanted an answer as to what made her 'throw the towel in' on that last night.
I wanted her to 'Man-up' and tell me. Frustration, but not anger leaked out.
I asked her,
"What do you mean, when you mention commitment? what's your interpretation of it."

She simply answered.
"A long-term arrangement."

I quickly replied,
"I'm not looking for a commitment only a relationship where over time we would get to know each other at our own pace..... and yet I was quickly pushed aside, with you looking forward to a 'commitment' with the soon to be divorced Paul."

Sophia took umbrage with that, and retorted,
"I am not looking for and could not give a commitment to anyone at the moment as I have only just been released from one and I like the feeling of independence."
She followed that with,
"I'm so sorry if you feel that I have hurt you.... I never said that I loved you."

That's right; she never did and I have never said she had, or asked.
So why has she suddenly brought this up.

A tangent thought immediately flashed through my mind.
When she mentioned that this 'Paul' was *'soon to be divorced'*
I thought about what she said to me;
'I don't want part of you, I want all of you, always'.
If this 'Paul' was a real-life person after all, and he was going through a divorce, then she would be looking at a commitment from him and for her, to give one to him, simply because she CAN have 'all of HIM'.
In my mind, that stood to reason, if that were the case.

I was hurting when I asked her straight out, but I felt I had to.
"As Paul popped back into your life, you pushed me aside for him, what would happen if I suddenly came back into your life. Would you push Paul aside for me?"

Her answer confused me, it did not seem to make sense. It did not answer the question.
"No, I have made a decision for now, and I'm sticking by it."

Is there something I'm not hearing... *'for now'*?

What did she mean by that?
The way things are now, even if Sophia was to turn around and say, 'All I want is a break from you, to clear my head, to ask myself what I want', I would have felt it was the end of the line anyway.
Could I believe she would still 'consider me' after her break from me. And just how long would that break be anyway.

Would it be long enough for her to either start afresh with someone else? listen to outside influences?
Would she be content just to leave me 'dangling' with the hope of a reunion, and then conveniently carry on with her life and I'm forgotten?

I'm am simply, and honestly afraid of losing her.
And I have to seriously ask myself – why am I so afraid?
And as the Lord is my witness, I don't have the answer.

Something keeps telling me to stay close to her, but I don't know why.
I will be truthful. I am confused with this feeling. Because I do not understand its reasoning, if that's the correct wording.
So yes, maybe a complete break IS the best way. The only way.
I wish I could discuss it, or have my own heart to heart, with someone.

But, I left it at that. I was deflated. I then continued our conversation with more non-descript 'clinical' banter.

It was apparent she wanted a clean break with no questions.
She wasn't prepared for, nor wanted, these 'attacks' on her, from me questioning her, wanting answers.
And that's all I wanted... answers, not a fight.

I was hurting so deep inside as it was, I could not, and did not want to add to it.

I needed to clear my head and try and sort out this mess. I needed to get away.
I quickly decided (after a phone call to see if it was ok to stay there) to go to my Cousin, and her family in France.
Now 'that's' what I call 'getting away'. But it wasn't running away.
A drastic measure, possibly... but away from it all, most definitely.
I messaged Sophia.
Just why I did I do not know., there was no ulterior motive behind it.

Daft as it may seem, I think I told her out of courtesy.
I also told Sophia's friend, Soo, though not out of courtesy, but out of friendship, for we had many online chats about many things. And she also seemed genuinely concerned for me, for my well-being even before Sophia and I got together.

Claire wasn't overly bothered, but wanted to know *"Why so sudden?'* and *'How long for?*
A barrage of questions, I mumbled something about a fortnight, maybe less and that It's harvesting season and they are short staffed. This was accepted – I think.
I thought back to my situation only three or four years ago or more.
I doubt I would ever have had the confidence to act so 'impulsively' and with little disregard for the outcome... whatever that would be.

It was a mad decision to take at any-time.
I knew I would be welcomed and that they would find room for me to stay, but that is not the point.
I didn't really like the idea of just dropping in on them, intruding on them with my problems like this.
I have no doubt Marie felt that 'something had happened' when I phoned and just told her that I just wanted to get away from everything and clear my head for a short while.
And I know Marie will not ask until I am ready to talk about whatever is troubling me. I'm sure of that.

For over twenty years I had occasionally asked myself, is it cheating to have a relationship with someone whilst you are still married? What defines cheating?
Some (religious?) people say *'it's a sin' even just thinking about it'*.
So to them its when that first corrupt thought enters your mind, that's when the sin starts. And not from the deed. We are all lost.

And who decided a lifetime was the length of any relationship? We know it's not the case and whilst some people think that marriage should be forever, the reality, as we know it, is that it was a man-made creation/definition of a relationship.

There is no "till death do us part" even in the animal kingdom, with the exception of a few species, so why do we feel that the human race should stay together for life no matter what? We are often unhappily married and yet we do stay 'together' for appearances sake. Just how cruel and soul destroying is that.

So why do people stay with each other? Is it usually out of fear?
Fear we will not be happy if we leave. Fear we will not find love. Fear we will be alone. As rare as it may be, is it because they truly love their partner and want to make it work? In reality, it's one-sided and a cruel exception that can only lead to even more hurt.

We often ask ourselves, as to why people come into our lives.
There is always a reason, and it is Karma.
And for good or bad, there is absolutely nothing we can do about it. People talk of Spiritual togetherness or love. But we can't feel it or experience it whilst we are alive, can we?
And so, it's a one hundred and one percent *'Que Sera Sera'*.

CHAPTER 35
FRANCE, BOMBSHELLS, DECISIONS

All was still 'calm' when I went away for a few days in France and my family over there. I needed to speak to Marie and ask her for advice. I desperately needed someone to talk to.
I was still very confused by what had happened over the last few days, how quickly everything turned around.
Claire was of course totally unaware of all that had happened.

I had helped out in the Vineyard a couple of times before, plus I always try to help out when I am over there, no matter the season. And now Rene has just purchased another small B&B, I will be kept busy
My intention was to spend the next twelve days, trying to clear my head.
I just pray, it works.

Clair was capable of looking after herself, and Graham was there to help if needed. In truth she preferred his company, and he too loves a drink.
Whether she felt something was odd, she never gave an impression, but she made sure Graham took me to the airport. Was that to make sure that I WAS actually going?
Where else would I be going for Christ's sake.

Why is Kitten having this effect on me. Yes, I care about her, a lot actually, but I'm not in love with her.
I need to bore Marie with it all. See if she can help and resolve the problem... and me.

The flight was smooth and the high-speed TGV was... fast, very fast. A train change, to the somewhat slower version followed. Simmone picked me up from the station and drove me to the vineyard.
Oh, she is one scary driver. It was late, but still remarkably light for the time of year when we arrived. It looked fabulous.

Marie is a great Soul to talk to, and Albert is a man who knew how I was feeling. Yes, Marie was fully aware of Sophia and even said that, *'despite Sophia's agenda and apparent lack of sincerity'*; she still wanted to meet her' one day.

Marie actually 'scolded' me for allowing myself to get into this situation so quickly, but layered that with,

"This girl must be so very special to you, yet you are hiding from her."

[I could never understand what she meant, that is until a couple of years later in December 2018].

Marie also insisted that she has a good feeling about Sophia, despite what has happened, but she never elaborated.

However, she did say that my inner feelings must be shown, and that I must admit to them, to find any peace. That I may have to decide between my inner feelings for Sophia or my friendship, because there is a chance I may never have both.

What inner feelings?

I hadn't a clue what the Hell she was talking about? Can't be love. All she kept saying when I asked her what she meant;

"It will come, it will come."

Marie bloody infuriates me sometimes. But that's her way.

I asked Albert as to how he and Marie got the time off from the University as it was still term-time. He told me that Marie and he were on a six to eight-month sabbatical and were enjoying every minute of the break and that they had come down to the vineyard in the September. They may even come to England next year.

[I had no idea at the time, that they were hiding a devastating secret from Simmone and Rene, their family at the vineyard … and from me. And it wasn't until early the following year that we all found out].

A little later, whilst having dinner the following day, Marie told me that she had put my new confidence and a powerful spiritual determination solely down to Sophia, '*her actions, her possible love and just by being there, have done wonders for you*'.

I cannot deny that she has been good for me, but I was cautious regarding the new-found confidence thing as this started before I even met her again.
So I cannot see any direct connection there.
But to Marie, it was very different and she explained,
"I strongly believe it started to grow back within you the moment you found her again. Despite your age and what you have been through over the years, you still have a lot to learn about yourself, and you still have a lot to offer her and give others".

Marie loved to make these types of statements; her students loved them as well... she wanted people to seek deeper into themselves, open their minds to what is and not what was or what if.
Though I have to say, I do worry about Marie sometimes. Albert doesn't, though. After all, he knows her better than anyone.

But her words,
"I strongly believe it started to grow back within you the moment you found her again".
That did make me think, be it for a short while. Was that possible?

Simmone, on the other hand, was a little more 'vocal' about Sophia's actions. But that's my Cousin, bless her.
Marie continued, using her Profession, her humility and her in-depth knowledge of me, and said,
" Things have now run their course, but that is not to say another course could not be found, in time.
But this new course would have to be on terms founded by compromise, a neutral zone, and from there a better understanding can be forged, and from where matters of the heart especially, are concerned.
Both sides have to admit to themselves and each other, that what is done is done and what is in the past cannot be undone, ever, but by remaining neutral with compromise and receptive ambitions, positive things can and will come from it. It's not a one-person thing; both sides need to want it."

I wish now I had listened more carefully and taken her advice. But I was stubborn, bloody stupid and blinkered.

From day one, and through the initial sadness, both Albert and Marie said they were astounded by my increase in confidence and how it had improved so much since they saw me last.
Was that really almost twelve months ago?
They both asked jokingly, *"Is Claire still alive?"*
I had to smile. Both Albert and especially Marie do not like Claire one bit.
Marie has said for a long time that Claire is stifling me, slowly suffocating me because of her own insecurities.
She is stripping away my confidences in wanting me to be like her.

I had tried to work on it, to improve matters at home, but yes, I knew Marie was correct...

Whilst there, I was 'told' to make myself useful. It was Simmone's vineyard (inherited from her late husband), and the last of the late summer grapes had to be harvested. And I loved it, working hard, having laughs with the Family and the sisters and cousins of Simmone's late husband.

I cannot (to my shame) speak a word of French, but their English was pretty good and got me through any barriers.

**Then, on the 13th, a half 'expected' bombshell. An email from the hospital. I had Cancer of the throat (Laryngeal). They needed to do more tests as soon as possible to find out the extent, as the first biopsy proved inconclusive **

All five of us (Rene, Marie's Son, who came around, as I didn't see him on my last visit) sat in the kitchen drinking wine, eating a little and discussing the situation...

Marie knew that I thought Kitten might be in love with me. And she agreed - in part,
"Yes, I too feel she may be in love with you, but if she is, then she has panicked. For her, it may be too soon, she wants her

freedom, her independence, and because she has refused to discuss it with you, it has led to this mess."

Marie became very upset when I told her of the plan I had started to put into action.
She told me to
"Do not be silly, wait for the other tests."

I told her and the others there and then, of my fear.
"I seriously believe I will not be lucky a fourth time, and that there is every possibility I will not get through this."

Yes, for the first time in many, many months, I felt really down, not depressed... just down. My confidence seemed to be waning.

This Alex needs to bounce back before the 'rot' starts.

I continued, maybe over dramatically, but I meant every word,
"If there were even the slightest chance that Sophia had any positive feelings for me, they would have to be removed, permanently, and by any means."

Even Simmone and Rene were a little shocked by this, coming from their typically level headed, but often tedious (their words, not mine, of course) Cousin.

Marie pleaded with me,
"Do not do anything rash, that you will regret, you must wait for the new tests."
Albert understood, tried and succeeded in calming Marie down. But he too advised me to go with a great deal of caution.

To me, I was making amends by doing something wrong for the right reasons.
I may not be around long enough to be 'punished' further, but I may be able to see Sophia not suffering from another blow.
Christ, this was sounding more like a Shakespearian melodrama.

I returned home late on the 14th after doing a lot of rearranging to the train and flight and more than a little extra cost.

I was writing notes, plans and thinking hard en-route. I still had doubts, if I was doing the right thing?
I hope to God I am, and that Sophia still has feelings for me.
Because I would truly hope, that I will have destroyed all or any of those feelings for the right reasons.
And if not, may I never, ever be forgiven.
Dammit, if truth be told, may I never be forgiven anyway.

When I arrived home, I acted as if nothing had happened or was going to happen.
I'm sure I sent messages to Sophia, but she did not reply.
I carried on having the odd conversation with Angela, talking about her Mum and Angela's accident, and yes, about Kitten.
It was during one of these conversations that some inconsistencies about 'how' Paul and Kitten contacted each other again, emerged.
How they rekindled their passion for each other.
Who contacted who… and how?
According to Angela,
 "Paul was, and never will be on FB or anything like that."

And also, according to Angela, who seemed to know a lot more about Paul though whom she had never met or even spoken to than what Kitten had told me about him, Angela continued,
 "Sophia gave Paul her telephone number a long time before meeting you."

So again, who contacted who first.
Because, and again according to Angela, she continued;
 "I was as surprised as anyone when he got in touch, Sophia assumed he was back with his Wife and had had no contact for ages- he was off the radar full stop."

How would Kitten have assumed he was back with his Wife?
Unless she was in contact with him a long time BEFORE he reconnected with her and the month before Kitten met me.
It is a coincidence that Paul contacted her when he did and that is what brought Kitten's true feelings into focus.
Was this, the supposed contact, immediately AFTER Kitten split with me and when he is suddenly states he is in the 'last stages of his divorce'.

This is NOT making sense at all.

And so, if any of THAT were correct... then WHY did she suddenly drop Paul when she met me.
Because her 'true feelings for him' (as Angela put it) were rekindled when the phone call was made around the 28th September

According to Kitten herself, she was speaking to him right up until the 28th of the previous month – where was the love or 'true feelings' then?
So mystifying, or is there a more simple explanation?

This is getting so confusing that you sometimes wonder, as to just what was the reason for the question in the first place – or is that the goal, that you are made to give up on the question?

There are, have been, so many questions. But without answers they only lead to assumptions, to speculation – and that can lead to all sorts of personal misery or in some cases, happiness of sorts. I do find myself asking, should I have listened to the silence more, should I have stepped back from where I am now, and tried to read that silence?

CHAPTER 36
THE AIRPORT, A BIRTHDAY, MORE PLANS

Shortly after, I found out that Kitten was going to a Wedding, abroad, with Angela. I messaged her again, this time to say,

"If the Taxi to take you and Angela to the airport doesn't turn up, give me a call, no matter the time and I will there in about thirty minutes."

Sophia replied, thanking me and added,
" Everything is sorted out."

Some small chit chat followed.
It seemed that Sophia wanted us to be friends again, after stopping our chats the day I went away because they were 'worrying her'.
I so wanted to say 'yes', I really did want to stay friends with her but I knew it would be futile, and quite possibly short lived.
God it really did hurt to do this, but I did not answer her question.
I couldn't.
I wished them both a safe flight.

The next day... a big fail

The taxi picked them up at 5 am (for a 6 am departure for the flight!, bloody crazy)
I wonder who of the ladies came up with that brainwave of a plan.. oh well.
They also had problems trying to get through security?
And so they missed their flight by five minutes.
They had to return home and try and get another flight.
When Sophia told me online, I was fuming, but I told her,
" Whatever time your new flight is, I will take you… and you will get there in time."

At 2.30pm the same day they put their suitcases in the boot of my car, and we were on our way.

A fifteen-minute drive. With Angela sat in the back and Sophia, 'insisting' sitting in the front, even though I had opened the rear door for her.
What is she playing at? She is so contrary, yet can be so annoyingly disarming. But though the sight of her sitting next to me made me feel happy on the outside, the inside was a different story.

Whilst driving to the airport, she asked,
"*How are you coping?*"

What a thing to ask, what did she expect me to say? *'Yeah, brilliant, got a new girlfriend, love her to bits, she's great in bed...'* for Christ's Sake!]
Instead, I replied,
"*I have sorted things out, whilst I was in France'.*

Whilst my left hand was on the gearstick, she placed her right hand on top of mine, squeezed it and said,
"*I'm glad.*"

She then slowly removed her hand.

I thought to myself, was she patronising me, or was she genuinely concerned, or was she lost for words and covering up her own emotions.

We got to the Airport, unloaded at a no stopping zone; a security guy was about to walk over. I told him... "*Less than a minute*" and he stood away.
I wished them both a safe journey, kissed Angela on the cheek and was about to do the same to Kitten (yes, she was and will always be my Kitten)' when she (deliberately?) turned her head to face me, and I kissed her on the lips.
I was screaming inside, *'Oh for Christ's sake... go... walk away, please'*

I felt the dry, emotional lump in my throat getting larger as I watched them both walk away toward Departures.

With that kiss on the lips, was she possibly showing that she still has feelings for me?
But then, where both Kitten and I come from, friends who are really close often greet or depart from each other's company often do that.
But even so, in my mind I was thinking, it may be the very last time I would ever see Kitten again – in this or any other world.

I got into the car and drove away. I couldn't get my breath, I was choking. My eyes filled up rapidly. I felt the salty tears run down my cheeks.

For Christ's sake, I was sobbing, genuinely sobbing.

My head was spasmodically jerking upward. I turned off down a road and parked up near some shops.
I don't know how long I sat there for, maybe only a few minutes.
I calmed down, wiped the tears from my eyes and cheeks, then continued home.
I don't wish to ever have to go through something like that again.

[Though I knew the area where I parked up for those few moments, very well, it wasn't until the writing of this book that I realised just 'where' I had parked up.
Though it had changed a great deal in almost fifty years, it was still the same place... it was the Minister Parade]

Later that evening, Sophia let me know they arrived safely. With that, did she want to remain friends... *distant* friends?

19th. More tests on the throat, Good Lord

The next day and another 'clinical' chat with Sophia. I think we are both a little afraid to go for the repartee and retorts thing, but that's fine by me.
For no apparent reason she quipped in,
   "I will be seeing 'Paul' on my birthday"

   "I will send you a card." I replied.

"I don't want anything from you, not even a card. Nothing to remind me." She answered, sounding very abrupt
CHRIST!!, that bloody hurt... *'Nothing to remind her... of me'*, Even friends send Birthdays cards to each other.

That cut so very, very deep into me. It took my breath away.
Did she deliberately mention about her birthday and Paul to goad me into answering her. But she wasn't finished.
She continued with,
"We will be just having a few drinks and an early night."

'An early night' Why is she rubbing it in, hurting me like this?

I made the decision there and then. I have got to end this completely. Even though I don't believe her about this Paul, she is goading me, rubbing salt into the wound. I can't believe Sophia is saying this.
You don't talk about your 'new' lover to the 'old' lover' you just kicked aside for. That's so cruel, heartless, taking the piss.
And very, very deliberate. But 'why' say it. It was ... odd.

Maybe like me, Kitten can get flustered and tongue-tied, but that was so nasty and totally unwarranted all the same.
So I started... I made a skitting remark about her and Paul;
"So you will be having a nice surprise for each other then?
If there is absolutely no chance of us ever getting back together,
I would prefer you to end all friendship with me. Think of it as a mercy killing."

She then just replied that;
"I have tried my best to stay friends, but I'm with Paul now, and that's what I want."

WHAT! *'Tried her best?*

[Immediately I thought, is this, what she was leading up to say? what she had previously planned and brought the subject up? She, now the innocent victim with a clear conscience and me the bad guy, and I walked into the trap, like the bloody fool I am].

212

I made another skitting reply,
"I may never have been able to keep up with your lifestyle anyway, but maybe Paul will be able to fill that gap as well."

But then, I suddenly realised that even though the statement, to me, was true, it was stupid and childish to say it.
Then, in a micro-second something made me think and recant on those words and I immediately followed it up with a commitment, a vow, and one that still stands today,
"No matter what happens, I will always be here, if you ever wanted to talk. I will never, ever turn my back on you. No matter what you did or said against me."
She did not reply, nor when I told her,
"I couldn't fight for you as there would be no point and that I would only be hurting myself, whilst giving entertainment to others."

With every comment, every message I was giving, I hated myself more and more, but I felt it HAD to be done and as soon as possible.
I even contacted Angela the following day as well, and I was even unkind to her.
God, this was ripping me apart doing this; no one will ever know just how much and never will.

On the 21st. another test, this one nearly bloody choked me. Felt like a bicycle inner tube going down my throat.
And another PSA blood test

From this date up to the end of October, I kept sending Sophia messages, half-truths, non-truths... anything to make her more annoyed, more upset.
During the time I spent with Sophia I never once told her a lie or a 'fib, I couldn't, it's crazy, she seemed to have that 'power' over me. But now, I find I am having to do the complete opposite. And not telling her the whole story.

I contacted her two close friends and I am more than assuming, irritated them as well.
I think I even wrote to her Niece, now that, was so unwarranted.

It more than disgusted me to do it, but I needed as many of her close friends to say *'Get rid of him; he's no good for you'*.

I needed so desperately to become an evil person in their eyes.
As horrid as this may sound, It became easier to do this as the days progressed. Simply because I created another person within myself. A person, whom for the first and only time, would despise everything I stood for.

I even brought up Teegra, the soft-toy white Tiger I gave her, her Birth sign simply because she loved it.
I told her because she discarded me, she will want to get rid of Teegra, obviously because it will have reminded her of me. And that being the case I would want it back...' *it did not deserve to be thrown into the dustbin like I was'*. How sad and childish was THAT?

I so needed to get, and wear that 'UTTER BASTARD' crown.
And in doing so, becoming someone I knew I wasn't.
I was also constantly bombarding her with pleas to make up, to meet up, to teach her dancing.
She was nearing the end of her patience.

She posted on my Facebook page
'FUCK OFF.'

Now, she told me she would never ever say that to me. And so it was working, it was all going to plan.

At the end of October, I received the results of the PSA test of the 21st. It had risen five points, still not over the 'action' threshold, but something of real concern – to me anyway.
It was also confirmed on the following afternoon that I had T1 Throat (Laryngeal) Cancer and it was partially resting on my vocal chords. Thankfully it was still localised, though at 93%. It wasn't terminal, but stage two being imminent. Immediate remedial treatment was required

Oh God, it was the *'it wasn't terminal'* that caused me more heartache than if it had been.

I had pushed Kitten so far, there is no way I could say *'Oooops, it's all been a misunderstanding, sorry'* I had to continue with my plan to totally remove her from my life – though I always knew she would 'still be there', tucked away inside me.

But yet, two days later after the 'Fuck Off' message, she was **still** retaining me as her FB 'friend', just 'why' I do not know.

I can of course wild guess, and I did, and I prayed that this was not the answer because the outcome would hurt me even more than what I could have ever have contemplated or prepared myself for.

It is possible she could have some feelings for me, may even be in love with me, but she was also still very much in love with her late Husband.
She may have felt deep down inside that she was cheating on him.
But at the same time, she truly wanted to retain me as her friend.
She desperately needed time, a lot of time, to come to terms with things.
To learn to accept the past, to look to the future, and change.
And was this her reason for dropping me like a hot potato?

The reappearance of Paul was quite possibly a fabrication in as such, this Paul was indeed, Eric. Both having the second birth name, John
If this is remotely correct, was she too scared of herself to tell me?

A far-fetched wild guess? yes, possibly, but that may give answer to some questions – I could have stepped back given her time as was my intention.
If I wished to be lyrical and full of wishful hoping, then the lyrics to the 1960s song *'Give me time'*, recorded by the late Dusty Springfield would be the most appropriate in these circumstances.
But even so, no matter the reason or excuses made, it needed to change. I had to 'close my eyes', become cold, uncaring.

She had to be forced, to remove me as her 'friend' for the whole plan to work.

I messaged her if she would meet me in a café near to her late husband's business for a talk, nothing more. But it was my sole intention to cause a row. This would have been so bitterly cruel for the both of us, but in my mind, it had to be done.

I went to the café.

I was scared for what I had to do. Secretly I was praying she would not turn up, and I was relieved when she didn't.
The following day I messaged her a long note full of angst, self-pitying and remorse.

That 'did the trick', she finally snapped with these words I will forever see;
   "There will never be anything between us and no further contact in any way. I am blocking you."

CHAPTER 37
KARMA

WHAT THE HELL HAVE I DONE!

I have caused so much pain, sorrow. I openly wept.
The damage has been done, and there is no way of reversing it.
I had utterly fucked up.
But I did have to finish it off. It had gone too far, way too far.
A melodramatic, but necessary, 'Coup de gras'?
And yes, Milnzy. You shall wear your crown.
You have 'earned it'.

I had 'successfully' destroyed any faith, any trust or feelings this woman may have had for me. If someone could, at that moment, be nominated as the **'Worlds Cruellest Bastard'**, I would have won hands down.
The remorse I felt was indescribable. I had indeed, quite possibly destroyed the spirit of the most beautiful creature ever to enter my life, and I will never allow myself to forget the harm I had done.

**In mid-November, at my review with my Urologist, he stated he was concerned about my rising PSA. And the Radiotherapy treatment on my throat continued through November until the start of December.
A scan followed, and soon after, I was informed that there was no sign of any cancer tissue, and everything looks good. The words were bittersweet.
My recent PSA Blood test results showed a drop of two points, though only slight, and was in the right direction….. but.**

Early January 2017, I sent a letter to Sophia, telling her of the Cancer and my absolute regret and disgust of the things I had done.

[Reproduced here as it was sent, with only the names being changed]

Sophia,
This is a 'Come Clean' note... not harassment. I will keep this as brief as possible.
What I did to you was unforgivable and because of that I cannot ask for forgiveness, just understanding.

I will assume you have already been made aware of my throat Cancer from Soo, who was given the message in mid-November. By that time, I had already been informed it was not terminal, as I had first thought, but still required immediate treatment. But the damage and hatred I had caused you had already taken place. I now wish I had acted on the good advice I was given in mid-October.

In early October I still had no way of knowing if you truly still held any feelings for me. I could not take the chance. I was not prepared to let you feel any possible remorse or guilt.

You refused to remove me as your friend on Facebook. And because I could not remove you, due to the promise I made, I was given no alternative but to get you to hate me so much that you would have no other choice but to remove me. To my eternal shame, the plan worked and the fact I had to also use other people to achieve it, disgusted me even more.

I may have done some bad things in my life, but nothing will ever compare to what I had to do to you. And for my penance, the knowledge of that will stay with me forever.
It is a bittersweet irony that on December 7th I was informed the treatment was successful and that the Cancer had been eradicated. My voice box requires therapy, but is functional.
I am telling you this now, not only because a dear friend recently advised me to, but also because if our paths were to ever cross again I would not try to hide from you, as I would have done if I had not told you.

Alex

I did not expect a reply, and I never received one.

Has my Kitten had become her true self, a female Tiger woman, or maybe she always was, but lost her way for a short period of time?.

With them, there are no prisoners. Once they feel they have been betrayed, they often shun the offender completely, whether justified or not. They may become blinkered, almost bitter, their stubbornness to not see *'any other side other than their own'*, almost unparalleled, and if left 'unchecked', could affect their future mental well-being and attitude toward others.

In 2018 on the anniversary of Marie's death (April 20th), Albert was looking through her computer and found copies of messages she sent to Kitten after we 'broke up'.
He sent them to me.

[Reproduced below as it was sent, verbatim, with only the names having being changed and any quotation marks added]

December 09th 2016
Sophia I was told by Alex that you are aware of who I am, who I am in relation to him and what I am by Profession. It is understood that you have taken action on Facebook to stop all forms of communication between you both.
If this is truly the case then I feel that you should a find way to gain access to his FaceBook page. When there, read the post I read today titled 'Cancer Recap' as there are two parts which I certainly believe concerns you.
Why he deliberately coerced you into hating him so much and why he felt he had no choice. What you read in his post does not even break the surface. I can provide answers to theses questions and others that you may wish to ask, but only if you so wish it.
Marie

December 17th 2016
Sophia, Yesterday morning during a telephone call I made to Alex to discus my Family visit next year, I took the bull by the horns.
I told him I had contacted you regarding his recent Cancer Recap post on Face Book.

He was not pleased at all,he was quite angry with me.Iguessed he would be.
He said it would not be possible for you or your friends to see what he had written anyway because none were his friends.
My Daughter later explained to me what how this could be.I learn about Face Book every day.
I explained to him that you have the right to know the truth.
That he should tell you.for his own peace of mind and to hopefully, lessen your anger and bitterness toward him.He just said he would be arrested if he tried.I thought he made a joke but no.
You must really hate him.For that I cannot let this continue,it would be very wrong of me to do nothing.he does not deserve that fate.
Because of what Alex said I have copied what his post is here and after I have given some detail not mentioned.
My apologies if you read all this on a mobile,it will be many pages.Please be patient.

First some of my own thoughts. The story from how you two first met and how you came to get back in contact with each other is like a du conte de fees,a fairytale.My husband is statistician at Lyon said the chances for this happened like it did and if unplanned is unmeasurable,it would be in the millions to one for sure.
What makes it even more incredible is that Alex said all this time you both lived closer than 6kms from each other and at one time less than 1,this is so wonderfully unbelievable. But sadly this fairytale appears to have ended in a bitterness that should never have been allowed to happen.
If only your inaction was not so While listening to Alex and reading a few of the messages between you both which he allowed me to see,it was like looking and listening to the same person,a miroir imag,Jumeaux. This has both blessings and pitfalls.
You both did not realise this and so make allowances.
If you had,I am certain there would have been a different ending. Both of you need the heads banging together and settle your differences or go through life not knowing what could have been. Messages emails cannot resolve this you both have to look in the others eyes.

My own Son,Rene is married for eleven years to Angeline,they are the same age,one week apart and both from 1984.
They are so much alike.They have only three roads in their marriage. Fiery-Relax-Pasionate sometimes to pasionate I have to keep a water bucket close by.You have been good for Alex.
We all saw thedifference in him when he visited.Though he was hurting,he was more confident and there was a shine in him I have not seen for many years.I can only put this as your doing.

[EDITED COPY OF FACEBOOK POST DECEMBER 9th - CANCER RECAP #1 (reprinted in Book Two)]

Alex was with my Family in France when he received the news of the tumor.Something that he had already suspected.
He said to me he tried to tell you earlier but you would not meet with him.
Maybe this was a good thing or a bad thing I dont know.
He was calm.His words when he read the email were.'Jésus why now'.'Kitten cant see this happening' 'it won't happen'.
Both Albert and and I already known you as Kitten for many months. He had also spoke of your long time care for your late husband and you saying that you never wanted to happen again.
It then became clear to me why he said what he did.And why he created a plan and started to implement it when he suspected at the time and for a long time after that his Cancer was terminal illness.
He tried to save you from any anguish as he truly felt you still held feelings for him. Because of the quickly unfolding events he knew he had to become un méchant a villan someone you needed to dislike, hate.
I advised him not to do so but to hold until tests were done and any treatment was complete.He also chose to ignore my warning when he told me he knew of your weakness,heaviness he called it.and how he had to exploit it.
Because of a promise he made to you ? he told me it was the only way he could force you to remove him off your friendship ring,out of your life and free from any guilt you may have felt.
He had asked you to remove him before,but you refused to do so.So in his mind he had no choice.

It would be good if you can acknowledge that you have read this communiqué as there is no way of knowing you have. If you do not I will take that as Alex no longer exists in any part of your life.
I will not concern it with you again as there would be no reason. He knows he made the wrong decision but the lord is baring witness and I know he did so for all the right reasons.
The reasons doesn't matter to him, he made he says a vile decision that he will be reminded of for as long as he lives.
Maybe one day next year I would like to meet the person who for a short time changed his World for the better.
May you have an enjoyable Christmas and New Year
Marie

I was heartbroken. Marie tried so hard to reconcile us, and she never told me.
It seems Kitten never answered those emails either; otherwise, her replies would have been on Marie's computer and passed on to me by Albert
Albert, to this day, still mentions Sophia in our conversations, either online or the telephone. He still hopes that Marie's prophecy (if you wish to call it that, I prefer 'vision') will have substance.
And that the substance will manifest itself soon for, as he says, time is moving forward for all of us. I find I cannot disagree with him there and I hope so too, regarding the vision.

Her words still make me tingle every time I 'see her' saying them in my mind. I have always enjoyed puzzle solving, it's in my nature… as does Kitten's words *'don't read into something that is not there'* (but that is really, too ambiguous)

The following paragraph has been added to this chapter to keep with the continuity.

[Today, May 31st 2022 I received a phone call and later, an email from Albert. In the phone call he said that he had finally found the courage to read Marie's diary which she continued to write in whilst she was in hospital during her last days. He told me that within those pages there is a small paragraph concerning Sophia and myself, which he felt (as would Marie)

that I should be aware of. Albert then sent me a translated version of those few lines (I have only changed the names and rearranged the wording):

Vendredi 17 Mars 2017
And something else I regret. That I could not meet with Sophia. Alex had given me the phone number, but my pain was getting worse. I so much wanted to tell her of my thoughts, my spiritual feelings and understandings about her and Alex. I know I will never see her and I know I will never see my beautiful Alex again, not in this world. But it is my wish that one day all will become clear to him and he finds a way to tell Sophia].

X
1. EPILOGUE:

What you are about to read over the next four, possibly five chapters, may be confusing to say the least. It runs off in tangents, and you may lose track on occasions. My apologies, I was as confused as you, at the time, due to the events as they unfolded.

As you will have now read in the story, our very short time together ended in the most brutal of ways.
Though the end was 'planned', it came about through misunderstandings, wrong words spoken on both sides and very possible, total misreading of emotions.
And again, though it was planned, I never expected the emotional repercussions that would haunt me for more than just a long time after. It would be two years before I started to get any resemblance of a normal inner self.

Yes, I had a choice, another path to take. I could have simply turned around and walked away from it all at the very start after the 'break up'. I could have said to myself,
'Who gives a fuck if she feels anything for me, let her deal with it herself. She 'kicked me into touch' and 'ran off' with a past boyfriend without any thought for me...fuck her'

Even her best friend and confidante, Angela, acknowledged that thought when she told me to,
"Fuck her...walk away and off her radar."

(Or was Angela playing along, to make me feel better and walk out of Sophia's life and hers? A case of 'good riddance, with flowers'?)

Angela also said to me at the same time that,
"I think you have fallen hard for her, Alex, but she cannot return those feelings. When you told her you loved her she looked away purely for the reason she didn't feel the same. I know she

was very, very fond of you. But she has now found her freedom and she doesn't want to be a full-time carer again."
Yes, that was true, I had 'fallen' for her. But 'hard'? No!!

I very quickly replied to correct Angela that I had told Sophia that
*"Yes I said I loved her, but also that the love I had for her was a caring love, I never said I was **'in love' or 'loved'** her per se, simply because I wasn't'.*

Angela did not give a reply to that, and before she could change the subject, I quickly asked her;
*"What would happen if **she** needed a carer, someone to look after her?"*

(With my hand on my heart, I was actually picturing myself in that position and it would something I would not shirk from. What a bizarre thought, was it really my caring love?)
She answered simply,
"She would take herself off to Switzerland."

I was totally taken aback by that. Angela seems to say, and know, a lot about what Sophia would do, as if she were her spokesperson.

Looking back could I have said '*I am very fond of you*' instead, but surely, being fond of someone is ambiguous. It's like a tap that can be turned off and on at will. Whatever the mood takes you at the time. The caring love I had for Sophia could not be turned off. It was a permanent thing and something I could not explain...
In the end I chose instead, to do the so-called honourable thing and protect her...from me. And it ripped me apart doing so.
To go against everything my Father had taught me and everything I taught myself throughout my life, everything, including my integrity, I pushed it all aside.
It was my choice. I chose to do it without hesitation and I accepted the consequences. But the fall out was mind-numbing.

On the outside, I was the same guy, maybe a little vague or moodier than usual, but basically the same guy. Inwardly, the story was far, far different and darker.
I wasn't suicidal, nor was I morbid and certainly not vengeful. Those things never, ever crossed my mind. I simply could not believe what I had done, I was full of remorse and self-hatred.
I had indeed smothered Kitten, far beyond her endurance.
She was suffocating. She felt it was going too deep on my part, she could not cope with that idea and the fact I was married only made the matter worse.

It all came to a head on the 28th and when I saw her eyes roll, I knew then, that that was the end of our relationship – but I still fought on. Just hoping, praying for a miracle.

Sophia, will, of course, say she told me two or three times, she wanted us to go 'slower', that it was always me who was 'intense', and yet the very next time we met, we couldn't keep our hands, or lips, off each other.
But all the while, was she playing a game with me?
Now, that thought did cross my mind, not at the time, but later on. And there was added credence to it, when I thought back to how she spoke of 'Paul', as if I didn't exist, that I meant nothing to her, past or present.
And yet, she wanted to remain friends, but 'understood' if I couldn't manage that.
It may not have been her intention, but that felt so patronising. Here is a twist, was my 'wild guess' (page 215) in fact, nearer to the truth.

But through it all, whatever lies are said to me, by her or by others, I still have so much faith, so much trust, in her.
It's so hard to explain, it's just a deep feeling of trust, understanding and compassion that I have. Yes, I know, unbelievably crazy 'eh.
But more than just a 'maybe', the question I should really be asking myself is, does she still have any faith or even trust in me? Or more to the point, had she ever have any at all?

I simply could not deal with NOT seeing her, NOT being with her, NOT having contact with her, and it all started *before* that first kiss. And in all honesty, I still could not understand as to the reason why. But at that time (and still now) I felt there was something very special, something so very different about her.

From that very first moment I saw her on the bus. And from when I found her again many, many years later, I knew that I had to keep in contact with her. So yes, even before that first kiss.

You may ask, is there the possibility of reconciliation, just wanting to be real friends again and not just the '*Hello do you want to be number 1985 in my friend's list*'.

I feel I have to say '*It looks very doubtful*'. And that hurts me beyond words.

Yes, it does take 'Two To Tango' as they say, and I fear only one of us will have the courage and faith to want to dance.

But, is it not true sadness, that she so wanted to learn to dance for real, and with me, as her Teacher.

Or were they just words she spoke, to appease me.

Some might say, *'Good, you are now being realistic'*.

But to be perfectly honest, a true realist bordering on fatalist?

I would not have been around to write this book as I would have listened to and followed blindly, the 'advice' given to me by the people with my best interests at heart, the 'Professionals'.

But for both Sophia and I to get together one day, talk seriously and become true friends, would be more than a dream come true, and one I am clinging on to, even though all hope appears to have gone.

For if you don't have hope, you simply don't have a future, you merely 'exist' in an already dead World, awaiting your last breath.

But no matter what any future may bring, there is one thing that is for certain and will never alter.

I was not able to fight (metaphorically speaking) to win back her affection, though I did try in my own clumsy, mixed up way.

For the past five years and more, Sophia, by her silence has apparently made it very clear that I would be wasting my time in even thinking about it.

But no matter what happens in the present or in the future, I will take her corner to defend her name, to protect her if you will, and with all that that entails.

In today's World, that may appear to be an over-the-top and an out-dated value, but it's with such, that I have come to value Sophia, my Kitten.

A value that has become, beyond just words.

And there is no higher value, that I can think of, or would want.

Defending her name has only happened the once, in either 2018 or 2019, and in a pub I frequented, someone who knew Sophia, made a disparaging and intimate remark about her.

Ok, the guy had been drinking but I felt that it was said with the intension for me to plainly hear it, knowing I was stood almost next to the person. Why? Hell knows, jealousy maybe, because one of those two people I had told about me dating Sophia had obviously told him. And as I had learnt earlier, he fancied Sophia. Anyway, it was dealt with in a subtle way that got 'the message across' with a little cutting humour.

It 'could' have caused an altercation, but I don't think he grasped just WHAT I said to him. It made his friend laugh though.

I did wonder at the time if this person was the mysterious 'Paul' as certain events would have tied in.

There is a question I have asked myself – and just the once. If I had had a happy contented marriage, would I have allowed Sophia to enter it like I did.

The truthful answer is yes.

Because deep down inside of me, I felt I could NOT have stopped it and I knew there was (and still very much is) something very special, very different about her – and I was proven right.

2. AFTERMATH:

In the telling of our time together, and the events that unfolded, it became, at times, almost too painful to write.
And I truly felt that I could not continue.

But the foil to that was our banter online. It was incredible, almost unbelievable, how two people could 'bounce' off each other and from the word 'go'.
Believe me when I say, it was like molten lava from a Volcano - it was unstoppable. Quick-fire repartee and retorts.
I think back and can burst out in laughter at some of the friendly point-scoring bouts we had, of which only a small number have been mentioned within this book. But believe me, when I say, I have never in my life had so much fun, had so much love and total enjoyment talking to someone as I did with Kitten. It WAS magical.

Offline we were often 'quieter', sometimes a little too quiet, as I felt that I had to force a conversation from Sophia on occasions, but that could have been worked on over time.
But alas, I was not given the blessing of that – time.

For a long time, and believe me, it did feel like an eternity; I felt sorrow, I felt despair, I felt anger. I was ripping myself apart, from the inside out, over what I had to do to get Sophia (and her friends) to hate me.
Yes, I felt it was justified because of the throat cancer, but I had to do things, say things that went against everything my Father had taught me, the self-discipline I had taught myself. My whole persona changed. It needed to, to succeed with the plan.
Maybe things could have worked out better. Maybe we could have ended our relationship later than we did. Maybe Sophia could have worked through my Cancer with me.
So many maybes. And the World seems to revolve around them.

If only Sophia would have opened up and just talked to me, about us, about her. Told me her fears, what she wanted out of our relationship, if anything. I could have shared my fears, my hopes, and what I wanted, with her.

We may not have agreed, but it would have been out there in the open, and open to compromise and understanding.

As you may have gathered, I am a firm believer in communication, talking face to face, discussion with no 'heated arguments'.
Though, sometimes within an argument, the truth comes out... but if so, why not before?
I have questions I will quite possibly, never get answers to.

Since 2016, I have sent both a Birthday and Christmas card (more bin fodder as well, most probably) to Sophia.
And yes, even for 'that' birthday she spent with Paul, I did send her a card and flowers, to her doorstep. I didn't care that she '*didn't want anything to remind her of me*'. I'm not that callous.
I had travelled to Kitten's house on numerous occasions to 'post' notes, asking for contact. Dinner dates, pleading for reconciliation. I have talked about these as part of MY plan in Chapter 36, but all the notes were also acts of desperation, and hope, on my part.
I must have, to any sane person, come across as someone with a mental disorder.
I also needed so badly for her to know, just why I acted like I did.

I even tried sending flowers regularly from the start of 2017 (as Soo, one of her friends, had recommended it some weeks before). Yes, Soo was actually still talking to me as I knew her before I met up with Sophia.
I have lost count of the number of times I drove the forty-plus miles dropping off the flower's or the 'notes' until about the October, two sometimes three times a month, either very late at night or in the early hours of the morning when it dark at night and though light during the mornings it was before people woke from their slumber. I was petrified, that she would see me. But, and it's really no wonder that that didn't work either, and I had no doubt the flowers would end up in the refuse bin.

Fast forward some eight months after I took the video at The Ironworks.

I was preparing it to be uploaded to YouTube and something caught my eye, in the background. A little out of focus but still enough to gain my attention.
I zoomed in... and there she was... Kitten. I was 'stunned'.

Stunned, not by the realisation that perhaps she may have planned the meet-up, which considering the crowd's size and so tightly packed it may not have even have happened anyway.
But her very first words, the more I think about it the more I feel my assumption was correct, that she DID have a photo of me on her phone. There is no other explanation – is there?

What I saw in the video not only made me smile, it also made me wonder just what **IS** happening.
For the love of Christ, this was more, far more than coincidence surely.
I only took three minutes worth of video that day. Three minutes in the whole of the time I was in the Ironworks. Think about it:
Three minutes out of a possible three hundred and sixty (as I was going to leave at about 6.00pm anyway).

I started the video and WOW .. twenty-one seconds later, there they both were, making their donation, then standing at the back, further away from the stage. I would say twenty-five metres away. Now come on, that was unbelievable, incredible and also a little spooky.

And then, not realising what I captured on video, came the realisation that I could have so easily have turn around and walked away, in the opposite direction, into the main body of the crowd when I stopped the video.

But no.
I stepped forward, in the general direction where Kitten and Angela were, chatted to a Lady and ***then*** made my way forward, to where our paths were to eventually cross.
Breath-taking coincidences, by anyone's measure I feel you would agree. But as said earlier the chances were - immeasurable
Though I did wonder, if either Kitten or Angela saw me videoing and deliberately hung back to see which direction I was heading.

But I pushed that thought aside, because even if that was true, to have actually spotted me at that precise time and distance, with my face covered by the (video) camera, amidst all those people, and for me to have been in plain sight of them. It would still beg belief.

My two long-time friends, twins Athena and Christina had, in late summer 2017 sold their house in the village next to Rosemount and purchased one in Rosemount itself.
The house, to make it their own, needed decorating and internal work doing. I had done the same to their previous house, updating and getting it ready for the sale.
This work carried on until just before Christmas 2017 and they celebrated with an open house Christmas party.
Now, during this time I had stayed over at the new house for a few days on a number of occasions. Much the same in their old house.
It allowed me to relax, and breathe as well. And during which, there have been times I had to go into the village itself, even to within almost shouting distance of Sophia's house. I have always tried to be discreet. Though sometimes I did ask myself, '*why should I have to tippy-toe around*'?
If she should ever see me and I see her, I don't know how I would react. I don't know how she would respond. I fear that more than anything. I became wound up with apprehension, tummy fluttering, just thinking about it.

In January the following year, with profit gained from the sale of the old house and savings from the new, the twins purchased, on my advice, a small bungalow holiday home near an established holiday resort on the north-west coast.
This was to be an investment and would be long-leased to professional people. After quite some TLC and renovations carried out by all three of us, both houses became as the twins wanted.
The following month, I found out, purely by accident, that Sophia had bought the house in Rosemount in the summer of 2017.
As silly as it may sound to the reader, I was so elated.

Another though less incredible coincidence, it was the same period that the twins moved there

So maybe Sophia, too, had found that unique calmness and the warmth of the house, that it had given me the first time I saw it and every time I entered. I do truly hope so.
Inwardly, I wished her nothing but the very best and that she makes the house, her house, her sanctuary.
It was so very different from the house she shared with her late husband. Maybe this was a deliberate attempt to get away from the memory that brought, I wouldn't know.
I just hope she will find contentment and happiness there.
But I would still like to think, that her choice of her new house was due, in part if not whole, to the same feeling I had many years earlier. Maybe we were not that different.

Around the same time, and whilst driving through Rosemount with Christina and Athena, on our way to a Furniture store which was open until late, we passed a small convenience store which was still open.
The girls needed some fresh milk. Athena parked a little further up the road, about twenty-five metres past where Sophia lived.
I volunteered to get the milk. In reality, I 'wanted' to go... to see if I could see Kitten again.
And so, as I walked past her house, my eyes automatically turned to the direction of the downstairs front room window, and there she was.
She was curled up on the two-seater sofa, either reading a book (she had dark-rimmed glasses on), or watching the television as it was on, the glow of which lighting her up her face and body.

I hurried past, accompanied with a very sharp intake of breath, not wanting her to see me. I bought the milk and deliberately walked on the opposite side of the road, back to the car.
And whilst walking past her house, the twinkling of lights amongst the ivy on the house wall, caught my eye. I then slowed my pace to take a closer look and noticed the ivy had also been extensively thinned out. I instantly recalled that first day... and made a knowing, thankful smile.

Later, I mentioned to the twins that we parked almost outside Sophia's house. They knew of Sophia of course, but absolutely no idea she lived where she did, and so close.
That has been the only time I have seen her since the end of September 2016, and she looked as beautiful as ever. I have never seen her since. For certain, we won't be around in another forty-six years.

Two incidents happened during 2017 and 2018, not so much incidents but being very dull, numbing almost a sense of foreboding type feelings, that Kitten was poorly, and I do mean poorly.
I recall sending emails to Angela, but never got a reply.
It was not a good time for me. I had no way of knowing if Kitten was in a hospital or a clinic. There was no-one to ask.

Then at the end of 2018, I don't know how it came about – it just 'happened'. It came right of the blue.

And it hit me full in the face. I admit I was stunned, shocked by my own blindness. All the pieces of the jigsaw were now in place.
I was, I am, truly in love with this girl, this woman.

Bloody Hell!!

The realisation first, then the admittance, had the most remarkable, calming effect on me. It was quite unbelievable, as the previous two years had taken its toll, emotionally. I was inwardly, a total wreck.
I hated myself beyond description for what I had done. And with matters made even worse with not having any contact with Kitten, I was mentally and physically exhausted.

The past two years of frustration and angst disappeared.
A welcome 'slap in the face'.
Though my self-disgust, at what I had to do to make Sophia and others hate me, is still there as a permanent reminder.
I claim that to be my penance for doing the wrong thing for the right reasons.

But that wasn't the only blinding revelation.

Love and friendship…. I found I could separate the two where Sophia was concerned. Too late I know but….
Muddied at times, but yes, I could. And if I had possibly known back in 2016, that I was indeed, in love with this incredible woman, I have no doubt it could have helped with our time together.
But at the time I had no idea that I could have even been in love with her.

Now here is the strangest part (to me anyway), because I now realised, and accepted, that I was in love with Sophia.
I also accepted that that Sophia has chosen her own path, and one without me.
Deep down inside I felt that if she ever wanted for me to be a part of her life (again?), she would let me know, but only when **she** was ready. An old-fashioned girl or not, it would be Sophia who needed to make that decision, not me. I was happy for her and with that acceptance and knowledge, it calmed me even more.
But I needed to resolve many questions, for my own peace of mind and hopefully find some sort of closure.
There is much before, during and even after our 'relationship' that is deeply puzzling.

Had I have known, in 2016, that I was indeed in love with Kitten, could I have told her then? My thoughts now are, it may have been too soon at any time, and sometimes you don't have to tell someone... they know already, they 'feel it'.
But all the same, though they may 'know it', may 'feel it', there is something within the reassurance to be told it, to whisper it in their ear spontaneously and lovingly.

And maybe, just maybe, Kitten 'felt' this on our last night together. Perhaps, all that Kitten indeed wanted was a casual, intimate friendship... and just why I could not allow myself to think that at the time, I will never know. By her previous actions and words?
A question arises. Why could I never say *'I Love You'* to her, even on that perfect evening of the 21st? Was it because I didn't realise? or because I was afraid or thought incapable of loving someone so

deeply, and so therefore, completely blocking the thought from my mind.
To use one of Kitten's phrases, *'Too Late Was The Cry'*. Maybe so.
With this in mind, and all that that was happening (medically) in my life at the time I had come to the realisation that I had played a bigger part in this terrible ending that I had ever imagined.
So yes, indeed, too late, *far too late*.

Then, of course, yet another side emerges.

There was always the strong possibility that she was 'tired' of me by the time of that night at her house. She wanted something new. I just inadvertently provided the perfect 'get out clause'.
This has indeed been mulled over several times by myself, but the same things keep coming back; The heart to heart, the sudden 'party', the immediate reappearance of 'Paul' it was all too 'tied up nicely with a bow' to be true. And that is something else it seems, that I will never get to know the truth about.

The last note I 'posted' to Kitten (at the very start of 2019) was when I told her 'that I had just found out I was in love with her'. Not truly knowing if she cared, I felt I just needed to tell her.
Believe me, it was a great relief for me to be able to do so – even in a note.

And since December 2018, I have asked myself more than once, *'was it possible I loved her from that very first moment on the bus?'* This, to me, would mean Kitten was my first love, but could she have been my first and possibly, only true love.
It certainly wasn't just infatuation or curiosity. After all, why did I keep her in mind and spoke of her at every appropriate moment for all those years?

But, and this still amazes me no matter what reason I try to come up with; *'How did I recognise her all those years later?'*
There was absolutely nothing in her comments that would suggest she was THAT girl. That in itself was so totally utterly

incredible. I would love to hear a professionals learned opinion on this alone.

Could all this really be a part of a Chinese 'Red Thread'?

[Wikipedia: The **Red Thread of Fate**, also referred to as the **Red Thread of Marriage**, and other variants, is an East Asian belief originating from Chinese Mythology. It is commonly thought of as an invisible red cord around the finger of those that are destined to meet one another in a certain situation as they are "their true love"]

It is often said that being true friends *is* a commitment.
It's an invisible commitment from both sides.
It takes time, understanding, compromise, openness and truth, often having to bend like the willow in the breeze. Most, if not all, can only be achieved fully, with physical, face to face talks and interaction. It helps guide us in the right direction, the use of body posture, eye contact, and facial expressions – they all help us learn about the other person. So, all in all, we need to come to an understanding of each other's wants and needs.

And that's just for starters.
In our case, there is the added factor that we were 'lovers' at one point, and that fact, whether it's liked it or not, would be seeded into any friendship we may have in the future.
So it must be accepted, even talked about with both sides listened to, and from there, with understanding, we both can move forward, without regrets, to become and remain real friends.

This may seem odd to actually hear, but when you are in a physical, caring relationship…it is an absolute **must** for friendship to be present and active. Quite often, it is not. Friendship is more than pretty words.
In fact, any type of relationship that is devoid of friendship is shallow and superficial, unfulfilling, uncomfortable, callous and even cruel. It is wearisome to the body, the spirit and the soul.
But when you combine the two, life becomes more colourful, more meaningful, more purposeful and more joyful when we have a deeper intimacy with people who matter to us.

This last paragraph insight, though I believe to be so accurate, are not my words. They are from an Asian Lady writer whom I have the good fortune not only to know and have dined with on a number of occasions, but I am also able to call her my friend.

Kitten always said she could not provide a commitment to me.
I never, ever asked her to, but I offered one for her.
And always remember, love is not a commitment; it never has been, it's a feeling one has, and in my case, that feeling was solely toward Kitten.
The commitment I made to her was that I would never turn my back on her, no matter what she did or said, even if against me.
If she ever needed me, I would be there, for her, irrespective of any status I was in. She only needs to ask, or I am told of.
And that commitment still stands, and always will.
I never demanded, nor even expected the same in return, though I did have hopes that maybe… one day it may be so.
A commitment can be an unspoken, honoured promise, be it short or long term, from one person to another.
It does not mean a 'contract'. It does not mean having to stay together, sticking together like glue twenty-four hours a day, three hundred and sixty-five days a year.
It should never, ever be treated as or even thought of as some form of servitude sentence. Those are 'my' thoughts, my beliefs.

Step back in time a few months. It's mid-2018, with the dramatic drop and flattening of my PSA figures, I started to make plans to move and work as a Teacher of English (and Dance) in South East Asia on a minimum two-year contract, as, quite honestly, there was nothing left for me here and Clair would have carried on as normal.
Some could say that would be quite cruel on Claire, to leave for two years or more. All I can say is, you have not walked in my shoes for the last twenty or so years. Besides, I could come home every four months for a fortnight as part of the contract, plus Chinese New Year.
By December 2018 these plans were quite advanced. And yes, I was 'now' in love with Kitten, but as it stood, there was a
'til Hell freezes over' chance of ever getting back together.

She made a new path, one without me. I finally surrendered and accepted that, and with that, life had to go on. It will go on.

BUT in late January 2019, that all came to a grinding halt.

Something (or was it 'someone') was telling me not to go.
The feeling within the message being so extraordinarily strong.
And, as it turned out, not going helped to carve out a very different future for me and one I am so grateful for.

[There is now a time gap of a year, which is explained, in detail within 'My Seven Year Itch… with Cancer' hopefully you have been reading it, alongside with this story, from Chapter 11. Confusing I know – but this is the only way you can see how the two stories are inextricably linked].

On January 29th 2020, whilst reading 'Survivors' by Maggie Oliver at The Royal, and whilst awaiting my review as my cancer treatment was starting, I reached page 84.

An epiphany occurred.

It just hit me. It hit me so hard I lifted my head and just stared at the ceiling, then looked down at the book re-reading the words, not shedding a tear, yet I was 'choking up'. Stifle it… control it.
How long? I don't know, two or three minutes, maybe longer.
Past visions, actions and thoughts flashed through my head.

A lady sat at the same table, asked, *'are you ok'*, and *'it must be a good book'* I only half heard her words. I think I answered her; *'Yes, I'm fine, thank you. Yes, it's a good book'*, and then showed her the cover. She nodded. *'I have read it, so sad'* she replied.

In one single paragraph of just five lines, the mists cleared, and what had been staring me in the face for the last six years became 'obvious'.
I thought the jigsaw was complete in December 2018.
Little did I realise that the most important piece was missing.

But now, I had found that missing piece, the source (if you wish to call it that) of '***The Gift***'.
And what a time to find the truth.

I can reveal now, in this book, that '***The Gift***' was… Sophia.
It may be hard for many readers to comprehend, but yes, Sophia was more than the source; she WAS, she IS, '***The Gift***'.
And of that, I have absolutely no doubt. Everything points to that conclusion.
I am now convinced more than at any other time, that subconsciously she was always the vision, the goal. A vision and a goal I had no idea of, or for what it was intended.
The goal was not of Sophia being a physical prize, to be with, yes that would be so nice, but not as a 'prize', but quite possibly as some form of spiritual attainment?
This was something of which obviously I had no knowledge or understanding of at the time – but now!
It is ironical, that four years before, Marie said these words.
"I strongly believe it started to grow back within you the moment you found her again. Despite your age and what you have been through over the years, you still have a lot to learn about yourself, and you still have a lot to offer her and give others."

And even earlier, when I spoke to her about the events of the August Bank Holiday.
"Something deeply spiritual was happening, and for whatever the reason, it was inextricably binding the two of you together'. 'It's Kismet, but so much more. You two were destined to meet up again from all those years ago, make no mistake about that. 'Someone' has something really big planned for the both of you."

My dearest Marie, you KNEW then, just what that precious '***Gift***' was.
It was more than a regained, heightened confidence Sophia gave me. It was a determination. A purpose which all living creatures have inside themselves, the will to stay alive. But this was more than just self-preservation. Sophia was the catalyst not only for me wanting to stay alive, but also in keeping me alive.

I had heard Marie's words, but it never struck home, until now. The 'strange' feeling which I could never express or explain was the most important part of Sophia's '*Gift*' to me. To give me back what I had lost. And to give me another reason for wanting to stay alive?

By the time when Sophia came back into my life, my confidence was shot. At the time of the Cancer being in my stomach, I was drained;

I only had enough determination to see that part through.

Then came the strong possibility of Cancer in my left breast.
In truth, I did not believe I would see the year out. I couldn't summon up anything.
All the previous years of me being made to feel worthless had taken its toll. I didn't welcome death; I just 'expected it' to come, and soon.

A full year into my fight against Cancer (December 2014), I was becoming aware of an unexpected change in me, mentally.

Whilst I still had some extremely faint sparks of confidence left, I started to receive 'boosts' of 'something' that appeared far more profound. And it was something I had never felt before.

It was like confidence, but different. I couldn't put it into words that would make sense. I still can't. It didn't fade, it seemed to get stronger as the months went by. It was an extraordinarily good feeling.

It 'just appeared', like a *'Gift'* sent, and that's what I ended up calling it, '***The 'Gift'***'. And never was the time I needed it more.
It is what I genuinely believe, and all the pieces fit together.

Sophia, or the nickname that I gave and preferred, and the one she later wanted to hear '*when I was old and grey*', Kitten, had been with me, inside me all this time.

When her 'presence' thought I needed a 'boost', it was there.

And so Sophia, it would seem, may have been brought back into my life to help me beat the Cancer, not only helping to guide me, not only to push me when I felt lost or weary, but to give me something else to fight for... and in truth, I'm still not sure what that is, without any 'fanciful thoughts' of a future.

So maybe it really was just the confidence, the courage and the spirit to stand and fight though I cannot bring myself to believe it was that 'simple'. But WOW, what an incredible *'just'*.

So together, as a 'team', yes, a team, we both made sure I would still be here today.
Her *'Gift'*, her inner spirit, wanted me to stay alive.
I now have little doubt that somehow, Sophia may well have been subconsciously in my thoughts when I created my 'calling card' all those years ago.
But **'The Gift'** knew there was a more critical time ahead.

But something else happened with that event, that epiphany, in January.
Was I truly *in love* with her, or was this, in some way, part of the' plan' created all those years ago.
Was it for me to keep her in mind because my subconscious knew that she was the key for keeping me alive in time to come.
Was this at all possible? Sounds incredible?

I had wondered as to why I needed to see her all the time, too often really. Was it because I wanted to share my time with her or was it my subconscious telling me to *'keep her in sight'* and *'not to lose her again as she will be needed'*. Totally crazy and unbelievable.
And yet the crazier it sounded, the more plausible it appeared.

But as I mentioned earlier in the book, a spanner was thrown into the works and created an unexpected 'ripple'. Quite possibly something my subconscious did not expect or want. Emotions entered the equation.

And if they hadn't, then the break up may not have happened, well, possibly not when it did.
And because of that, the connection between Sophia and I was cut, and so may have been the subconscious connection between us as well.

This did dwell on my mind for some time.

I tried to fight against it, and said to myself that if this was the case, then why did I come to the realisation that I WAS in love with Sophia, my Kitten some TWO YEARS after we broke up. It just did not make sense at all.

By June 2020, I received the first indication, through a PSA reading, that the treatment to clear the 'final' Cancer, was visibly working. A further two tests in July and August confirmed it.

If only Marie, my Late Cousin, were here. She would have been 'over the moon' and I know what she would have said,

'Alas, you can never turn back the clock. You have to live and learn from the mistakes you have made. You can only live in the hope that whilst you may be forgiven, you can also learn to forgive, no matter what the reason or circumstance. And from these lessons, go forward with a better understanding'.

From past experiences, I have found that there has never been, or can never be, a time limit on learning.

Sophia's '*Gift*' defied everything, and it stayed with me for it to come to the fore once again, in possibly, what was to become my greatest ever physical, and mental, challenge.

But, through everything that has happened there is one very, VERY big part in all of this, for which the answer will never be known.

WHY ME?

Why was I chosen above anyone else?
There was Sophia's husband.
A husband of many years, terminally suffering from Cancer.
Why was she not able to pass her '*Gift*' to him and quite possibly save his life? Did he actually want to die? Was he so desperate to want to leave everyone, the ones he loved, once loved, cared for?
I was just like a passing cloud, with no connection, other than meeting her on a bus and talking to her for thirty, thirty-five minutes some fifty years prior. My life had no meaning to her.

So yes, I truly have justification in asking, '**Why me?'**

And yes, there will be readers, even friends saying... *'Rubbish'*, *'Impossible'*, *'Fairy tales'*, *'Total Bullshit'*, *'What planet are you on'*, a *'Suitable case for treatment?'* but in reality, there are many mystifying, 'spiritual' events going around us every day. It is only because we cannot 'feel' them; we are not part of them, we say they don't exist.

These are not to be confused with 'premonitions'.

There are so many instances where people have been affected by them,

'If I had turned that corner two seconds earlier, I would be dead, something made me slow down, it's a miracle'.

'If I had not stopped to help the child who had been injured, I would not have missed the 'plane, [that crashed]'.

'My judgement and training as a Fireman said I must turn right avoiding the dense smoke as I had no breathing equipment on, but something told me 'No, turn left' into the dense smoke ...and there they were, the two kiddies lay on the floor, collapsed. I scooped them up and got them out of the house. Thank God they are both ok'

These are just three events that actually happened and reported at the time - there are many more examples, some we just don't even stop and think about – we take for granted.

And for that reason, there is no real end, no real closure to this book whilst either Sophia or myself are still breathing the air. It's a never- ending book. But to this book, there will be no written sequel.

I am not a religious person; I don't follow any cults or mystics, I'm mentally sound (though some may argue that point). I'm just an everyday, typical type of bloke who has experienced something quite extraordinary. But I am sure the Buddhists would have an answer for it all.

Maybe someone like Freud could have concluded that this 'connection' and all its tangents I had with Sophia were due, in whole or part, to whatever I saw within Sophia, I possibly saw within myself. She was a subconscious reflection of me. And this had already been touched on with Marie, that we were 'so much

alike.' *a miroir imag,Jumeaux* as she would say when discussing our own similarities
It may be as simple as that... and then again, maybe not.

But it's more than fair to say, many others have had this connection with someone. A person in their life that was so special, they could not put into words as to just why, when asked.
August, has now become a very auspicious month in my life.
1. 1968, Early August, Sophia first entered my life
2. 2013, The first of the Cancers was confirmed
3. 2016, Sophia became a reality once again, after forty-eight years
4. 2018, I finished twenty-eight weeks with the Speech Therapist.
5. 2019, I became the first (and only, to date) recipient outside Barslow to have the specialist full Gallium PSMA PET/CT scan. The scan that found the Cancer that other scans couldn't.
6. 2020, And the end of the Seven Year Itch with Cancer.

And it was around this time in 2020 that I did a rather foolhardy thing.
Foolhardy? downright bloody stupid more like.

Lockdowns, due to the escalating pandemic, were in full force. People were dying. I was very concerned about Sophia, I couldn't help it. I still cared for her wellbeing very much.
I wrote a five or six line note to Sophia's Niece and husband expressing my concern that she may do something foolish and catch the virus, and asked for them to keep a watch on her.
Then, whilst struggling with the pain due to the side effects of my treatment, I drove to her old house, and posted the note into the external letter box.
Getting out of the car to post the letter was a struggle to say the least, I almost fell over twice and if anyone saw me, they would have figured me to be pissed (drunk), I then drove back home.
It may have seemed like a silly and 'not needed' thing to do, but I just had to do 'something', to tell her to keep safe, my nature I suppose.
I just hope I haven't embarrassed her or anyone in doing so.

I had previously been informed in July of 2020 that due to the side effects of the cancer treatment, there is little hope of me being able to dance again.

I then recalled many years before, that I was informed, due to an injury sustained in 1979, that, in time I would never be able to walk, unaided, again. With only the 'fusion' of my left ankle, though far from guaranteed, could prevent me from the possible use of a wheelchair in the not too distant future. I refused to have the operation.

I proved the 'white coats' wrong, and I will prove them wrong again.

By the time of Sophia's seventieth birthday, I felt I needed to send her an 'extra' card. And other than the cursory note I had sent with the previous Birthday/Christmas cards, stating *'it's just a card, nothing more nothing less'* I sent along, a very special 'Thank You' card, along with a note that read….

A BIRTHDAY CARD
Nothing More – Nothing Less
and also a 'THANK YOU' card
For A Reason
You Would Never Guess
(Never as in a lifetime of Sundays & £5 bets, that I could never collect)
You can destroy the card(s) if that is your choice, but you will never destroy my thanks.

Because of how our time together ended, it seems I may have been and always will be, portrayed as the 'bad person'.

I was (am still am) treated with disdain, like a Leper by her friends. Yes, there is some justification in that, because it's how I wanted it to finish. An ending I did not want to happen. A little self-pity?

And I have little doubt, so as not to upset Sophia either through her instruction or the closeness of friendship, those friends have refused to make any form of contact with me.

And in doing so, I am now being denied any chance of being listened to in my defence.

There were mitigating circumstances which people, her friends, maybe even Sophia herself, have no knowledge of.

Come the Christmas, the Country was still in the grip of the Pandemic. Yet people often disregarded even the most basic of restrictions, and became seriously ill or in some cases died. I was once again concerned for Sophia's safety. Along with the Christmas card I hand posted I also included a note to the front.

I KNOW YOU WILL DESTROY THIS CHRISTMAS CARD

..BUT PLEASE
FOR THE SAKE OF THOSE WHO KNOW AND LOVE YOU
FOR THOSE YOU KNOW AND LOVE IN RETURN
FOR THOSE WHO LOVE YOU AND WHOS LOVE CAN NOT BE RETURNED
THEY ARE ALL PART OF YOUR PRESENT AND THEY ALL WANT TO REMAIN A PART OF YOUR FUTURE

DO NOT TAKE ANY RISKS THIS CHRISTMAS AND NEW YEAR, NO MATTER HOW TRIVIAL THEY APPEAR.

THOSE THAT LOVE YOU CARE FOR YOU
ALWAYS REMEMBER THAT

Sophia loved socialising with friends and family. I felt then that it was the very least and the only thing I could do. I could never regret doing it.

At the end of December just prior to New Year's Eve, I decided to try and rectify in my defence, some part of the misunderstanding (too light a word I know) that had taken place, by posting Sophia, the complete story of my fight and 'victory' over Cancer.
It was the same story I had been posting, as and when it happened, in diary form on Face book (but for reserved viewing) and also a covering letter which included a synopsis of a very early unproofed version of this book, via recorded mail delivery.
The hope being was that she would read and understand the reasoning behind my severe, cruel actions towards her, thus creating a bitter end.

It was also my intention, with her consent, to follow that up with a short part-proofed manuscript of my (future) book that she could draw opinions on, and inform me of any corrections.
I told her of this in another letter I sent at the start of January 2021.
If she was hurt by the manuscript, I would seriously have considered not getting it published. She was 'in the chair'.
Sadly, another fail, as the recorded letter was never signed for.
This may, of course be down to the new rules on mail delivery people have to abide by during the Covid-19 pandemic, and that many recorded letters would not require a signature.
So, I will never know if she received it, never mind actually read it.

[Due to not hearing from her, the short manuscript of the book which I was going to send to her, was destroyed – or so I thought.
In April, Christina sent her the copy, totally by mistake.
She was mortified when I mentioned in passing, that I was both sad and happy that the copy was destroyed. And she had to admit otherwise. She either did not read or could not find the yellow post note that I attached to the manuscript.
Most of the work had been created at their house, in case Claire should come across it. Both Christina and Athena were the unofficial 'keepers of the scrolls'.
I suspect Sophia will either leave it unopened or realise who it is from, rip it up and throw it into the rubbish bin.
Oh well, what's done is done].

As the New Year dawned I took my two dogs out for their first walk of 2021. To them, as it was to me, just another day.
And within five minutes, we were on the frost-covered fields.
A dusting of snow layered the top of the frost, giving the ground that 'full moon at night' look, at 6 am, it is still quite dark.
Huan picked up the scent of a Fox, whilst the other, Zhen-Zhen, never stirred from my side, much in the same way as she has done since I found her at five o'clock in the morning in May 2018, tied up to a compound steel gate, emaciated, little hair, with no food or water.
Humans can be so very cruel.

And so, whilst walking on that crisp New-Years Day morning, Kitten just entered my thoughts once again, only for a few seconds, as she always seems to do, with no prompting or inclination and at any given moment in time. It is both spooky and yet so calming, one could say beautiful even.

A few days into the New Year (the 9th), and out of the blue, I received a text from Sophia warning me not to send any more letters or notes.
She stated she had all the unopened letters and notes in her possession. And that if I sent her anything else, she would go to the police.
I phoned her back straight away. Her phone rang three or four times, and during the possible fifth - it went dead
I then texted her back.
It took ages as I am bloody hopeless at texting on a phone. I tried to explain why I needed her to read the manuscript.
I sent the message, she did not reply.

A very short time later, the word **'unopened'** hit me.

If that was true, that might well explain her perceived hatred toward me, and why it continued.
I'm sure I told her about my throat Cancer within those notes, and how I honestly thought that I would not be 'lucky' and survive this time. I didn't do it for pity. I was not playing for her sympathy. I was just being honest.
I asked for understanding and possible reconciliation, but not forgiveness – even I knew I didn't deserve that.

On the 15th I sent a letter to Angela explaining the contents of the original letter and the more recent one, and also Sophia's text. I asked her, pleaded with her, to ask Sophia just to read them. And nothing more.

But from all that, a question arises. Again, if true, why has she kept all my notes and letters?

Was she/is she thinking of 'vengeance'? To use these against me at some later date, as she texted me or was there another reason?

With continuing hope, to clear my 'bad person' name. I sent another recorded letter to Angela some time later. Again this was not answered.
I finally succumbed to the realisation that they all did not want to know me.
Basically, I was like a Leper to them. It was like a closed shop, a secret masonic society. I could not have any 'hearing', any justice.

And THIS is yet another reason for wanting this book to be published. Though, I will possibly never get to know if she has read this either.

On more than one occasion, I have seriously wondered if my actions may have done more damage to Kitten. By that, I mean her mental health.
Yes, there may have been other factors which I do not know about but she appears to have r*eally* wanted to retain my friendship, but I pushed her away. I had to, but she felt betrayed.
She had physically given herself to me, and I 'betrayed' her.

During the Spring of 2021 I find I'm wondering about this again, because that very same dull heavy feeling I had in 2017 and 2018 has come over me again. There is no one to ask. No one is prepared to share the truth with me. It's so heartbreaking.
From that second contact in 2014, and up to this book's original creation in late 2021, I have never discussed Sophia with anyone.
No one, other than two people (both known to her), and even then, I only mentioned that I had dated her a few times and that we got pretty close. And to Jennifer, whom I trusted implicitly, both then and now.

Would it be futile to hope, that one day Sophia may accidently, or other, start to read this book?
But what would say when she realises it's about her.
'For fuck sake, doesn't this sad bastard ever give up'?

Those could very well be her words, and with that I would have lost any chance of reconciliation.

For in reality, could that be what she wanted me to do after the emergence of 'Paul'. Simply, to give up.

Maybe I lost the reality of any reconciliation a long time ago, so what further harm or torment could befall me with the book?

I know I took the wrong path, but I still firmly believe I did so for all the right reasons and I have no reason or inclination to think otherwise.

And if she never really had feelings for me and just used me, then both Marie and I were totally hoodwinked, conned, made fools of.

But even through all that. I still have the strangest faith and trust in her. And for the life of me, I cannot explain how or why.

I am still in love her with her, I will always be in love her, no matter what she says, no matter what she does, no matter what she becomes and no matter what she has done previously.

There is no hidden agenda in the writing of this book.

I have been totally honest with my explanation for doing so.

It's totally out of my hands regarding any form of reconciliation.

I have tried in the past and failed.

Only Sophia has the key to open the door.

One half of me says; maybe she never will, especially if she were to read the book – which may well prove to be the 'death knell'

Whilst the other half says; that in time, she may come to the realisation by herself and possibly contact me.

All that aside;

In the Spring of 2022 I shall be taking my first tentative steps toward a new adventure, but on an old path.

A path I have not trodden in almost fifty years. And I am waiting, in anticipation, with wonderment as to where it will lead. For new adventures to unfold as the coming years unfold, when another life starts to blossom and show itself.

So, what could the next five, ten, or whatever many God willing years may lie ahead? I certainly haven't got the faintest idea.

Who knows if the Cancer will come back. If it does, it does, and like before, I will fight it. I might lose that fight, but a fight I shall give.

Nothing in life is guaranteed and to use the well-known saying *'shit happens'*, it happens to us all at some time or other, doesn't it.

But that would bring into question any possible future relationships, even with Sophia.

Anything can happen in the meantime. I could also be run over by the number 75 bus tomorrow, with Kitten as the driver.

I certainly have no intention of becoming a recluse.

Yes, there will be reflective periods I'm sure, but I will strive not to become someone who says *'I'll do that...tomorrow'* or *'I'll see my friend...tomorrow'* scenario and in turn become a self-inflicted house-bound shell.

In the past, I have helped two people break out of this mould. It's not a nice place to be in, trust me, it really isn't .

So, unless Kismet has another surprise in waiting, I will possibly travel this path alone. Though, in truth, I will never truly be 'alone', as I still have my dreams, my hopes and of course, new adventures to either look forward to, or to avoid.

I already have something to wish for; a vision, something to strive to; a goal, because I don't want to just 'exist', I want to 'live'. And I'm doing just that, now.

As for any future relationships?

Could I share what life I have left with another woman, be it short or long term?

As hard as it may be for some to understand, the answer has to be a very cautious 'no'.

For one, I am well aware **'The Gift'** has not made me invincible to Cancer and it could possibly return. And if it were, I would prefer to work through that on my own – and my gut feeling says, I will beat it again.

Secondly, if Sophia were to ever enter my life again, I could not ignore her. I would be drawn to her, like someone pulling me on a roped. Yes, I could hold my distance, but my feelings for her could never change. And any astute partner I may have at that time, may see this.

The question is, could they accept it.

I fear that I would not be able to explain to anyone just why and how I have this bond with Sophia. It's not just the two greatest feelings I have for her, that of love and caring, it's something else, far deeper and for the life of me I don't know what it is.. and it's **that** that keeps playing on my mind, I can't help it.

Thirdly, though not really an issue for me, but may be one for any future relationship. My libido.
Whilst I am in the very same situation I was prior to my intimate relationship with Sophia. I also find that my desire for actual sex (the act of lovemaking and well fore and after-play) has been of no interest. There was no *'ohhhh that was good, let's keep on doing it'* after Sophia and I stopped seeing each other. It was almost a 'no one can or could ever replace her and that feeling of being close to her'
Since the recent treatment I again have been blessed, but it's still as it was prior to Sophia – will it, won't it, be ok on the day?
Sophia was, I would like to feel, aware of this and did not expect *'the earth to move'* (I smile at that), but would or could a new partner?

Also, I would have to question not only myself, but also Sophia, as to just **why** has she re-entered my life. And that would mean some deep discussions need to take place. In reality, to find out what we both want, what we both need from each other. No pre-conditions just an open and honest discussion to seek harmony for us both and with each other.

Sophia has become a gigantic void in my life and one I would want to try and close up by becoming friends, true friends.
Yes, I would like to tell her that I am in love with her, but being true friends is as important. If she were to ask, then I would tell her the truth.
But she has created her own pathway, and has walked past me.

And then, of course, there are my memories. Never as good as the 'real thing', but the highs and lows in my life that I wish to carry with me.

I have lost so much, but memories are everlasting. And I will always carry the memory of Kitten, with me, for the rest of my life.
When we reconnected after so many years, when I cupped her face and kissed her mouth, the many times we held hands and the night of the 21st – the vision and the words spoken.
And even that last night together.
It seems she will be forever in my system.
But with any happiness, sorrow is often interwoven.

I have nothing tangible, nothing what-so-ever, to show I was once even in the company of Kitten.
A photograph of us both together would have been so beautiful, but as fate would have it, and maybe in Sophia's mind, happily so, there were none taken.
But even so, Kitten was, and still is, remembered as the girl on the bus on many occasions from 1968 through to 2014.
And since Winter 2018, it has seemed to be more so, just why I do not know. Maybe because that's when I realised that I was in love with her.

But, and for no rhyme, nor reason, and totally out of the blue, as I have mentioned before, she will push her way back into my life, I see her in my thoughts for the briefest of moments.

But sometimes that becomes reality.

Since the end of 2018, and through my cancer, I have led a life virtually free from any angst surrounding Sophia.
She was on another pathway, and I have accepted that.

Then on February 8th 2021, there came a shock to the system. Sophia re-joined a group on Facebook, a group she knew that's where I was not only an Administrator, but also the Host.
I was confused. Was she looking for a way forward, to reconciliation?
If it was, I was never to find out.

There was no photo ID in her description and her profile did not show up. After discussion with my fellow administrator of the

group we allowed her to stay, even though it went against the group rules.
Within a few days of Sophia re-joining, a member who had joined a few weeks before, placed a very personal, malicious post on the group site.

A post with no basis of truth concerning the two admins.

Within the hour the post was taken down and replaced by a post from one of the Admins apologising to anyone that saw the offending post, and stating also that there was no truth in it.
The poster, who was later found to be a male using a female s name and ID, was tracked down by Facebook and suspended.
A couple of days later around the 17th, Sophia removed herself from the group.
More trials and tribulations indeed.

Recently, in late Spring 2021, I was walking the dogs. I stopped to chat to a man I knew, and out of the blue, a vision of the solitary photo that I have of Sophia, but along with the spoken words *'remember me'* was in my head.
Incredibly, my subconscious was playing games with me.
But for Christ's sake -WHY??

This is the first time that a vision of Sophia has been accompanied with words. And it took me aback for a moment. I was quite confused by it.
But then, and not for the first time, I became concerned.
I later checked the photo, and then realised for the first time, a conscious connection.
The photo was taken at the dinner she prepared, it was the only photo she liked, and it was the same night she said

"I don't want a part of you... I want all of you, always".

That memory, so warm, so vivid, and yet, so beautifully annoying, but WHAT was the reason behind the words 'remember me.'
Was it a statement, or a question?
Was she ill, God forbid, dying? There would be no one to ask.
What was my subconscious trying to say?
It can be maddening, that I am forever searching for answers.

So, yet again, as suddenly as she arrives, she leaves, often leaving a void, an empty feeling for a brief, but very noticeable moment.
This has happened a number of times. It's as if she is 'haunting' me, in a non-malevolent way, letting me know she is 'still there'.

Is my subconscious deliberately keeping her memory alive, just as I did for all those years after the bus journey. But why, OH WHY?
...And it seems, there is absolutely nothing I can do about it, almost like a bitter-sweet penance? or is something else going to happen

I'm now in deep thought, not because of what Sophia, my Kitten, has done for me, but the fact that she may never get to know.
Though I had thought for a while, this may not really be a bad thing.
There is no way I would want to embarrass her even more than what she may be for even knowing me.
Hence the writing of this book.

Because others had praised the other part of the book **'My Seven Year Itch with Cancer'** in which they spoke of it being inspirational, when it was 'real-timed' on my Facebook page.
And though to understand the interwoven events, it has to be read with **'The Girl On The Bus'** it had to be read as a 'stand-alone' and may possibly help others blighted with the horrible illness that is cancer.

But, and sadly there is another side (just why is there always another side?). Sophia may see the book cover and most certainly, if the back were to be read first, realise the book was about her. She would then take deliberate action to remove that vision and the memory from her mind – if she hasn't already done so, and totally bypass the book.

It would bring back memories she wants to forget. She does not want to be reminded of because it would make her angry, it would make her sad. And of course, hope to God nobody 'recognises' her.

Simply because I entered her life when I did, it doesn't matter that she entered mine all those years before, because she always said she 'could not remember'.

Did I hurt her that much or was it, is it, something else? As the song goes "There are more questions than answers" (Johnny Nash 1972)

Marie, your prediction, your premonition, that;

"Someone has something 'big' planned for the both of you (us)",

Had it already taken place?
Has it yet to come?
I simply do not know.
But if it is to happen, then I accept it as part of life's tapestry that is being woven for me (and possibly for Sophia).

Now some may say Sophia must have or had, a Svengali-like hold on me or that I was completely besotted, obsessed by her.

I can tell you now, neither was the case. Yes, Sophia pressed all the right buttons, but I was an open-eyed, and a totally willing, if not a sometimes surprised, partner.

I am still intrinsically tied to her – but WHY is that?
And for what reason. There MUST be a reason, surely.

I have always had red lines which I would not allow myself to cross for myself or anyone else.

And with Sophia, I was never asked, nor ever felt I needed or even wanted to do. I felt safe with her.

As I have mentioned before, my subconscious may well have been 'telling' me to keep her alive, in my consciousness and for all those years after our first encounter.

The possible reason for this may have been already established, as part of a 'plan', and that the plan was for us to almost certainly meet up again.

But was it really a form of Kismet? or something greater.

Even before we physically met again, I now know that she had given me **'The Gift'**.

So why was there a need to take this to the next level.

How was I to know that later, as previously mentioned in a past Chapter, Marie, my late Cousin stated that someone has 'something big planned for us both', not for me, not for Sophia, but for us both.

But then, though we parted, *'The Gift'* remained, inside of me and miraculously served its purpose once again, a few years later.

And also, but not in line with Marie's statement, instead of Sophia's memory slowly fading over time, my subconscious was doing its level best, in its determination, to keep her very much alive.

As if there may be another part to all what has happened, and that it has yet to show itself.

All this may appear 'fanciful', but at the same time thought-provoking and as for Marie's statement? not so as wild as it may have been first thought.

But I cannot, I will not, afford this to become some sort of 'fixation' in my mind, I will be curious of course, but I wouldn't allow myself to become either depressed or obsessive or even both, God forbid.

And even more so now, because I know what *'The Gift'* was, what it is and what it has done, for me.

And in knowing this and the very possible collusion with my subconscious I would have no reason to suffocate her with my presence or attention should we ever become friends again.

And if she were to (and if not already), found a love with whom to spend the rest of her life with, yes I will sigh, but I will not have lost her because she will always be in my heart.

And for that, I will be forever thankful.

3. CONCLUSION... *if there really is one*

And so, at this time in my life, I have come to the rather obvious conclusion that someone *('up there?')* must have had, or perhaps, still has, a plan for me.
Either that, or maybe just thought I was 'worth it' enough to send to me a living 'Guardian Angel' (not too strong an accolade given the circumstances).
But whatever the reason, I know that I will never meet or love anyone like I love Sophia, in this or any other lifetime.
She was and still is, unique, a very special woman indeed.

With finding the final piece of the jigsaw in late 2018 I thought I had the answer to my actions and thoughts over the past two or three years.
The event of late January 2020, proved just how wrong I was.
Now some may think my love for her would have become even stronger from that date, but it hasn't, and I totally understand and accept why. And so will you, if you have read this book with an open mind.
My feelings for her were beyond what we acquaint as love, and it's a feeling I cannot explain and yet I feel I may already know the answer but afraid to say or even give it serious thought.

I cannot say how things would have turned out if I had been given a 'second chance' in her life. I cannot say what would have happened three years down the line when Cancer struck again.
But I can say, I could not have stood by and allowed Kitten to go through that torment, that helplessness or that sorrow again.
But I at least, would have given her the option, irrespective of Angela's words of 'warning'.
"...Had for many years been her husband's carer, she loves her new-found freedom now and that she never wants to do that again'.
It is ironic, almost like a Greek tragedy. Looking back on the two paths to choose and my possible selfishness in not telling Sophia about my Cancer until the January, it may well be that Sophia did have deep feelings for me, or even love, but wanted her freedom – in reality, she could very well have had both.

It was indeed there for the asking.
Wishful thinking on my part? - maybe too much thinking.

Then there was of course, the Cancer.

And because of those uncertainties, to have had our time together end when it did, and not 'how' it did, may have been a blessing.
And of course, did I get it so drastically and tragically wrong in believing she had honest and true heartfelt feelings for me?
There is every possibility she may just have wanted an 'arrangement', where she could enjoy her freedom to do whatever she wanted, when and with whom she wanted, with no emotional entanglement, and I totally messed it up.

But this book is not just about an apparently one-sided failed love, even though the evidence is so strong, and so seemingly valid. This story is so much more. It's about a girl, a woman, who more than anyone, and more than once helped to save my life, and in doing so, extended it. She gave me the extra will, the extra determination, to survive and in the most unbelievable and incredible of ways. What is heartbreaking, is that I will never be allowed to even say 'thank you', to her face.

I am not going to idolise her, other than speak only good of her name. Nor will I place her on a pedestal, other than to look up to her for what she has given me. And I will never slight her to others, I have absolutely no reason to, To me, she will always be Sophia, my Kitten and everything else she has been blessed with.
My mind goes back to my thoughts when I asked Angela about a carer for Sophia if she became too ill to look after herself. And for me to be the one to care for her.
It would not be a sacrifice, to coin a very old phrase, it would be a 'labour of love' and that, should it ever come about, is the absolute reality, the truth.
Whatever Sophia may think of me is immaterial, and whatever my status in life is, is of no consequence. I would be there – for her.
And so yes, after all what has been said and done, I have a lot to be thankful for, a heck of a lot more than most, yet no words of gratitude to Sophia could ever, would ever, really be enough.

Unbeknown to her, she gave me '***The Gift***', and unbeknown to her, either in this life or any other. It is my wish, my hope, my dream, that someone will find a way to pay her back in kind, and in doing so, acknowledge my eternal gratitude and in a small way, my everlasting love for her.

I only hope that one day, Kitten will get to read this book, and halfway through, **not** say "*Can't be doing with this, too heavy*"

And finally, if I had known about the 'plan', and how it would affect both our lives, the hurt as well as all the joy, would I have stopped seeing Sophia? walked away, never to see her again?
And not knowing what my future would hold?

Initially I said yes, based purely on emotions.
But because there are so many variables, the question is hypothetical. Each part producing a question within a question, therefore the only true answer I can give is '*I don't honestly know*'.

4. AND SO, TO THE FINAL LINE

A very apt page header, because there is that book I mentioned earlier that I had read, 'Now Voyager' and at the very end of that book, the now-classic final line.

'Don't Let's Ask For The Moon. We Have The Stars.'

There have been many suppositions as to what that line meant. But I would like to think it, hopefully, meant
'We Cannot Yet Have A Permanent Relationship, But We Will Always Have Our Memories To Go To Sleep With For Now'.

The same could apply, in part, to our time together, except in this story I was given something more tangible than memories. I was given '***The Gift***' which more than helped, to save my life.
And that's why my relationship with Kitten ended up being something more than just the '*Moon and Stars*'.

But for the briefest of moments in a lifespan of years, I actually held the Moon, the whole of the Moon. And as much as I still have the memory of the Stars, and as bright and beautiful as they are, nothing will ever compare to seeing and holding that Moon above me.
And I cannot help comparing it to the words of the bitter-sweet love song by Buffy Sainte-Marie, 'Until it's time for you to go'.

I have no idea how life treated Sophia, especially in her later years. The pressure she was under would have been immense. But as sure as night turns to day, and given even half a chance, it would be my choice and one I would gladly make, to 'share' both the good and bad times past, present and future with her, so that we may in some positive and lasting way, help each other.

Because that deep spiritual feeling I have for her, no matter what, it can never be broken or become faded and wilt with in time.
But, as there are no guarantees that Kitten will ever come back into my life and I can't live my life waiting forever, so I will carry on having a life, enjoying it and simply say, 'Que Sera Sera'.

On a much 'lighter note', halfway writing this book, I was (jokingly) going to call it *'I Fell In Love With My Guardian Angel'*. Oh for God sake!!, for one, it sounds like a crass B movie title, and for the other... it would have pre emptied the story.
But no, the title is very apt, and the correct one to use, as more than three quarters of the book is about her.

SPOILER ALERT 'A'

It's now December 20th 2020, and I have decided to complete the story of 'The Girl On The Bus'.

I really didn't have the heart, nor the courage, to finish the 'story' which I started in June 2017 and had a 'completed' 15k first version a month later. Even though I remember the laughter, the unspoken good times, you cannot get away from the fact that it all ended so abruptly, and then carried on to a hateful finale, from which the repercussions are still being felt today.

Remembering all those moments brought out mixed emotions. But because of the encouragement from two or three people on another subject, my cancer, and unknown to them, a matter irrevocably connected to this story, I took more than one deep breath and put 'pen to paper'.
We are not getting any younger, and it needed to be written down before the mists of time take over and clouded my memory. But there is one memory I will never allow myself to forget... 'that' look on Sophia's face, those words spoken, on the 21st September.

In January 2018, my computer totally crashed. I could not access the hard-drive. Specialists quoted very hefty fees for retrieval - but with no guarantees. I lost everything, my medical notes, digitized personal papers going back fifty years, FB files, photographs and memories. Good fortune was that Part One of this story was worked and saved on a separate thumb-drive/memory stick.

I have only one photograph of Sophia. A 'grab-shot' taken the night of dinner in her house. No make-up, a hint of a smile and 'those eyes'. She said she liked it, so ironically, that it is the only photo I have of her.

[Footnote: June 2021. 70% of the crashed hard-drive has been recovered. Many items lost, but now and because of that, many important memories and conversations have been be added to this book ~ November 2021]

SPOILER ALERT 'B'
　　　　This formed part of the catalyst that set off a heartbreaking chain of events a very short time later.
Some months later, I looked back and could not help wondering.
Did she mean those words? Did she ever really intend on saying them in the first place. Was it 'really' a case of 'in the heat of the moment', was she really that good an actress?
Did I completely, disastrously misread the whole situation?

5. THE REAL BEGINNING?

There WILL be many readers who will STILL feel that all the 'coincidences' mentioned within both parts of book one are a 'bit too much', almost a fairy-tale like fanciful.
Believe me; I will swear on oath, on any Holy Book you care to put in front of me, they all happened, and as they were written.

And if you feel you have heard the last of them, read on, the final most jaw dropping 'coincidence' awaits you.

If you do believe in such a thing as Kismet, then you will also believe that both Sophia and I were destined to meet again all those years later.
But what 'upset the applecart' and created, almost certainly a ripple in events that was something quite unexpected (then again.. was it?) happened, emotions came into the equation.

Some might say it was that first kiss at La Tosca, but that could be countered with my gamble to contact her from the restaurant. Because, if I had just allowed myself to believe I had been deliberately 'stood up' earlier that evening, and gone back home, then the events that unfolded later that evening would not have happened and quite possibly may never have happened in the days that followed or in fact, ever.

I believe that the many 'coincidences' that have occurred, were more than that, more than just 'coincidences'.
These were moments that were meant to happen, whether people choose to believe it or not.
It was indeed Kismet, but it seems to have ended up being so much more than that.

And if the following does not convince you, then nothing ever will....
I always thought the story of Kitten (Sophia) and myself started with that bus journey in the summer of 1968
But unknown to me... or to Sophia, it may well have actually started ten or possibly eleven years earlier. Read on.

I believe it may have been the Christmas of 1958 that I appeared in a junior school play, for the first and for the last time.

I played the part of a woeful King with severe tummy ache (I had to groan – a lot). During the play, three or four 'physicians' came with remedies to cure this terrible 'illness', none of which worked.

Finally, the Chef/cook came on, and apologised for giving the King 'indigestion' from the large pie he had baked earlier. [It was so good, that the King ate the whole pie].

The Queen calls for the Executioner, and I shout '*Off With His Head!*' (my only spoken line) at the very end of the play, and with that the poor Chef is 'dragged' off stage screaming [to laugher from the audience].

Then, we all took the customary 'bow', our parent's and family all clapping – as they do. Bless them.

I was to learn, some fifty-eight years later, that less than one and a half miles away, at the same time, another play in another school, was taking place.

Kitten had found and put up a photo of that very same play onto her Facebook page. It was a school group photo of the Nativity, where a little girl, of the same age was playing the role of the messenger, the Archangel Gabriel.

I don't know how she came to have it, was it taken by a teacher at the school during one of the rehearsals, by one of her loving parent's possibly.

That little girl was Sophia and her friend then, and still is today, playing 'Mary'.

A little girl that many years later, went on to change my life forever, when unknown to herself, she became the 'giver of the message' (in this case – ***'The Gift'***) and an 'Angel' once again.

Even when I learnt of this, it wasn't for another four years, until January 2020 that the full significance of this simple event was realised. And I became almost numb, speechless.

And so, if you cannot see the unbelievable similarities within the storylines of the two plays, the 'actors' who played the parts, with what happened almost sixty years later, then...

~ May 21st 2021

It was at this point I believed the book to be finished or, at least as far as it could go.

How wrong I was.

6. AFTERWORD: THE 'WHAT IF'

It's strange how the mind tries to resolve issues by constantly looking at unexplored and often implausible avenues. It's always a case of 'What If..' and it's 'What If' I put before you now..

There is no doubt the most significant **what if** has to be, **what if** I had not got that bus, had never met Sophia back in 1968. Would life have been any different for the next forty-five years? Would I have taken the 'white coats' words as gospel and followed them to the letter, and the cancers eventually taken over my body and I would be in the ground somewhere. It's the plain truth.
You have read the book, so what do you think?
BUT I **did** meet her on the bus, **and so**;

There is one **what if** that could in fact answer many questions. Could she actually have remembered that first time we met, on the bus and then later thought, as things progressed that there is something more to this relationship. After all, she did say a few days after we met at the Ironworks that *'we have history'* – or was that just a casual remark? a strange phrase to use all the same.
Maybe I'm reading into that too much.
She did say later that I should *'stop reading into things that were not there'* and it's well known that phrase quite often means *'not to look any deeper because the truth will unfold'*.
Could she have been unnerved, even frightened that she could even remember that first encounter. Why should she remember such a short meeting, something she may have done many times before, and since on a casual basis.. **What if** indeed.
And this ties in with the following 'what if'

What if Sophia was struggling to come to terms with her Husband's long illness and subsequent death? I have mentioned this in a previous chapter. It seems we have both lost one's we love and whom can never be fully, if ever, replace. We both rushed into something we could not really control. I more so it

seems, but then was there something else at work regarding my actions. And that still troubles me to this day.
But, let's be honest, we were both at fault, there is no blame game to be had, no percentages of right or wrong to be had.
And so, **what if**, she truly wanted to keep her friendship and her feelings for me, alive, but at the same time was afraid of the consequences. And she finished with me because she wanted time to clear her head and THEN decide. But I stupidly did not see that.

So **what if**, and without condition, I held out a hand filled with only love, caring, friendship and understanding, as building blocks to help build trust, honesty (and possibly a different future). Would she take it? Either in full or in part? but take it all the same.
Now THAT would indeed, be the 64,000-dollar question.
Because, through any not-so-good times, be they past, present or future, I would rather have her in my life than not. Full stop.
Our hands are there to be held on to, for as long as we both want them to be, for as long as until it's time for either one of us to let go. *(Buffy Sainte-Marie 'Until it's Time For You To Go').*
If it happens, then it happens and if it doesn't? I can do nothing else but accept that as well, Que Sera Sera.

And so, I ask you… *'isn't that something worth pondering over?'*

Running off, on a tangent for a few lines;
I'm wondering (perhaps a little too much again) about if years, 2014, 2016, 2018, 2020, are not just biennial years covered within the latter stages of Book One.
They are all quite defining years within the relationship of Sophia and myself – but every two years, uncanny.
But what of the present year? 2022.
I'm heading for a new start in life, walking a new pathway of my own making, also the book is (hopefully) to be published, all that's for sure And it's still only February.

And talking of the book, and Marie's suggestion that there may be a bigger plan, concerning the both of us waiting to happen.

Maybe it's not something 'physical' in the broadest sense, but it is something tangible – by that, I mean this book.
And within that, there lay another **'what if'**, and possibly the ultimate one.

Long after both Kitten and I are dust, this book may be on someone's bookshelf and deemed a 'good read', another person may read it, and it may resonate with a connection from their past or even present. And in turn, it may even answer their own questions or uncertainties.
Or maybe someone becomes a sleuth, and curious to find out who these two protagonists really were.
It may be in digital form or in a book store or a long-lost box of memories, waiting to be read.
But the story of our time together will forever be out there, until the Earth itself turns to dust.

Even though I am still looking for answers, I maybe should stop looking at the '*What ifs*' even if they are of a casual nature and not wishful thinking...
And concentrate more on the *'What Is'*.

~ *February 07th 2022*

7. FOOD FOR THOUGHT
a - 'A Friends View'

With the book completed, a PDF copy was given to my long-time friend, Jools, for her honest opinion. Continuing the books ethos for honesty and openness, below is the full 'review' as received from Jools. Printed with permission

Once I started reading this book I could not put it down. I found it so fascinating, so strange and created a lot of personal inner thought. I found it beyond my understanding of Kismet or even Karma come to that. I pleasantly found a quite different you. With the Karma and Kismet being so pronounced, and gaining your permission, I have now passed on the PDF to Naimish, for him to read and study.

As you know, I am an avid book reader but I don't think I have ever had so many tears of sorrow, tears of utter joy and all dispersed with laughter and smiles.

Alex, you often, and deliberately, give the World a completely different picture of yourself. A person who is; cuttingly direct, deep, often cold, even aloof. I had the same opinion for quite a while, until you very slowly started to let down your shield.
My thoughts on this are, that you were afraid to show the real you, because you were afraid others may see it as a weakness and possibly use it against you. And yet, with Sophia, there was no shield, no armour, you allowed her to disarm you, from that very first day you met.

Your childhood was far from the best for many reasons, and my heart went out to you. There were memorable chapters and events I cried for you as much as smiled and laughed. But nothing gave me more tears of joy than the time you spent with Sophia.
From that moment at the railway station when you cupped her face to when she told you she *'didn't want a part of you'*, but wanted *'all of you, forever'*, those two events alone sent tears of joy down my cheeks. Without sounding voyeuristic, I could

visualise it all happening. It was all so beautiful.
But it was the ending with Sophia that both shocked and intrigued me more than anything. I never expected it to be so deep and cutting.
The way you both bonded from the very start, it was the perfect chemistry. You appeared so content with each other and yes, some work would be needed for that contentment, that security and honesty to grow even more. Just being together, as a couple, not as in marriage, you outwardly appeared to be a force that would be forever going forward. Sadly, it appears I was to be proven to be so wrong.

Since I first read the line, a burning question has been inside of me;
Did Sophia actually 'roll' her eyes, both up and then to the side or did she just look side-wards?
The meaning, the act of such, can be quite different.
The upward roll of the eye often means *'Oh, what an arsehole'* whereas just the sideways movement could mean *'No, please, I'm not ready, not yet'* or *'Oh God, what have I done'*.

Alex, Sophia was a recent Widow who had just come out of a long-term marriage, sadly, from one that for the previous twelve years or more was not, by all accounts, of the best. And it's this that that may of panicked her. My thoughts are that she wanted to try and live life as free as possible. And if only she had talked to you about what she wanted from this relationship and what you could offer. You both could still have enjoyed a deep, lasting friendship.
But the reality was, in what actually did happen that night.

Though your story finishes in May 2021, life continued and in the January of the following year, Soo, Sophia's friend
re-joined the group we are both hosts to. You told me that you were pleased when you reformed your friendship with her, as you both seemed to get along fine even before your relationship with Sophia really took off. And that you always understood Soo had to make the choice she did.
Soo said that she had lost contact with Sophia for the last two years.

But then, two weeks later, Sophia also re-joined, and this was the last thing you expected.

Sophia came back on (almost) the exact same day that she came back onto the group, the previous year.

You said you found the connection for the dates, but you never elaborated to me. Maybe one day you could get around in telling me?

You were curious and confused, not knowing what Sophia wanted. But, once again, and as suddenly as she appeared, she disappeared. Sophia 'blocked' you once again on Facebook on the 4th of April, and then on the 7th, removed herself from the group completely.

You told me you had asked Soo to send Sophia a PDF copy of the book, if she felt it would help. And Soo told you, after contacting Sophia, that she seemed to want to move forward and that she made no mention of the book when told about it. You can only trust in what Soo had told you, to be the truth.

Now, some onlookers could take that one of two ways, they could say that she wants to move forward in her life (as do you), and slowly get over the loss of her late Husband and the ties that are keeping her attached to him. Ties that that are stopping her having a normal life, and that may also mean, for your book as well.

But for other onlookers, they could take it that you, Alex, have been wiped away from her memory. Basically, you have never existed.

You would have never been allowed to be even a part of her life, to enjoy what she enjoys, her friends, her lifestyle. And you could not be seen to have any emotional ties with her, or she with you.

She is obviously a self-obsessed, good time woman, with certainly none or little empathy for others, someone who has a 'friends with benefits' (with little emphasis on the 'friends' part). And with that lifestyle, you can bet it is all too easy to become addicted to drugs either illegal Class A or B, or over-use of medicinal prescription types. And as for the book, well that is a complete figment of someone's vivid and wild imagination. Who is the author again?

God forbid, that any of that last paragraph is even remotely true, because I have been witness to that hedonistic lifestyle, and it totally destroys people, destroys any true feelings they may have had, real relationships and happiness. They become shells lacking any form of true worth, and they convince themselves that their life is, 'normal'.
But, you being you, your open hand would still be there, for her to grasp and hold on to and with a total, unconditional faith in her.

You are not naive, Alex nor do I feel you were besotted by her.
But I cannot get over just how much she meant to you.

You mentioned that you had asked Soo only a few weeks ago if Sophia had been poorly recently and that her response was a very emphatic, 'No'.
But, Soo did mention to you that Sophia had told her that she had recently (?) suffered a life-threatening illness, Sepsis.
You knew the gravity of this, and you were extremely concerned, also annoyed that no-one considered you worthy enough to inform.

Even so, you surmised that this illness may have been anytime from Winter 2020, because during the very early Summer of 2021, you had a terrible 'gut feeling' something was wrong, with Sophia.
The same feeling you had more than once a few years back.
I remember you were angry then, because Sophia could have been in a clinic, or a hospital somewhere, and nobody would have had the decency to tell you even though you had asked her friend, Angela.

You also told me that you strongly suspected what part of the body was affected by Sepsis, the possible reconstructive surgery and emotional after affects that would have followed.
What I did not tell you at the time, was that Soo had also told me, in confidence, just where it was.

You often made the quote to me about people, or their actions, that other gauged as 'not up to standard', *'Imperfections are only perfection in disguise'*. With Sophia, I truly believe you saw a beauty, far deeper than her physical form.

And to finish wish, and for the life of me, I still cannot get over just how you knew it was Sophia all those years later. It's so mind blowingly incredible.
So, let's see what Naimish makes of this and also another matter I know that has been troubling you for the last two years.

You already know that I would love to see a happy outcome to all of this, but you also know I have reservations about Sophia and yet you have so much faith in her to do the right thing, whether that hurts you or not. And I find that so beautiful.

I'm leaving it there, because I have something in my eye, again.

~ April 30th 2022

[During the course of her writing her thoughts, Jools suggested I have a meeting with a friend (one whose Wife I had met some time before) who not only was a qualified Psychologist, but also a long-time and respected Rishi practitioner. She hoped, with the meeting, it could help resolve a number of issues I had struggled with over the last five or six years regarding both Sophia and myself. As it turned out, more than one meeting was required. And they proved to be more than just informative. A lot more].

b – 'Revelations & Realisations'

Below is a transcription summary of the findings from two audio recorded sessions, held during May 2022 and undertaken by Naimish Pandit. Naimish's professional background is that of a practicing Psychologist with over thirty years' experience. He has also been a Rishi practitioner over an even longer period.
The sessions were to concern themselves with the periods directly connected to Sophia, though a number of the

questions seemingly irrelevant, were later to be an integral part of the revelation, the realisation that followed. Naimish was to give me the best of both Worlds.
With permission given from Naimish and later, a fellow Rishi colleague, is the following summary of findings *(italics)*.
The more I read, the more it adds validity to my Cousins words.

Alex, an admission from me. When I started to read your manuscript (given to me with your permission, by a mutual friend) a few days ago. Whilst it did gain my interest, it was not until Sophia first came into the story, and your life that I felt then, that something quite significant was indeed happening. And then, as I read on, many years later when she came back into your life, in the most extraordinary way of ways. That you knew instinctively it was the same person, my interest grew beyond my expectations. And my keenness for wanting a meeting with you. But it was not until I read about your visit to your family in France, that I was totally taken aback.
*You were related to **the** Marie Leblanc. Let me explain*

I had attended a series of lectures held by Marie and other learned associates in both London and Lyon, between 1998 and 2002. Her direction and foresight was inspirational. She was a respected advocate of thinking outside of the box, throwing away the traditional narratives within our profession. To embrace the lesser-accepted methods which were rarely talked about in the Western World, as a source of learning and practice.
She told all to look to the East, to open up our minds and hearts.
I and a number of others, thought at the time, 'Now here is a Western woman who not only accepts, but also endorsed the practice of the likes of (my field) *Rishi'. And so, when I read your words along with the quotes from your Cousin, I was flushed with a sense of humility that here, sat before me was a member of her family, asking me for assistance. Her tragic and unexpected death in 2017 came far too soon. Your cousin Marie was a remarkable, exceptional woman.*

It was during the second session that it became obvious that the bond between you and your Aunt was quite strong and if not for

circumstances, you would have made a formidable team, had you chosen a similar path to hers.
With your permission, I would like to put forward this case study and my findings, for submission to the open forum section of the next bi-annual conference that is to be held in 2024.

SUMMARY OF SESSIONS HELD DURING MAY 2022
Taken from audio recordings and handwritten notes made at the time.
(The original summary now forms part of a later review of the original recordings and notes made in October 2022, which was taken with another Rishi practitioner, Dr Gordonsdale whom by profession, is a qualified Psychologist and licenced Hypnotherapist)

As Sophia has not been a study of mine, I can only present my findings and informal summary of her, based on what you have presented to me, and with my many experiences with such situations. Therefore, my thoughts and findings about Sophia cannot and should not be treated as absolute.
Alex, you have told me that you are aware and have knowledge of 'Yin-Yang', and where opposites often collide and also combine. But how are you with Spiritual connections?

I am not sure how far you have delved into this, but I am more than convinced it has crossed your mind, and what I am about to say may come as a surprise.
I feel deeply that you, or rather the masculine (Yang) side of your subconscious also wanted to end the relationship with Sophia. And for quite possibly the same reason as Sophia.
At first, I assumed it all revolved around the 'Gift' that Sophia gave you, The 'Gift' did play a very significant part, but not solely, as it is now understood to be intertwined with something much deeper.

And I feel your Cousin, Marie instinctively knew what that was. She could not tell you at that time simply because you had to 'play-out' the story by yourself without any outside influence.
To have told you then may have changed everything - even the writing of your book.

After my initial summary which you received, I was still troubled about some of the aspects of what we talked about, and also with the reading once again of your original book.
After telephoning you in the September of 2022 with my intentions, I consulted with long-time friend and fellow Rishi colleague, Doctor Gordonsdale. Who like me, is a fully qualified Psychologist, and is also a licenced Hypnotherapist who specialises in regression.

In late February2023 another session was arranged at a mutual friend's house and at your request that friend was present. This allowed more study into specific events surrounding the events after the last time you were together, of which have now been added to this summary.

It is now of my, our belief, that you and Sophia have known each other in previous lifetimes. In what capacity, I cannot say, but I feel it may have been close.

Spiritual partnerships can transcend time and space. And what you are experiencing now may be just as easily be the continuance of your spiritual journey with Sophia. As much as it could be the final stage, where you both become as one in two Earthly bodies through each of your separate Yin's and Yang's. There are no guarantees within this or any other lifetime, but the bond would grow stronger with each receptive pulse you receive. Dr. Gordonsdale has told me that, with your acceptance of course, he would like to pursue this a little more, possibly through regression. I leave that with you both to discuss.

This finding would also give more clarity and understanding regarding the multitude of 'coincidence's' you had, concerning Sophia.
And gave rise to Marie's Husband, Albert to say that the resulting factor was immeasurable to which I can only concur as it is the natural way that Spiritual connections are made. And of course, with Marie's immediate explanation when she said 'something very Spiritual was happening'.
You knew as well, but chose not to be fully convinced.

*Even that first physical meeting with Sophia. That was planned.
If it didn't happen then, it most definitely would have happened sometime in the near future.
What you did not know, and neither did Sophia, was that a receptive pulse was sent out on that day. And from that day a heightened connection was made – and has stayed with you, within this lifetime, ever since.*

*Quite remarkably, you intuitively touched on something with the observation of the Christmas plays that you were both in as children.
I have concluded that it was then, that the first Spiritual connection within this lifetime was made.
The timing, the parts you both played within you respective plays and the content. These were too significant just to be later deemed as mere coincidences.
Spiritual connections are never one-sided; there always has to be a pulse sent by one, and received by another, forming a receptive connection. There are never multiples; it's solely one to one in any lifetime. That is the foundation to the saying, 'you were made for each other'.
There will be many doubters I know, but there is everything to conclude that it is more than possible. A pulse was sent, and received by one of you, but you were both far too young and innocent to have felt it and even if you did, not realise its significance.*

*Let us step back into time, this lifetime, and that bus journey;
With that first known meeting with Sophia, you instinctively chose to drop your shield and allowed her, for the briefest of lifetime moments to completely disarm you and enter your life.
You could have only done this only if you were absolutely sure of the person you **knew** you could do this with. And the only way could have known this would have been if you had known this person in another lifetime. And you knew this because of that pulse from a decade before.
So, did she too, let her shield down on the bus?*

An interesting question, to which I do not have positive answer. But there is every reason to believe that she did, why else would

285

she speak to you first, if not to strike up a conversation with a total stranger.
Her subconscious was evidently telling her to do so. Because of the same pulse.

And then there is the 'Gift';
Your sub-subconscious already knew that your Cancer was within you, and growing, a long time before you intuitively knew, and before it was officially confirmed later by the Doctors.
And after it was confirmed you fought bravely to defeat this terrible disease and again when another Cancer was discovered shortly after, but it took its toll on you, both mentally and physically. And it all started to fall apart when there was a suspected third cancer.
And it was at that time, you seriously thought your time was possibly coming to an end.
And then, almost as if a call was sent out for a miracle, Sophia reappeared in your life.
Sophia held that 'Gift' in her very being.
And that' Gift' was her confidence, her positiveness, her courage, and it could be said, her life-source
Sophia sensed this, and sent out an extraordinary strong pulse to you.

*Her pulse, the Spiritual connection, reached out to you once again. That is why, and how, you knew with all certainty that the girl on the bus and the girl on Facebook were one of the same. By the fact of your own admission, you knew the answer even **before** you actually made any form of contact with her. It is of my opinion, that not only did Sophia send the pulse so she could help you, but also for you to help her as she was going through a very difficult time with her husband. She needed your support.*

And from then on, the pulse, the bond, appeared to increase dramatically when you were both together and this is how it is meant to be, how it moves forward.

That last meeting;
I put to it you that on your final night together, that this is where a juxtaposition happened.

Sophia's sub-subconscious already knew of the 'Gift' she possessed and it knew it was to pass it on to you, and you alone, when it was 'requested'. And when that was done, as far as her masculine Yang was concerned, her mission was completed.

And so, upon hearing the word 'love', Sophia quite possibly then heard nothing else. The realisation that the person stood in front of her was real, and that he had very real feelings for her.
Her subconscious put up her defensive shield, as it had its own agenda. It's not that she did not want the affection because I have no doubt she, her feminine Yin did, but her Yang was telling her to be afraid of the unknown, the possible consequences.

And yes, I suspect strongly you were indeed already (Spiritually and emotionally) in love with her, but your masculine Yang subconscious could not allow you to feel this. You did not realise then or possibly even now, that your love for Sophia was in all probability created in another lifetime. And so that is why your words to Sophia were all, as you said, jumbled up.
Those 'jumbled up' words were your Yin, the feminine side of your subconscious. It was fighting back, trying to override the words and thoughts created by the Yang, and to stop you creating the break.
But it failed.

Your consciousness had no knowledge of what was truly happening, that is, until you were on your way home that night and even then, with only the slightest of hints. This led to even more confusion and uncertainty on your part.
But Sophia's subconscious had sensed what the Yin was trying to do, and basically, her failing Yang stepped up a gear.
It knew of Sophia's true feelings toward you and needed the break up to happen, it only saw black and white. It wanted this lifetime to be like the previous, never concluded. And so, the reason it immediately put up her defence shield.
This had happened before. When asking you, on more than one occasion, to 'slow down'.
That it may well have been an admittance of her true feelings and not, as you may have thought, a criticism of yours.

It may have also happened when she often said, she could not remember the meeting on the bus, for if she had then she might have started to question other events, and come to realise the connection between the two of you was very real.
And that's the last thing the Yang would have wanted.

And so, it was, that her subconscious took control over her conscious thoughts and acted upon them.
She had given you what you needed. There was no now need for continuing the relationship.
At the very same time, your subconscious knew the plan created by the spiritual connection had worked, the emotional side was a hindrance. The masculine Yang had won the day. But it wasn't finished
After all, did you not say previously that you realised you were suffocating Sophia and after that night you were going to back away from her and not actually seeing her for a few weeks.
You now had the 'Gift'. And you were going to stop (for a while?) seeing Sophia. So where was the issue?
So yes, a juxtaposition happened on that last night together, two stories, one ending.

Many Psychologists will formulate their own views on the above and of what follows, but discard anything they do not wish to understand simply because it is outside of their own narrative.
The Rishi have always believed that in many ways the subconscious often trains the consciousness to do its bidding without the host realising it, and not the other way around.

Because you both are so much alike, more alike than you could have possibly realised at the time, your subconscious knew what her reaction would be on that last night together and you was ready for it, but your consciousness understandably, reeled from it.
But then, whilst The Yang's plan continued to work on you, and it had won the day with the break-up, it now wanted to finalise it by locking the door for this lifetime.
You, in your openness but now we know naivety, wore your heart on your sleeve where Sophia was concerned, and this was manna from the Heavens to the Yang, it was your weakness.

You were becoming understandably emotional. You were rightly confused with what was going on around you. Sophia did not want to answer your questions. It became almost a war between your Yin (who wants compromise) and the Yang (who wants full control) and this is not uncommon.

In France, news of your cancer came. This is when something quite extraordinary happened and it is my belief that your closeness to your Cousin was behind it.

The force of her Yin reflected onto yours and in turn allowed you to create your own plan of fading away from Sophia, slowly rejecting her so that she could never feel any guilt or remorse when and if at a later date she found out about your new cancer. Your plan for an honourable and admirable atonement for what you were to do, however misplaced it would appear to others, was put into place.

The stage was basically set. And by the time of driving Sophia to the Airport, both you and your Yang felt Sophia still had feelings for you and your feelings for Sophia were cemented. It is, in my opinion the moment your Yang and Yin came to a compromise that would allow you to carry out your plan without hindrance. But it wasn't 'quite' finished; it wanted one last chance of controlling your emotions. And that came at the time of Sophia's birthday.

What Sophia told you about not wanting anything for her birthday that reminded her of you was hurtful, but understandable. But to then tell you just what she was going to do on her birthday was, and I agree with you, unwarranted and contrived - but I feel there were guarded elements of truth within it. She wanted to remember only her late husband on that day and the birthdays they shared together.

Your Yang rolled the dice... and it partially worked. You became upset and angry for as you said 'rubbing salt into the wound'. Shortly after, the Yin influence came back even stronger. And made you aware that you needed to cut ties with Sophia and

quickly. Before your Yang had chance to come into the equation again.
But to do so, you would have to become a different person, and it would hurt you immensely.
You were far from being a Martyr. For you there was no option; it was the only thing to do. And for a reason you were not aware of.

And so, without a thought for your own personal consequences, you pressed the 'self-destruct' button, so that Sophia would not get hurt.
Though, even you or anyone else would not have realised at the time, the angst and self-inflicted hurt you were about to endure.
*But now that I know more about your psyche, I feel you would **still** have 'pressed the button', even if you had fully known.*

A question that crossed your mind, possibly more than once
Could Sophia have, or is, emotionally, in love with you within this lifetime
I cannot say for certain, but why not.
There were many instances, based on her actions and what she told you in those intimate moments together, that can either confirm this or in the very least, lead many people to believe so. Like you, Sophia could have fell in love with you in a previous reincarnation. And intuitively, fallen in love with you, in this lifetime.
Whatever the reason or doubt, she never told you she was. That could have been the fear of the unknown as mentioned previously.
.
You are inquisitive, a seeker of truth and one of the most astute subjects I have had the chance to work with. And with that in mind I feel that what follows may well have already crossed your mind.
*I mentioned earlier about **your** Spiritual connection to Sophia, that it is, very much in evidence. Though Sophia's toward you appears shrouded for the most part, but when it has shown itself, it's been incredibly strong.*
Sophia's connection looked to be, at unique times actually greater than yours, but for the rest of the time I feel it may have been suppressed, and quite possibly, by her own self.
It is not an uncommon occurrence.

She is still uncertain, and I suspect, very much afraid of what that connection may mean if she were to become aware of it (more on this within the summary).
It can be a very emotional and daunting experience for some, as they don't know where this deep feeling is coming from.
They become afraid of the contentment it often brings. It is tearing down their natural inbuilt defences.
And their real true self starts to show one minute, but not the next. And this could very well explain some of your actions, as well as the actions and words from Sophia, during your time together and after.

Confusion is often the hidden reality.

When you were in touch with each other before you met up again, you wondered just why you were so relaxed talking to her, you were totally open.
The answer was right in front of you.
That disarming affect that manifested itself when you contacted her so many years later, was simply the continuation of that bus journey. Sophia had already stripped you of your defences on that bus journey all those years ago. As you have, more than possibly, done to each other in previous lifetimes.

When your subconscious finally relinquished and allowed you to realise, at the end of 2018 that you were (emotionally) in love with Sophia you were shocked but at the same time had such a calming effect on you. It could have released you to this emotion two years before but it needed you to become a better person through your anguish. A strong case of 'being cruel to be kind'. And I believe it worked

And the Gift that was put to incredible use with your subsequent Cancers, is quite possibly, still inside of you today.
And when you consciously found, at the start of 2020, just where this Gift came from, it was another great shock and as you said, the last piece of the jigsaw was now in place.
(But with it, another jigsaw was already forming).
Inwardly you now doubted that the love you felt for Sophia was real. That it was somehow, all part of the plan.

And this has obviously troubled you very much, ever since.

Alex, your love for Sophia was certainly not created by the plan, nor was it by your subconscious.
Those first strange unexplained feelings you said you felt, and in truth, felt uncomfortable with, grew into something much deeper and it began to scare you.
But at the same time gave you, inwardly, a warmth, a comfort.
The truth is that those feelings had transcended all Earthy aspects, and it's become a deep, spiritual love, far deeper than any emotional love. And once fully understood, it can lead to a very calming, but unexplained experience, as it did you.

So yes, Alex, the love you have for Sophia is as real and as strong as it can ever possibly get. And it is both Spiritual and emotional.

You have already shown just how far you would go to protect her. This was no self-pitying act; it was as pure and natural as the rain coming down from the sky.
And this was not the only time, was it Alex?
This protectiveness you have for Sophia is something that cannot be erased, no matter how hard you may wish it gone.
*It is quite obvious that Sophia still is, a Spiritual connection, whether she chooses to believe it or not that is. And **that** will always be the case. Sophia is here to stay, as she has been in your past and as she will be in your future.*

I hope the summary so far has answered another question that has, for so long troubled you.
Why could Sophia not pass the Gift to her husband?

That Gift was always meant for you, and you alone. There is no guilt in feeling as you did, that her husband needed it more. Those emotions you felt (unknown to you) were in truth aimed at Sophia. You did not wish to see her struggles and anguish.
If it had meant to be, then it would have happened many years ago. And only if her Husband was her true Spiritual partner he would have been receptive to it.

This may appear to be a very cruel statement to make And I can understand you may well be troubled by this. That you have quite possibly taken someone's place.
But it was meant to be, and neither you nor Sophia had any control on the outcome.
It certainly was not a failing on her part, quite simply because she had no conscious knowledge of the Gift within her. Her own subconscious would not allow her this knowledge.
But remember this Alex; your connection within this lifetime with Sophia goes back to the Christmas festivities. That connection, for all intents and purposes has lasted a lifetime. And a long time before she met her future love, and Husband. Need I say anymore?

You are quite right when you have said, in the past, and as it may be still, that Sophia has no knowledge of her part in saving your life as far as you are aware. This, I can quite understand.
My thoughts are that her subconscious may not be allowing her to comprehend any part of the connection as she may not be able to reconcile herself over not been able to help save her husband, and then to save you, a total stranger. Her shield is simply preventing it being known to her.
She may well suspect something, but even though she mentioned it first herself, Kismet, she cannot yet open her mind fully to all what that it implies and has shaped many aspects of her own life (and yours) not only in this lifetime, but the previous ones as well..

The question now arises, and it is a very important one. If she were to become fully aware of the Spiritual connection between you both, how would she react?
It is assumed that even now, she is still unaware and so it would be a lot for many to take in, and she may become afraid of facing the reality of truth, and simply turn her head away.
It may come slowly, by her own violation, for her peace of mind, curiosity and with a sudden totally unexpected realisation.
It will shock her.

Alex, you had in the past queried those 'coincidences' concerning Sophia. They not only puzzled and confused you, but they also raised concerns.

The replies, the thoughts you gave to those questions, were a lot closer to reality than you could have ever imagined. Such is synchronicity, which I believe Sophia may have felt as well.
I also have a strong belief that your sub-consciousness was letting out little clues so that you were able to accept that Sophia has control of any Spiritual, and now emotional future you may have together.

The path you say you are about to embark on shows humility, openness and an honesty not only to yourself, but also to others.
Some may say it's only a self-pitying sacrificial act of no importance, but nothing really could be further from the truth. Those with open minds know this.

In my learned opinion, both you and Sophia have been blessed certainly within this lifetime, and that, if it becomes a reality again, you both should accept and explore that blessing, together.
I believe, should this happen; it will be a third attempt of joining together. You will have learnt so much both during and after your second, that it can only lead to your joint and individual betterment, in all of life's arenas; Emotional, Mental, Physical and Spiritual.
Grasp what you find with both hands, nurture it, for it is Kismet, and yet for you both, it has always been so much more than that.
Take time to get to know each other with every fibre of your being. Learn from each other. Neither of you will regret it
And I know what you are thinking, but it can never be too late.

A short while ago we had a conversation regarding 'Twin Flames'.
You are very much of the same thinking as your cousin, that this Twin flames, also called 'mirror souls' are terms used to describe a relationship ideology rooted in new-age spiritualism. And that it borrows heavily from the Rishi and other aged reasonings, but then it dissects and creates its own teachings and seemingly, its own agenda and purpose.
I can only agree with your assumptions.

And I feel I must state now, for the readers of this summery that the findings you have read so far and those that follow, are not connected with the Twin Flames spiritualist thinking, ideology or agenda.
Yourself, and your Cousin previously, raised doubts about the sincerity and truth-finding of this relatively new concept. It can be construed as a loose veiled concept based on an age-old theme, one which could easily lead people to think of it more akin to a new age religious sect. And, of course, that can appeal to many seeking some form of guidance.
The allurement is a strong one, but one you have found to be uneasy with, and to keep firmly at arm's length.

During the sessions and also our talks, both face to face and on the telephone, you sometimes tended to lapse into thinking of what may lay ahead. It would be wise for you to try and resist this as much as possible. Visions are one thing, reality is another.
Sometimes we can manifest our visions and then, sometimes our visions are something we can sense.
And so, remember. This is all this is about what you can sense, and not about what you see. All too often what you see can be an illusion.
What you sense, can never be an illusion.

*So I ask you, Alex, what do **you** sense?*

No matter what happens in the future, and though you both never realised it at the time, you have each met, literally embraced, and physically joined with your Spiritual partner.
Though apparently brief, few people have had the honour, and blessing, of ever being in that position.

A cautionary final word with the ending of this summary.

Alex, you may well have found your only true, Spiritual and Earthly love, but Sophia must in turn, also free herself in both mind and body to find you.
She may well be trying to forget you. And in doing so she may become adept at burying emotions which don't fit with her social paradigms.

*But, in time, her love for you will bring her back into your life.
She will not only come to understand those feelings, but to accept and embrace them as well.
But I must reiterate - there is no time limit for this to happen. It is totally out of your hands.
It is Kismet, in every sense of the meaning. And if my initial prognosis was correct, remembering Sophia has not been a study of mine, it will eventually happen, and of that I can assure you.*

*Because of what you have mentioned before and the knowledge you have gained since, I know you will accept compromise.
And by that, I mean not being together as a traditional earthly couple, but sharing with each other, a part of each other's life. Enjoying each other's company as and when you meet.*

And so, I am pleased that you have now have that understanding and that you are living your life freely with that knowledge, and as people often say – 'just roll with it'. Who knows what tomorrow will bring.

~ February 20th 2023

Well, that certainly is an eye-opener, and so much to take in.

But it has eased, quite possibly resolved, some personal issues.
And if I were a lesser person, I could use the findings as an excuse for any negative words or actions made toward Sophia.
But that would be a total cop-out, because it was me, as a whole person, no matter how it's dressed, and as Sophia saw it.

Therefore, I have accepted it as such.
And now, as it stands at this very moment in time, it is unlikely that I will see Sophia again, let alone talk to her, so there would be no point in even thinking she would reconsider.
And I wish, with my whole heart and body, it could be different

I have fully acknowledged the **Gift,** which gave me the extra confidence and with it, the will to live.
But I now find myself asking;
'If this connection is so real, then is Sophia the sole purpose for which I am still alive?'

And if so, to what end? To be with her again, in this lifetime?

Yes, in this lifetime, there, I have said it.
To think all that has happened between Sophia and I, the torment, the hurt, confusion, misunderstanding, lies and deceit, the love and deep caring has been created by those two 'extra-terrestrial' comedians who go by the name of Yin and Yang.
These two should be 'stand-up' comedians or making films in Hollywood or something... anything.
Ok, this is my way of dealing with it – humour.
And if it wasn't so serious, it would be laughable.

It's not that I want to believe it; it's more that I can believe it to be more than possible.
Yes, I am angry, but angry with myself, because the Yin and the Yang IS within us all, and as Naimish say's we just have to roll with it and accept what it does. Because we have no way of knowing, we have no control

Is it so incredulous for anyone to believe that they, and others, may possibly have lived in another body in previous lifetimes?
I have never really thought about it to be a sceptic.
And yet, when I look back on all that has happened, the unexplained feelings I had towards Sophia, the overwhelming number of 'coincidences', was I possibly right all along, that there was something very special about her.

There are many things we take for granted and truth, that are based on past events and only as hearsay, that later became written about.
What's the old saying? *'If you tell a story and keep repeating it, people will eventually come to believe it and it becomes 'fact'.*
This was quite easy to perform in ancient time, but I wonder just how many of these stories and that includes religious ones would

stand up to scrutiny if started in the here and now. But then again, we now have 'Spin-Doctors'.
Talk and tales of the 'here-after' have been around for centuries.
They have been used in times of war, in times of suffering, to ease the fear of death in a person. That only their Earthly body will fade away, but the Spirit will continue. Within some sects and faiths, it also became a form of control over the masses – do as we command or your Spirit will perish with your body.

We have all had experiences of '*Deja-vu*' and try as we might, we cannot remember where that something happened previously.
People are reported to have lived previous lives when subject to confirmed regression. So, could there be truth in it, as these people were later proved to be 100% genuine.

'Past events in previous lifetimes can trigger our actions within a present lifetime'.

Yes I have heard this, but as with the great many people of the here and now, I cannot help but feel that the present, my presence in *this* lifetime is the most important.
Though, at the same time, it would be interesting to know how we have evolved, within our own self, our own spirit. Maybe I am closer to my cousin that I have realised and Naimish saw this.

The question is;
Would I EVER be ready to embrace the full realisation as to what has happened and what is still happening as Naimish seems to think I am?
More to the point, do I want to be ready?
And is there any point in 'being ready'? Because from what has been said, I and others, have absolutely no control of these types of events, present or future. So why would I concern myself with them? Besides that, I'm into the last quarter of my lifespan, a bit late for a 'life-change'.
But all the same, I do accept and in a growing way, understand what has happened and what is still happening.

And with that, the knowledge that if I were never to physically see or hear from Sophia again, the deep spiritual and even emotional love and caring I have for her, and have had (so it may seem) in a previous life or lives, will forever continue into the next lifetime and the next lifetime after that, and so on.

To many this seem a bit of a 'hit or miss' affair, but then we would not know this would we – because we are mortals?
The Yin and Yang is very true and very much with us in our daily lives and many believe that these are the spirits that transcends time and space and create the *'Past events in previous lifetime...'*
All confusing, and as I mentioned earlier, I'm slowly trying to understand. Maybe I should have studied with Marie, or even just allowed myself to open up and talk to her more before Sophia came back into my life.
Or would that knowledge led to a totally different outcome when Sophia did come back?

It seems we may be constantly striving to find the missing piece of the jigsaw, life's jigsaw – but for what purpose, a Spiritual union?

Well my jigsaw puzzle has taken (by all accounts) over sixty years to complete... but then again, to believe the previous short paragraph - is it REALLY complete? Or maybe, I ALREADY have the final pieces in my hands, but I now have to wait and just see where they fit.
Ahhh well, deep sighs all around... ha-ha
But that's for a possible future, back to the here and now
Four years ago, when I (finally?) acknowledged my love for her, I also understood and accepted that Sophia was creating her own pathway, one that would possibly, never include me.
Yes, I'm a romantic at heart, and so I ask, is there such a phenomenon as a 'happy ever after' love for anyone?
I like to think, and hope that there is, or at least something pretty damn close to it, and if not for me, then for others around me.
There IS one thought that has very recently entered my mind. It is a thought that envelopes the past with the future.
With the book completed. I started to read it for possibly one last time before it goes to the publishers. I was pleased with it.
Then I got to the bottom of page 225 – and froze. OMG.......
I recalled when talking to Angela soon after the 'break up' and

Angela stated that;
'I know she was very, very fond of you. But she has now found her freedom and she doesn't want to be a full-time carer again'.
How the hell did I not pick up on those last ten words?
Was Angela repeating what Sophia may have said during their 'heart to heart'?
Was is just a general 'independence from everything' or did it spring from a concern Sophia had about my cancer?
If so, then that would mean that she has very strong feelings for me (maybe she knew she was falling in love with me), and that she could not emotionally put herself through the same experience she went through caring for her late husband?

Is there the possibility that both Sophia's Yin and Yang's subconscious had known as what was to come over the following three plus years, and the Yang deliberately steered her away from a continuing, possibly deeper and lasting relationship leading to (possible) heartache once again?
Whereas her Yin wanted Sophia to take 'leap of faith.

In a macabre way, the 'Yang' was correct and I also was correct in my thoughts that if we continued our relationship, how would she have reacted, especially with the last cancer in 2019.
The cancers of course, are well documented in both parts of this book as was the success in fighting them.
And as I have also mentioned, and stand by, that after the first two, the only reason I am still living is more than remotely due to Sophia. She may have even been 'involved' with my recovery with those two as well. Who knows?

It's ironical that directly after Angela said those ten words I asked about a time Sophia would become ill and would need care?
I would have been there, without a second thought, irrespective of my status. And her answer was that 'Sophia would take herself off to Switzerland' *(for assisted Euthanasia to take place)* (page 226)

We all die, yep... it's true folks, we do.
I cannot predict my future health, or how long I shall live for on this mortal coil we call Earth, but I shall keep breathing the air to my best endeavours and hopefully without assistance.

Personally, having someone for whom I care for so much, to be there at the side of me – at any time really, not just my passing. That would be a beautiful loving vision as I close my eyes.

A reality is that that person may have already passed on, or they would find it too much to bear witness to when the time was to come.
If still alive, I would be able to see it in their eyes. And it is then that a discussion must take place. A discussion and understanding to ease both our minds and souls.
And until such time, if it were to arise and all being well, the freely given, natural care one person gives another be they friends or lovers, relations, Brother or Sister, Husband or Wife as they grow older is something I (and so many others) would accept with gratitude, appreciation, and with love. If that is not possible, through whatever reason, then you simply circumnavigate – there is always a way to overcome such issues.

And from words spoken, should Sophia decide to take herself off to Switzerland, well, that would be her choice. A choice I am sure she would make for the right reasons and all things and people considered. I would hope, should we become at least friends once more, that she would allow me to accompany her, and witness her passing.
To witness not in grief, but with a feeling of joint contentment. That Sophia has found her peace, and that I may have the chance to cup her face for one last kiss and say to her before she finally closes her eyes;
   *"We **will** see each other again".*

Because, if what has been spoken about before is true, and I have no reason to discredit it, then I say it with the knowledge that I have never lied to Kitten.

But before that possible eventuality, be we as friends or not.
I truly believe we will both be around, both pleasing and annoying people for quite a few more years to come.

And I would strongly suspect Sophia would simply say
'all that from ten casual words, you are reading far too much into something that isn't there'.
Yes, maybe I am reading too much into things. Yet when you consider all that has happened concerning both Sophia and I over the last few years it, does tie in and of that there can be no doubt.

But, as there has been a red card on communication, if the above is remotely true, and whilst I find myself walking a new path, I also find myself in the same position with Sophia as before.
All thanks to those two bloody comedians called Yin and Yang,
But I honestly believe it will all come good, sometime in a future

But the reality is NOW, and another chapter is being is being amassed as you read this. I am fully embracing the life which lies before me. I am facing each new day as it comes, enjoying music that gives pleasure to many, meeting new people, seeing old friends, dining out. Whatever lies before me, I will face. And in times of stress I can also look back on the memories, the good ones to bring a smile, but always remembering that is just what they are, …memories.

Memories aside, there is one thing that will be forever certain. Though I may not be in Sophia's life in any foreseeable future, but if she were to re-enter mine, either as a whole person or still unsure, she would be welcomed like no other person alive. And yet silently, because the love I have for her, is unconditional.

For as I have said previously, I could never turn my back on her as I have no reason to do so, and I sincerely doubt I ever will have a reason to in any future or lifetime that lay before us.

I can only visualise a future within this lifetime, I certainly could not predict one. And so therefore I could not give this book an ending, not even a fanciful, fairy-tale one.
It would be so wrong of me to do so, it would also end up being a lie – and I have not lied in this book, and I have never lied to Sophia, my very special Sophia, my Kitten.

So, with questions that only Sophia could answer, because of the recent revelations made, and of course what had gone before, I now feel that this part of the book has now come to an unresolved ending.

But there will be many 'here and now' smiles and (future) memories in the days and years ahead and I shall accept each and every one as they come along.

And, as mentioned before, why can't we both take a leap of faith and work on a compromise. And then both move forward 'taking it one day at a time'

And finally, a couple of thoughts;

Just how would she react, to be informed that we **do** have a history, a history going back lifetimes?

She is level headed, but even so and for her own reasons, she may think it's too much to actually believe in, and she is having none of it. She may also feel of course (like I do) that there is nothing we can do about it. So, let those in a future life try and sort it all out.

And thinking about it, maybe that vision and that goal I have had for a long time is actually more than that. And if that is the case, there is *still* nothing I can do about it – but give a knowing smile.

After all, it's only Kismet… *isn't it?*

~ March 12th 2023

Footnote:
August 15th 2022, Zhen-Zhen crossed over the 'Rainbow Bridge' aged only eleven.

For those four short years she was with me, she never once left my side. And for those four short years, I welcomed her company.

BOOK TWO

MY SEVEN YEAR ITCH ...with CANCER.

The Unbelievable Link With The Girl From The Bus.
A Link That Defies Logic And Perception.

THE STORY BEGINS....

JULY 2013 - JUNE 2014

In early July 2013 (6th or 7th), I was in the final stages of booking my multiple flights to, and within, South East Asia and 'something' made me stop.

I felt something was 'wrong'. I immediately made an appointment to see my GP.

Two days later, in the second week of July, my Doctor asked me what I 'thought' it was. Something made me say *'Prostate Cancer'*.

He went through a long list of symptoms associated with this particular illness, and because I said I had none of those, he insisted that it was just an 'age thing' and nothing to be concerned about. Many people would have agreed and left it at that. I did not...

And after another two days, three phone calls, and another visit, and only when I stated that I would take the matter further did he perform an Index examination. The results, according to him, were quite average for a man of my age, and to concur, a PSA blood test would follow.

In mid-July, around the 15th and after a PSA blood test at Smedley General Hospital, I was back in to see the Doctor. The reading from the blood test was high, but not to him alarmingly so.

After verbal persuasion, he made a referral for me to have a biopsy at Smedley for the third week of July. This was quickly changed to Gloston Infirmary, some eight miles further away, two days before the appointment date (Sunday 21st)

I suspected, even then, that I had Prostate Cancer.

Three weeks after the biopsy, I went for an appointment in mid-August (the 13th I think) at Helmton Hospital.
I was informed at the hospital that it was 95% Cancer positive, and if it had been left maybe another six months, it could well have spread outside of the prostate.
I was given two treatment choices, Radical Surgery or combined Chemo-Radiotherapy, combined because of the high percentage. Radical Surgery is the removal of the Prostate Gland.
I opted for the latter. The Chemotherapy tabs (Temozolomide?) started in September. Then Bicalutamide followed by Prostap hormone injections and anti-sickness tabs in November and December. And finally, the Radiotherapy in January-February.

Claire (my wife) did not appear overly concerned; it may have been because she didn't know what to do. My Son was the same. My Daughter, on the other hand, was anxious and concerned
Other than buying me some pain killers, little interest or concern from Claire or Graham. Let us be honest, other than a positive outlook and words of comfort, none of which I did receive anyway, just WHAT could they do? Nothing, it was out of their hands. But once again, it was Zoe-Ann who was able to show the most concern.

At the end of February 2014, an MRI scan had shown a number of lesions/black marks in the Stomach.
According to the Doctors, this was not secondary. A relatively new treatment of direct injection was prescribed for four sessions into the area of each lesion over the next two weeks.

Once again, little concern from Claire or Graham. But again, in their defence, what could they do. It would have had some comfort if they would only talk to me about it, but they didn't. For all intents and purposes, I was 'on my own'. Zoe-Ann was becoming a little more relaxed about it, but she still phoned every 2nd or 3rd day. Bless her for that. I was becoming inwardly very despondent. My inner confidence levels were, by now, almost non-existent after years of abuse. My determination to keep fighting the Cancer had all but drained. I wasn't in a good place. I seriously wasn't

The follow-up scan in April could not detect any lesions. And in the summer of 2014, my Family Doctor of almost forty years retired, and a Doctor Jowett from within the practice, has taken over. A lot of hair loss, but not total, as expected. Now growing back slowly.

JULY 2014 – FEBRUARY 2015

By late August 2014, I noticed that my left breast was starting to swell and harden behind the areola.
Both the swelling and the area of the hardening became more extensive as the weeks went by. By this time, I was becoming more than curious, I was becoming concerned.

It had all the symptoms of MBC (Male Breast Cancer), and I was fully aware of the meagre survival rate. I was verging on being scared. Due to personal reasons, and certainly what I had been through the last twelve months or so, my confidence levels were at almost zero. I had been pushing and pushing. I was mentally exhausted... but not done.

I clearly remember thinking, as silly as it seems, 'what a time to happen. I have just found some old friends, also a girl, whom I met only once some forty-six years prior and also Lynn Cohen. It was like someone kept pressing the 'restart' button.
I digress I know, but what a time to think about rekindling old friendships. But it's giving me a rest bite from the pressures I am under.

I made an appointment to see my Doctor at the end of November.
As it was a Practice and my listed Doctor was not available, I was seen by one of the others. She informed me that she 'had seen this in many men of my age' and recommended Emugel.
"Are you sure?" I queried.

"Yes, nothing to be concerned about, I have seen this many time in men of your age." was the reply
.
On the way home, I was thinking '*Nooo... not having it, I'll give it a week, ten days at most*'

After almost two weeks of using the Emugel, the symptoms had not subsided, and I telephoned the practice and spoke to my Doctor.
After some insistence, he arranged a referral to see a consultant (Miss Nasir) at the Acute Breast Service unit at Helmton Hospital.
Again, little or no concern at all from Claire or Graham. Zoe-Ann on the other hand was quite concerned though, as she knew how serious it could be for a Man. My Daughter proving and showing once again her true caring side. Her own life at that time was going through a messy period and yet her concern was for me.
I was still not in a good place. I truly thought I may not see the year out.

It's strange to look back and think I wasn't overly concerned. Yeah, I knew about the one in three mortality rate, but my optimism and a little extra confidence from somewhere had kicked in.
The tests were conducted over two days, in February, and a consultation took place a few days later.

They said it wasn't cancerous from the off-set, but they were quite concerned when checking my treatment history that
I did not have the required Radiotherapy to the chest.
It was said to me that this procedure of one (or two) sessions is standard when having both Chemotherapy and Radiotherapy
so close together. By not having it done caused swelling of the blood vessels and subsequent hardening behind the areola, aggressive, alarming, but certainly, non-fatal.
There was also pronounced signs of Gynaecomastia, but only in the left breast.
Tamoxifen, though not 'licensed for use', was recommended for a three-month treatment.
For the most part, it has worked with only a very slight swelling evident to date.

Looking back on all that had happened, what could have been…
Has it been down to my stubbornness, not to accept the word or advice of a 'white coat', a Doctor, blindly?
Had it just been just an overwhelming desire to literally 'survive?' or was there something else, something that can't be explained?

And just where did this extra hit or *'Gift'* of confidence come from?

At the end of the day, I'm just glad I disobeyed my Doctor and have had both the issue and my fears resolved.

MARCH 2016

After several reviews, I am now officially in 'remission', and although my PSA is still rising – albeit relatively slowly, the prognosis is good, according to both Urologists and Oncologists alike, and they assure me that I will still be around, for quite a few more years to come.

So, even though I will be around annoying people, and hopefully, giving them the occasional cause to smile, I must never lose sight that I have been given a remarkable 'third' chance of continuing my life, in much the same way that I had been accustomed to (both good and bad.).

But whilst there are no certainties in life, and that the Cancer will always be there, it should not make me, or anybody, complacent and ready to accept the word blindly off even the most eminent people.

My investigative nature has always been there, but my confidence in my abilities and worthiness has not.

There have been many setbacks over the years, but I have felt a more profound, more substantial confidence growing inside of me for the past eighteen months or so. I say confidence, but it feels 'different'.

I cannot be sure why this has come about, but I am pretty confident, looking back, knowing what the catalyst could have been from, finding my 'lost' friends. The timing is the same.

For sure, it could not have come at a better time. It somehow made me extra wary of the 'experts', their professional suggestions and pieces of 'advice'. It also gave me an incentive to look beyond their words. It felt like it was 'pushing' me.

And I'm pleased to say I feel a whole lot better for it, both physically and mentally.

Now, this may sound a little crazy, but I have a strong feeling that I'm quite possibly alive today due to its help.

The following updates were posted on Facebook verbatim, for 'friends only' to read.

CANCER UPDATE #1 - December 9th 2016

This update is the first and hopefully, will be the only update in response to 'The Request' put up by a friend to help others talk about their Cancer experiences. The initial reaction to 'The Request' is due to Leila's memory, a remarkable young Lady still being painful in my mind, five months after her passing.

For Leila and the many other people, both men and women who put off going for check-ups.

For those who are at the early stages of cancer. For those at the latter stages, may your God be at your side always.

Your life is precious, it always has been, and it always will be.

And as for me, I had NO SYMPTOMS, absolutely NONE... and yet.

Maybe, it was directly a side effect from my previous treatment, I don't know, but it coincides time-wise.

Shortly after (less than a month) from when I finished my Chemotherapy/HRT & Radiotherapy treatment in February 2014, I noticed that my voice box was weaker. It was breaking up. Nobody gave me an explanation. I just took it as 'it happens'. Annoying, but I lived with it.

Then from late 2015, I felt as if there was something in my throat when swallowing. Through the weeks and months that followed, it was still there. The symptoms and affects, increasing

Around the second week of September 2016, it started to become somewhat more painful, it created a genuine concern.
That, along with the niggling cough, which had been more noticeable, and irritating, over the last month.

Shortly after, my Doctor informed it that it was quite possibly due to a severe cold virus strain that had recently started up.
Not being fully convinced of this explanation, A week or so later I 'requested' if I could have an x-ray of my throat, as I was becoming quite concerned.

Due to me having a 'something in the throat' issue from a while back, he (almost reluctantly) agreed, and made the referral.

Two days later, I had an x-ray. Then less than a week after the x-ray, I received a letter, and an appointment, from Smedley General Hospital to see a Dr. Murray, a throat specialist, five days later. WOW... I thought at the time, this IS unusually rapid service.

The Doctor performed an 'eye watering' Nasendoscopy (camera and light passed through the nose to the back of the throat) and after what seemed an eternity, but in reality, maybe less than a minute, he said he 'found something' and that he was going to take a sample for a biopsy.

At that very moment, my mind flashed back to the biopsy for my prostate. I started to have a 'gut feeling' as to what the results were going to be, there and then, but I was still feeling optimistic - just.

My confidence, though going through a seemingly low period due to a personal issue, thankfully, did not allow me to become morbid. But however optimistic I was, the reality or a possible reality, set in.

I started to prepare for that singular eventuality because I genuinely thought I wasn't going to be as lucky this time. I tried to be as rational and as strong as possible. And in the main, I felt that I was. My renewed (?) confidence was still there.

But individual personal decisions and choices about my future, or maybe a possible lack of it, had to be made, and in a small way, I consciously started to play them out in early October.

Then, on the morning of October 13th, whilst on a short break in France visiting family, I was informed (via email, by request) that I had a tumour in the throat, though the biopsy was inconclusive as to what stage/level.

This news reacted on me more negatively than with the Prostate results in 2013.

Yes, I had a feeling it would be so, but I knew that even though I was determined to fight it and hold it off for as long as possible, a particular situation had to be resolved.

This would involve me taking on a different persona. It was a vile position to be in, but in the end, it had the desired (though not truly wanted) outcome and the situation was resolved.

The tests that needed to confirm at what stage or level the tumour was, were carried out between the 19th and 26th of October.

Everything was now moving at a faster pace, and in retrospect, I am so thankful.

A case of 'being in the right place at the right time?' I'm not so sure. Is this yet another extraordinary coincidence to add to an apparent growing list?

On the afternoon of October 31st, it was confirmed that I had T1-Throat Cancer and partially 'resting' on my vocal-chords. Thankfully, it was still localised, though at 93%. The previous, more serious concerns proved unfounded.

A few days later, I was telephoned to inform me that a cancellation had left an appointment open, and that I could take it, but it was in Lee, a few miles further away, at another Hospital. Not an issue. I said yes [let's get it done], my confidence levels rising ten-fold.

The treatment continued through November, with the Radiotherapy being completed by the start of December..

During this period, I had a review with Mr. Bold, my Urologist, in mid-November. He was a little concerned that my PSA was steadily rising.

At the previous review, he should have mentioned that then. I certainly did, to which he retorted, *'It was only a blip'*.

Yeah, right, so NOW, it's NOT a blip, and he is concerned?

He arranged another review and another PSA blood test for March next year (2017). As if I haven't enough on my plate.

After the Radiotherapy finished, an x-ray and invasive test quickly followed at Smedley General on the 7th, and the following day, or may have been a couple of days after, I was informed, by telephone, that the cancerous tumour had been removed and that everything looks good.

A full report would be sent to Mr. Bold and my GP. And a further scan next year will determine if all the cancerous cells had been eradicated.
I could not get over what can only be described as a whirlwind of events over the last 3-4 months.

The relief was good, but a reality suddenly hit home,
I was saddened and very angry because the decisions and actions I took to fulfil them were so very much the wrong ones. I totally messed up, and it's something that I will have to live with and be reminded of for the rest of my life, but in doing so, I am also learning from it.

(This was posted along with a 'Happy Christmas' card)
December 24th 2016

'As most of my friends on Facebook are already aware, the last three years have been, to say the least, traumatic, with two Cancers and a 'near miss' plus the latest Cancer in October, which I honestly thought may have led to being 'one too many'.

Thankfully, all these are now entirely under control or have been eradicated. So much so, that I can wish you all a very Beautiful, Happy Christmas and a Joyous, Safe New Year, and I will now be able to do so for many years to come'.

CANCER UPDATE #2 - March 12th 2017

In the third week of January 2017, I had my yearly MRI Prostate scan at Smedley General. I think by now, I have attended all the Hospitals within the Hospital Trust Area

At my review at the start of March, Mr. Bold stated that if my PSA goes above a certain level, he recommends I have radical surgery (removal of the prostate gland).
He assured me that there *'was nothing to be concerned about as it's a straightforward and standard procedure, and it will lower my PSA considerably'*, as, in his learned opinion, the gland contained the cancerous cells.
I asked, *"Are there any other types of treatment available to me?"*

He answered that *"There are none."*

Something deep inside made me wary. His reply didn't convince me, don't ask why (maybe it's that 'feeling' again). I just felt uneasy taking his word and going down this route.

I informed him, in a quite positive manner that,
"I am not prepared to make a decision at this moment and I prefer to wait."

He said he was *'ok'* with that.

What with the ongoing recovery for my throat Cancer, and his pushing for radical surgery on my prostate, it wasn't confusing, just very annoying. I needed to think very carefully.
But my optimism and these extra bursts of confidence I have been getting are making me want to push forward all the time, like they were guiding me. Weird

Within twenty-four hours after the review, and doing some research online, I found out about trials being carried out at the BARSLOW ROYAL HOSPITAL, which involved laser treatment and freezing.
I telephoned Mr. Bold's secretary with the news, and a couple of days later, Mr. Bold telephoned me to say,
"I have only just heard about these, but after checking, all the trial places had already been secured and as you previously had both Radiotherapy and Chemotherapy, you would not be eligible for the trial anyway."

He reiterated that radical surgery was the best option.
I still wasn't convinced.

After his call, I did more research over the next day and eventually found the confidence [thank you (?) yet again] to telephone Mr. Grayson's team at the Barslow Royal Hospital.
I explained my situation and my concerns. They informed me that they would get someone to phone me back.
What followed next left me totally amazed, humbled and full of respect.
Around two hours after that initial telephone call, I received the return phone call.

The caller introduced himself as Luke Grayson.

For the next hour, whilst we talked, he explained all about the ongoing trials and new testing equipment.
He showed interest in my concern regarding Mr. Bold's persistent pursuance for radical surgery.
He said he was pleased I am *"The sort of person who did not resign themselves to the first option."* and, in a concerned way, questioned the 'only' option I had been given.
He then said,
'Mr. Bold was wrong in suggesting that you was not eligible because you had previous treatment, as a number of those on the trials (which was indeed fully taken up) *had prior treatment'*.
He also went on to inform me that, *"All those on the trial were from the Barslow area because that is where all the procedures are taking place. This was purely logistical, as the patients needed to be available for any further tests or consultations when required, quickly."*

He finished off by saying he would send me the full details of the trials literature via email (which he did), along with a Patient registration form to be filled in when a date can be found.
This appointment would be for an assessment only.

The next day I telephoned Mr. Bold and informed him of my lengthy telephone call with Mr. Grayson. This created a surprising reply.
Mr. Bold stated that he *'knew the Doctor personally'*, yet a short while back, he had only *'just heard'* about the trials (which had been going for at least eight months prior).

He then went on to say, *"If you didn't mind travelling to Barslow, [over 200 miles] at your own expense, I would contact the Doctor."*

Now, this was a change coming from him. Though it was my feeling that he was not pleased that I had the audacity to 'go above his head' and contact the team at the Barslow Royal. But, at the same time, he may have been glad I was off his hands even if for a short period. All down to budgets.

A few days later, I received my appointment to go to Barslow for the assessment early February 2017.

A simple interview, other than the blood, urine, and blood pressure could have been done 'online' with the tests done locally, but it was good to meet a few of the team.

I was to learn that Luke Grayson was a leading and highly respected figure within the field of Cancer treatment.

From a full MRI scan report taken in late January 2017, there are *'no signs of tumours anywhere in Prostate, Bladder and Rectum'*.

The MRI scan shows a volume of less than thirty and density calculated at 0.04, which is' very good' for all intents and purposes.

There are, however, ill-defined PIRAD 3 lesions in the region, with apparent restrictions, and that a targeted biopsy may be helpful.

Also, a recently undertaken CaT scan has shown there are no Cancer cells in the left breast. And no re-occurrence of the Cancer in the Stomach or Throat…., yessss !!

"Getting an appointment to see a Speech therapist may prove to be a long wait, as they are few and far between."
So said Doctor Khim at my assessment, in February 2017.
[I never realised I would still be waiting in twelve months]

At the latest review in the second week of March 2017, with Mr. Bold, he stated that,
"I am reluctant to perform a biopsy on the lesions in case it disturbs 'anything'."

He did, however, confirm that along with Mr. Grayson, and myself if agreeable, there would be a twelve-month observation period during which time Mr. Grayson will be kept informed of all tests and reviews.

So, as at this moment, I feel fine with no physical Cancer-related issues. Though whilst it's still in the 'back of my mind', it's THERE where it stays, until otherwise.

In this country, we are fortunate to have in place a Health Service, whilst far from perfect, and is often financially abused by non-

citizens of the country and sometimes even its own consultants, it is still deemed one of the best 'at point' health care systems anywhere in the World.
I have been MORE than fortunate, having gone through Prostate, Stomach and Throat Cancer, plus that Breast Cancer scare, and still walking this Earth.

It was as if there was an undefined reason, a meaning to it all, a reason why I have survived, and others have not.
Kismet?
I am not pious when I say this, but I have the strangest feeling that I may already know the reason, but I dare not tempt providence by mentioning it.

And whilst I try and do the Spock thing and 'Live Long And Prosper' I humbly accept with open arms what a very special person in my life said to me not so long ago, *'Let's take it one day at a time'*. Though not said in relation to my illness, it was, and still is a good reminder not to rush into situations or make rash statements, whatever the honest reasoning behind them are.
In truth, looking back maybe I should I should have heeded those words and stepped back. But what is done, cannot be undone.

CANCER UPDATE #3 - December 3rd 2017
Whilst I'm upbeat about the whole thing. I start this update on a sombre note.

My Cousin, Marie, was less fortunate than I.
She and her husband (Albert) came over to England from their home in France at the start of January 2017. She became very unwell. I had already been made aware she had Cancer in the December, after my visit to France late last year.
I never allowed myself to think it was 'that' bad, as Marie was so close to me from the time we were children.

I kept positive on the 28th when I took them for breakfast whilst on the way to the airport. A lovely little bistro, south of Hamilton I had been introduced to by a friend sometime before. I didn't allow the thought to dominate my mind, that this could be the last

time I would have a real conversation with her and the last time I would ever see her alive.
She died on April 20th from Cervical Cancer. And my mind wandered back to another time, but to that same airport. A terrible and heartbreaking coincidence.

I have been keeping in contact, via telephone and email with a member of Mr. Grayson's team in Barslow, and it's more than fortunate that I have. Because from the very start, it was apparent that information was not being received from Mr. Bold, as they 'could not access his system?'
That issue was very quickly resolved, with me sending the missing four blood test results via email.

At my review with Mr. Bold at the end of the first week in October, I made it known to him about this *'lack of communication'*. He replied that he would *"Look into it."*
What would have been the position if I had not kept in contact with the team in Barslow?
Would they have eventually contacted him? A year is a long time for observation, when there is no information to 'observe'.

In late November, the recent 1st annual throat scan has shown that everything is 'normal' and the Cancer has not returned.
The PSA readings are continuing to rise, but the full blood test later this month will give a clearer picture of what the next procedure may (or may not) be.
I am not unduly worried or concerned, thanks to my optimism and this pushy confidence. Just where did this ' *'Gift'* come from?

Though it's always there at the back of my mind, it does not affect my day-to-day life or lifestyle. The boost to my confidence (I mentioned this a while back) seems to be still with me, and it is indeed helping more than words can express..
What is affecting me is connected to the recent Cancer by a dotted line and something I touched upon in the 1st update (December 9th 2016). Whether that issue will ever get resolved, I do not know, but it has not stopped my positive thoughts.

CANCER UPDATE #4 - May 18th 2018

Well, certainly a lot has happened since the last update of December 3rd 2017.

As people are now aware, I do not give a running commentary week by week. I only provide an update when 'I' feel it's the right time.

I was due to have my regular check-up with Mr. Bold in January, and an appointment for a scan was to be made at the same time if the latest PSA reading showed an increase.

But before this, I received an appointment to go down to the Barslow Royal for tests.

I duly went to Barslow again, had a couple of blood tests and gave fluid samples, plus lots of paperwork... and that was it.

I was a little disappointed again, but I was content in the knowledge that I was now getting treatment from two sides. Or so I thought.

The expected date for my appointment with Mr. Bold came and went, no letter or telephone call.

My first appointment with the Speech and Language Therapist was set for the second week in February.

The number of sessions needed would depend entirely on my progress and just how far my therapist could take me. Each weekly session lasts forty-five minutes.

I received a report and appointment from Barslow. My PSA was doubling, not a good sign at all.

They wanted me to go back down for a three in one scan (Barslow Royal is the only Hospital in England to offer this procedure)

Come the start of February, and still no appointment from Mr. Bold.

I travelled to Barslow for the three in one Scan (MRI-Bone and Choline PET/CT)

By the end of the third week of February and still no appointment from Mr. Bold, I contacted the Hospital Scheduling Department.

I was informed that the earliest date I could make to see Mr. Bold was April.

After I made it very clear that I will NOT be waiting until April, because my appointment and a possible scan were overdue. They immediately put me through to Mr. Bold's Secretary. Two days later, I received an appointment letter to see Mr. Bold in the last week of February.

When I went to see Mr. Bold, there were no apologies from him when I requested a reason for the missing January appointment. He stated that he, *"Thought Grayson in Barslow was dealing with my case and making my appointments."*
What an excuse. What on Earth made him think that?
I abruptly replied that, *"As my appointment and subsequent confirmation letter from October 2017 stated that you would arrange an appointment in the January."*
His reply was unbelievable; he said in response that there was
"A lot of paperwork with your case, I must have overlooked it."

(WTF!!)
I just replied...
"That is just not good enough"

I figured he knew that I was more than just a bit 'annoyed'.

My personal opinion is that Mr. Bold was somewhat pissed off when I brought in Mr. Grayson, who 'outranks' him.
Don't forget, it was Mr. Bold who wanted to refer me to another Surgeon to perform surgery, and it was Mr. Bold who 'knew little' of the trials carried out at the Barslow Royal.
Do I hear the sound of Cash Tills?

Within a week, I received a twelve-hour notice for a scan at The Royal in Helmton at 8.30pm.
During this time, I was still waiting for the results and report of my three-in-one test.
Two weeks later, I received a report from Barslow. It stated that they compared the results from their scans with the latest scan (from Helmton, of which I am still awaiting the report) and that they wanted me to travel back down to Barslow for more tests as there was 'an anomaly in the shape of a Prostatic Extension'. They felt that this could be cancerous and be the reason for the acceleration within the PSA readings.

Once again, I made my way to Barslow, where I had a Cystoscopy (?) performed in the morning. The results came back with no issues.

In the late afternoon, I had laser treatment to remove the Prostatic Extension and full biopsy. Thank heavens for those soft railway seats on the travel back home.
A couple of weeks later, the results came back.
The Extension showed it to be 1.2% Cancerous, which, according to them, was within 'normal levels' (?) but what concerned them was that it's now apparent something else was causing the accelerated PSA reading.

They are also now, it seems, to be of the opinion, though not entirely convinced, that the high reading may be from living residual tissue left behind when I had radiotherapy. I made mention of this quite a while back (2015). Could these be the lesions Mr. Bold did not want to do a biopsy on?
They would wait until they see the results of my next PSA (after the recovery period).

It's not over, it never is where Cancer is concerned. But I'm feeling 'positive'. I have that deep unexplained confidence, a 'Gift' indeed. I also now have a vision of a future that may not come to pass, but without that vision, that goal, this journey may never be made. Maybe the message on my card is more profound than I have ever realised...

I cannot see you...
nor can I hear you...
... but I feel your presence.

CANCER UPDATE #5 - May 13th 2019

It has been an eventful journey with many twists and turns... even up to a few days ago.
I had my PSA and a full blood test taken in May 2018. The results came back a few days later.
The reading had dropped to 2.07, an incredulous drop indeed.
I now wait to see what the Barslow Royal Hospital review is and also Mr. Bold's opinion (if he has time to give one).
A PSA reading three months later created the same reading. This was indeed brilliant news.

After twenty-eight sessions, and the first week of August, the Speech Therapist could do no more and pushed me out of the door in the nicest possible way.

My voice was a lot stronger. I had to go back to real basics, and that I found very frustrating, but I worked on it, changed the dynamics in my voice, changed the tone and pitch through breathing exercises. I still have to be careful not to strain the vocal chords. But, touch wood, everything is looking and sounding good, no pun intended.

With my PSA dramatically dropping and staying there, I started making moves about going abroad to work as a Teacher. The following January, I was persuaded by 'something, a strong push to reconsider. I'm so glad I did.

In early February (2019), my PSA was up, quadrupled from the November reading of 2.12.

I contacted Barslow, and they requested I see them ASAP with an appointment for four days later.

I made the trip, did more tests.

I was told, like last time, that *'they could not understand why the PSA rose in such fashion'*, other than what I had discussed with them on a previous visit. But they had a sound theory. They said they would request Mr. Bold to have an MRI done and the results sent back to them as soon as possible.

When I spoke to Mr. Bold's secretary at the end of February, it was confirmed that an MRI had been requested, but by Mr. Bold (?). I also asked about my review, which was due that February. I was informed that," *There was nothing in the schedule for a review,* and an *'oversight'* had occurred. " (again?).

And a 'new' review was set for beginning of March 2019.

My MRI scan was set for the third week in April 2019, and the results being forwarded to my Doctor and Mr. Grayson.

I will admit, I was more than a little apprehensive regarding this particular scan, possibly a definite case of YES or NO regarding the Cancer.

Even though the thought of Cancer was on my mind during December 2018, I was in exceptionally good spirits.
Two things had recently occurred.
One was to allow me to see the light at the end of the tunnel, though being a legal issue, it may become Law sometime next year, 2019
...and the other was the acceptance of something that I had, quite possibly been in denial of for many years and even more markedly, the last four or five. Accepting it gave rationale to actions I took and was remarked upon previously in one of my updates. Accepting and making known the truth created the most astounding 'calming' effect within me. Truly remarkable.

In mid May 2019, I received the MRI scan results (via post) (though I had to get the full report from my GP a full week later). The Scan results showed no cancerous cells... It was the 'all clear'. But what of the slowly rising PSA?
What of the Barslow 'theory'... I await their response.

So, could this be the last 'update'? I certainly hope so.

I'm certainly no fatalist, as the last six years have shown. I'm an occasional idealist, aren't we all at some point. I am still a realist who still has hopes and aspirations, as any sane person would.
So for now, I am pleased to say I'm here, still annoying people... still helping people as best I can... and still loving life and people.

CANCER UPDATE #6 - November 16th 2019

I wrote in my last update (#5) '...Could this be the last 'update'? – I certainly hope so'
Murphy's Law strikes yet again…. It WASN'T to be.
So much has happened (yet again) since the last update.

First, a little more background about the work done by the Barslow Royal Hospital clinic in Barslow.
They have been doing trials of a revolutionary new type of
scanner for three years, the Gallium PSMA PET/CT.
This is, I am led to believe, a German invention that is already in use in a very small number of specialist Hospitals (four in Europe,

one in the UK and three in the USA). These are all Private Hospitals and charging upwards from £11k Sterling per scan.

The Barslow Royal Hospital specialist unit finished trials in the Spring. These trials were on behalf of the SHS (State Health Service) to make them as proven and as cost-effective as possible (SHS budgets).

[It was finally given the 'all clear' in the F\all (Autumn) 2019].

The PET/CT scan taken in January and previously in Barslow were not of the PSMA PET/CT variety but the standard Choline type. Patient numbers had already been allocated for the trials.

Five days after getting the *'excellent'* MRI scan results from my consultant (Mr. Bold) in May 2019. I received a letter from the Barslow Royal Hospital team stating they had noticed three, possibly five 'anomalies' just outside the prostate area, and that an appointment had been made to see me in Barslow in mid-June 2019.

On the day, I travelled once again down to Barslow. Several new tests were outlined from that appointment, with the final one, a PSMA PET/CT scan taking place sometime in August.

And so began regular trips to Barslow in June and July for yet more tests and another MRI/Contrast scan ending with the PSMA as mentioned earlier in mid-August as SHS patient number 12. You would have thought I would be extremely apprehensive at this crucial period, but I wasn't. If anything, I was in 'good spirits'. My optimism was high, as were my confidence levels. Even the team in Barslow commented on it.

Because I had already made eight trips down to Barslow since I first contacted them in November 2016, they asked me if I would prefer the review via the telephone. This would be beneficial to me as to make the journey for only a possible ten-minute review seem pointless. I agreed.

The review, a couple of days later was conducted by Mr. Grayson himself.

In a nutshell...

The good (1) – Because of the PSMA PET/CT scan, they are 100% certain there is no reoccurrence of the Cancer in the Prostate.

The bad – The PSMA *'showed extensive Lymphadenopathy in the external iliac areas and retroperitoneum, which were avid..'* The Pelvic Nodes, and it was this that was causing the accelerated PSA.

The good (2) – Because of this newly developed scan, it had recognised Cancer cells in one definite, possibly two Lymph Nodes, but both at the earliest of stages, 1 (TxN1M0), there was low Cancer activities within another region close by, but again, stage 1.

Mr. Grayson also informed me that if conventional scanning had been used, the Cancerous Nodes would not have been detected until a high Stage 2, and more commonly, Stage 3 level.

There is an 'extra' good – (from the full report received in the September) Confirming that I have no other Cancer cells in any part of my body and, with that, no reoccurrence within the Stomach and the Throat cancers either.

The full results were emailed to me the following day, but my Doctor and Mr. Bold did not receive theirs until seven to ten days later.

Mr. Bold, for some reason, then arranged for an NM (Nuclear Medical) Bone Scan for last week in October.

It's 'not the same' as the PSMA Pet/CT scan, but the primary results are the same.

This seems a waste of money and stops another person on a waiting list from receiving the necessary treatment.

When I informed Barslow Royal Hospital, they too were a little confused but expected the same results.

And the results which came back showed – 'no abnormalities.'

After an appointment with my new Oncologist (Dr. Dale) in November, my treatment leading to Chemotherapy has begun.

The following day, the results of my latest PSA showed a high five-point jump. I immediately informed Dr. Dale and (for perusal) the Barslow Royal Hospital.

So there it is… and I'm ready for it. A case of *'Bring It On'*.

The two footnotes below were posted to my face-book page on the 18th November 2019, two days after the posting of the 6th Update.

Footnote 1: A member of the Barslow team mentioned in passing that the MRI with contrast in Barslow was a completely new concept/ idea. They went on to say that scan combined a standard MRI, with the PSMA. And this scan will go on trial starting in the New Year. What I had was the testing/setting up on the scan proper. I was, in fact, one of several 'Guinea Pigs' to test this new concept out. Once again? I was fortunate to have been in the right place at the right time. And this is how I came back with a 100% clear bill of health regarding Cancer of the Prostate. The new scan is for detecting cancer cells at a far earlier stage and preventing most of the unnecessary and costly surgery in the removal of the Prostate gland.

Footnote 2: I looked back a couple of years and realised EXACTLY what would have happened if I had not had this strong feeling, this '***Gift***' inside of me to be outspoken and demanded a different approach. The Consultant would have referred me to have my Prostate removed, when there was no cancer there. And the Cancer in the Nodes would still have been there, undetected.

CANCER UPDATE #7 – JANUARY 30th 2020

This is more of a 'strangeness and spookiness' update… read on... you may understand where I'm coming from if you have been reading the previous updates.

At the end of January (29th), I went to The Royal for the blood tests and review before the Chemotherapy (two days later).
I arrived about thirty minutes before my appointment, only to find a delay of up to forty-five minutes for the actual review.
Within ten minutes, I had had my blood test. Now the long wait.
It was fortunate that I had brought along some reading matter.

After watching the Documentary and knowing of the events sometime before, I had (just) purchased the book 'Survivors' by Maggie Oliver.
I was reading through it from the start. It was very absorbing and sad.
Then I came to page 84.

As soon as I read the five-line paragraph near the end of the page.
It hit me, it hit me so hard, I just sat there dumbstruck.
I found the answer to the real source of '***The Gift***'.

Unbelievable, totally incredibly unbelievable.

Shortly after, I had the review.
Whilst talking to the Urologist, I mentioned my PSMA PET/CT scan and the MRI Contrast, and I am pleased that from reports, it's now come online for all SHS patients at The Royal.
He gave me the same vague look Dr. Dale, my Oncologist, gave me.
He stated '*The Royal had not got it 'online', maybe later this year, but he heard it was available 'in the South'* (which was rather obvious because of my report). He then went on to say that he *'was quite excited about the report, as were the team, as the treatment usually given, would be altered (from 9 sessions to 6 and one or two other changes) and that I was the first patient who has the PSMA scan to be treated at The Royal'.*

This got my curiosity going yet again. And as soon as I got home, I did some more research.
He was, indeed, correct. The Royal has yet to go 'online' with the scan – they, along with five other hospitals, had been given the go-ahead to do a short six-month trial (ending in June 2020). But this was later cancelled due to the Pandemic.
I sent the link to a member (Claudia) of the team, at the Barslow Royal Hospital.
Late the following day, I received a reply.
They were surprised the schedule had been changed and could have been why there was a limitation (of 160) of SHS patients they could scan, and it was to be reviewed in summer 2020.
They are the only Hospital offering these scans on the SHS.
The reason I was the 'first patient The Royal had' was simple... all the other patients were from the Barslow area. This was to keep them all within a short travelling distance if they needed to be called back.

Claudia also mentioned that the reason for this was that when I first contacted the team, I did so personally, and they only reply to Hospital referrals.

Mr. Grayson overheard the conversation between herself and another team member, and he became curious. And so it was he who telephoned me back. Readers of my Cancer Updates will know the story from thereon. Another coincidence - or was it?

CANCER UPDATE #8 - April 15th 2020

I started Chemotherapy treatment on the last day of January after taking 3x eight steroid tabs (Dexamethasone). I then had to self-inject over seven days, 480mgs of Filgrastim (which boosted the immune–white blood cell) system.

And that's when things started 'going wrong'.

After the fifth injection, I started becoming unsteady on my feet, a sort of vertigo? Then the white flashes began. People's faces were totally 'whitewashed', in fact, anything with a bright surface. This was very evident when I walked out into the sunshine. It was as if a torch was shining into my eyes. I was disorientated. Anything white lacked detail and was blinding.

After the sixth, I also started with diarrhoea, which was something to watch out for over a twenty-four-hour period according to The Royal's medical book I was given.

The following morning, I noticed traces of blood, and the more I went to the toilet, the more blood was produced. I took the final seventh injection at noon, and by 2pm, pureblood was being seen when I went to the bathroom. I was haemorrhaging. I phoned the local Hospital, explained the situation and within twenty minutes, an ambulance arrived.

As I lay there on a trolley bed at the hospital, on oxygen and a drip, I felt scared, and I do mean scared.

I thought at times, for '*Christ's sake I ain't going* [dying] *like this'.... 'Why go through all I have done, for it to 'end like this'.. no... It ain't going to happen*'

My natural survival instincts were kicking in, as was 'something else'. Again, I cannot explain it; it was both in my physical aspect and very possibly my subconscious.

I was in brutal agony and I have a high pain threshold. For over seven hours whilst waiting for a bed, I was in a corridor then a triage side room.

Claire came to see me and stayed a couple of hours. I told her to go, as there was nothing she could do. I think she was relieved to go, as I was doing the 'Macho' *'I will be fine'* bit. In reality, I was far from fine. I was fighting hard, fighting the pain and an initial thought of not 'surviving'. Those initial thoughts was taken over by a strange calmness, and an inner voice telling me that everything was going to be alright eventually, and not to worry. Where the Hell did that come from? But it was working.

I was in isolation within the Infectious Diseases ward of Smedley Hospital for four days, during which time having lost over a litre of blood. I was given blood transfusions and later a 'drip'.

The doctors who saw me were very concerned that my White Blood Cell reading was 22.5 (my usual reading before this was 4.5 or 'normal') even though they were made aware of the injections I was taking prior to my Chemotherapy.

The cause, the Consultant put the heavy bleeding down to on my discharge form was, 'Inconclusive, possible bacterial infection'? and then sent home in an ambulance. Lost over a litre of blood and its 'Inconclusive' A case of 'white coats' sticking together?

Not an experience I want to go through again, all the same

By the time of my next visit (for blood test & review) at The Royal, I had started losing my taste buds, slight blurring of vision and continual pins and needles sensation in my feet and fingertips.

My blood test then (and on all subsequent visits proved satisfactory), though the Consultants answer to my question *'would it be normal for my white blood cell reading to be that high, as the Doctors did seem somewhat concerned'*, he stated (with a smile?) that the *'Doctors should have known the injections would give a higher reading'* and that *'there is nothing to be concerned about'* .... Hmmm.

Spending four days in a Hospital, Doctors knowing about the injections and losing a litre of blood is nothing to be concerned about.... Jesus Christ!!

The second Chemotherapy session went ahead a couple of days later,

The side effects (other than the 'white flash outs' and blood loss) started almost immediately during the seven-day injection course.

Along with the after-effects previously mentioned. My thighs, arms and back, along with my knee joints, started to ache. The pins and needles (later found to be Peripheral Neuropathy) were getting stronger, making my walking slower and painful. Plus making the picking up of individual items with my hands almost impossible.

As time went on leading to my next blood test, these symptoms became progressively worse.

After the next blood test and during my review, I asked the Consultant if these symptoms were regarded as *'normal'*? He very briefly explained *'each patient is different and reacts differently to the treatment'*. In other words, he hadn't a bloody clue.

The third Chemotherapy session over, and again, during the taking of the Filgrastim injections, any lessening of the side effects quickly passed by.

After walking only short distances, I was becoming breathless, having to stop for a couple of minutes to 'catch my breath'. Walking any incline made it even worse.

The pain to my thighs was getting stronger. My balance was becoming noticeably unsteady. Dressing, at any time, was becoming an experiment in agility and balance.

I was that concerned, that I typed and hand-delivered a letter the start of the third week of March to Dr. Dale at The Royal, asking if all this was 'normal'. Was it possible that I may be allergic to either the steroid Dexamethasone or the Immune booster injections Filgrastim? Was there a blood test or something to find out?

Leading up to the fourth session, full restrictions created by Covid-19 were already in place. I took the blood test and received a telephone review a couple of days later.

I was asked then, *'If I wished to carry on, even though the risk of infection by Covid-19 was by now, far greater'*.

Even with side effects, and the Covid-19, I was willing to carry on.

I was already taking stringent precautions both at home and when I ventured outside. Since the end of January, I had been wearing surgical masks and social distancing. I have also used hand sanitisers for the past four-five years.

It was a real struggle walking to the hospital and the corridors for the fourth session in the first week of April. I became extremely breathless whilst walking, and the pain to my thighs and calves, almost unbearable at times.

After the fourth session and the injections, I found I could only walk ten metres or less before I had to stop. All the other side effects had increased as well.

With the side effects, in my non-medical background opinion becoming more severe, I wrote and hand-delivered my second letter to Dr. Dale via the hospital a week later.

On the second week in April, Dr. Dale replied – by telephone. Over three weeks since I sent my first letter of concern. She said she had received both letters.

During this telephone conversation, because of the severity of the side effects she said that:

"I am pleased that you had done four sessions, I feel that might well be adequate (or words to that effect) in removing some, if not most of the cancerous Nodes."

She also stated:
"There was no test available to see if you are allergic to the steroids or the injections."

I did not have any background information regarding the amount or level of Docetaxel used during my treatment; otherwise, I could have asked if the dosage was too strong.

A Small World: Whilst at one of the later sessions I sat facing another part of the ward and about eight to ten metres away lay on a bed propped up by pillows was a Lady (I guessed about my age) fully 'wired up. She was wearing a colourful full bandana and was chatting to a female friend (I assumed) with dark hair (?). The 'patient' looked so familiar, but for the life of me I could not place who she was. Quite possibly someone from many years prior. Earlier, I also saw the owner of a Newsagents I used to go into some fifteen years ago and we chatted for a short while.

CANCER UPDATE #9 - June 1st 2020

Nobody could give me a timescale when everything is back to normal, most of or even anything.
Weeks, months, years and even a starker, 'never' was muted by Dr. Dale during the telephone conversation in the April.

I decided to do some medical research and investigations as I believed someone has 'mucked up somewhere' hence the original 'alarm bells'. After finding more information about the medicines used, I wrote to the Barslow Royal Hospital team.
I was not surprised to learn that the 150mg dosage of Docetaxel was thought to be 'higher' than my circumstances may have needed, but within the standard range based on current and historical information on my weight.
Figures of only 75-100 mg of the Docetaxel were mentioned for at least the first two sessions. But as they had no authority of direction, they could not intrude.
So, in other words, it was highly likely that I had been 'accidentally overdosed'. It was a bit late for blowing trumpets, but my 'alarm bells' proved right yet again – but painfully so.

Earlier, by the start of the second week in April, I was in excruciating pain in my feet and legs, I had not had more than two hours of sleep a night for the previous four nights, and the pain relief was not having a great deal of effect. I took a gamble (after some research) and purchased two Bregg T-Scope leg supports (modern-day Callipers).
The relief though limited, was instant.
These have now been worn on and off (mostly on) since then until the end of May. Now it's like the 'Forrest Gump' clip where he runs and his callipers break away. I'm far from running, but they have indeed helped to stabilise my balance a great deal.

To ease the pain in my legs, I finally got an appointment with my Doctor (so difficult during the pandemic) in May, and was given a 'one-off' injection to my knees and ankles. This, along with some Furosemide tablets (to ease the swelling).
This created good, short term results in pain relief to the knees and thighs; though the numbness is still there, it had no easing effect with my toes and fingers... oh well.

Taste buds are almost back to 'normal', though my love of chocolate, coffee and other 'goodies' seems to have significantly diminished (hope not permanently)

The continual numbness and tingling sensation (like grasping a handful of nettles) have lessened a little, but I still have difficulty gripping or picking up items, like eating utensils.
Also, I am walking a little stronger and longer, but still with the 'wobbles' (which still happen even when not walking). I'm a little overweight (by about 4kg), and my hair on my head is very, very slowly coming back, though I feel it will be 'sparse' for life's duration, Que sera sera. Mind you, it's also an excellent excuse to occasionally wear my Fedora's and other hats to keep my head warm and dry.
So, in a nutshell, I feel I am improving.
I have mentioned before that people are suffering a lot more than me, and for that mercy, I am grateful.
Mentally, my inner self, my well-being is more important as my outward physical appearance.

CANCER UPDATE #10 – August 2020

June 2020. Is The Seven Year 'Itch' Really Over?
At the beginning of June 2020, I received my recent (29th May) full blood test results. They showed that my PSA readings were at a level they class as, 'undetectable'.
The Chemotherapy treatment 'appears' to have removed the cancerous cells in the Lymph Nodes. Only another scan will prove that. And such a scan I will be pushing for at the next meeting with Dr. Dale in October.

The quarterly treatment I have to take also reduces the Prostate levels, so it's still 'up in the air' if the Chemotherapy has done its job. And so, combined with the report from the scans and treatment undertaken in Barslow, which could not find any cancer anywhere in my body, except for the Nodes, I will assume that this time around, I am now in 'complete remission'.
I have waited for two more full blood tests to reinforce the (end of) May results before posting this notice on Facebook...
On the third week of July, I was given the results of a recent scan, x-ray and EMG on my lower limbs and feet. And it was what I

expected, irreversible nerve damage resulting in peripheral neuropathy. This will I fear, affect any future artistic merriment on the dance floor.

Others have told me that I have always shown a positive and confident attitude to this illness.
Outward appearances can be deceiving. And s are extremely good at doing that, giving little, if anything, away.
There was that one horrible time though, in 2016. A time when I thought my 'luck' had finally run out, with the throat cancer.
Outwardly, to many, I was just the same, but inwardly I was so different.
A long time before, I had been *'Gifted'* (no other word describes it), a more profound boost to my inner confidence. I can't truly express the feeling, but it was to prove an extraordinary catalyst toward my wellbeing as it grew within me.
A short while later, I had to make decisions that were totally against my normal character (I have briefly touched upon this and the repercussions previously). The newfound 'confidence' that sustained me during this time has stayed with me through both challenging and enlightening periods since.
I do not know how long it will last, but one thing I am now confident of. It had been *'Gifted'* to me for this extraordinary time in my life. And as that time is about to pass, and if that extra inner confidence fades with that time, then so be it.

This 'Journal' of my fight against Cancer is for the memory of my Princess, Leila, a very special Lady. I will always miss talking to you, your smile... and you really did 'light up the room'. It is also for all Men…?
Men need to get rid of their 'Macho-ness' and have a regular check-up that includes a full blood test. The blood tests at least twice a year. Do it not only for yourself but also for your Family, your Wife, partner, and lover – do not allow them to grieve before time.

August has now become a very auspicious month for me.
1. 2013, The first of the Cancers was confirmed.
2. 2018, I finished twenty-eight weeks with the Speech Therapist.

3. 2019, When I became the first recipient outside Barslow to have the full PSMA scan, the scan that found the Cancer that the other scans couldn't.
4. 2020, The end of the Seven Year Itch

Yes, a very auspicious month indeed, and more so, if events from Book One are included.

AFTERMATH…...

OCTOBER 12th, 2020.

Another review with Dr. Dale during which he wanted to know *"If the PSMA trials were still ongoing?"*

It's becoming very evident that Dr. Dale appears to have little faith in Mr. Luke Grayson's work in Barslow. Based merely on the fact that there is very little evidence that the work with the PSMA actually 'prolongs' life.
I don't feel it was ever proclaimed that the PSMA would prolong lives. It did and still does detect cancer cells far earlier than standard CT/MRI scans. This was proven on my last MRI scan, and my consultant gave me the 'all clear'.

So, the fact remains *'if something in the scan had not been picked up by the team in Barslow shortly after, and if I started taking my PSA blood tests once a year as prescribed over two years PRIOR. Then it might have been in May 2020 that the PSA readings could have been through the roof and would have been left to my GP to try and arrange a CT/MRI scan.*
It almost guaranteed that that scan would NOT have shown any cancer cells, simply because the Cancer was NOT in my Prostate but the Lymph Nodes'.

I put all that to Dr. Dale, and all that was said in response was that,

"If it had not shown on the scan, a referral would (?) have been made for a body scan."

In other words, and as far as they are concerned, the Cancer would have been found '*eventually*', and treatment started.
I then pointed out,
"Yes, it could have been spotted, but at what level would it have been by then and could it not spread even further and created a stronger and longer Chemo course of treatment."

The answer given was astounding (to me)
"Nobody knows that for sure."

Words utterly fail me with such a reply. I was stunned.
Finally, I just had to ask about a follow-up scan.
The answer to that was,
"There is nothing planned."

I had emailed Claudia (part of the team in Barslow) a couple of days after the interview. She said Dr. Dale is correct. 'There is little evidence yet because they were waiting for funding to start up a second scan review program'. Claudia did NOT say, but implied...,
'Just WHAT did this Dr. Dale want. To be convinced that the PSMA is better at detecting Cancer than any other known scanning system in use in UK hospitals?'

I have since gained information as to the reactions of the clinical staff at the Royal and also that of Dr. Dale when talking about the treatment I received at Barslow and its progress and in particular Dr. Dale's recent 'questioning'.
It does NOT make for good reading, it's very political and (to me) questions the ethics of those involved.

I have said it before... I am so glad I was given the confidence, determination and the courage to go above everyone's head, and yes, in my case, I truly believe by doing so, my life (what I have left of it anyway) ain't going to be cut short by the attitude of the 'white Coats'.

A referral for x-rays and possible minor operation on my feet – calcium build-up

OCTOBER 29th, 2020.

With a strict regime of treatment of my own, I have continued to help correct my gait *[because having to walk on the sides of your feet is NOT the best way of getting around, never mind getting back into dancing mode]*. It is quite painful, BUT it's getting there. It is a case over mind over matter, but progress is being seen with the lessening 'wobbles'. Turning whilst walking or from a stationary position is still proving to be quite awkward, but with the somewhat unorthodox 'therapy treatment' and the stick's added security, it's working.

Ok, with due caution, and on the slower tempo, more sedate dances. But definite red flashing lights, where the high tempo dances like the Quickstep, Foxtrot or Samba are concerned. It's going to take time.

I have a particular personal vision and goal in mind. It will be extra special if both come to fruition. It will indeed 'take two to Tango' as the saying goes.

DECEMBER 05th, 2020.

During the ongoing pandemic due to Covid-19, the health services have been stretched and many surgical operations and treatments, both minor and critical have been cancelled and yet by the start of December I had not only had x-rays taken, but within ten days was having a double operation on my feet..

The surgical name for this type of operation is Arthroscopic Debridement and involves removing Calcium deposits/build up along the Metatarsal (in this case, the 5th, of both feet).

I arrived at the Hospital, just gone 6 am and back home by 1pm.

They had removed between 1 and 5mm of Calcium deposits which 'lined' the whole outside of the 5th Metatarsal, the little toe to you and me.

Though the surgeon would not say when asked, if this was a side effect of the Chemotherapy. She did say that in all probability, it WAS caused by the constant walking on the

outsides of the feet, an unusual gait. The connection between this and severe Peripheral Neuropathy is undeniable.
I have been given some medication and informed there is no need to return. The surgery should heal between seven and ten days. Providing the feet are 'padded', she recommends some light walking exercise – but not bare feet to bare floors (too hard). If all goes well, a nice Christmas present.

DECEMBER 14TH, 2020.

Four or five people on Facebook have all suggested that I put all this in a book, as they saw it as inspirational and could be a source of hope and encouragement to other people who find themselves struggling to cope.
To do so would mean EVERYTHING would have to go in. I think I had mentioned before that there are parts in this seven-year battle that were only 'touched' on very, very briefly when their effect was, in reality, beyond words.
The effects was profoundly personal, and life changing.
To write a book would create gaps that were an integral part of
the jigsaw. There is only one way those gaps, the missing jigsaw pieces, would complete the story, but I doubt that will ever happen. But doubts are mere obstacles, meant to be overcome.

MAY 2021

The treatment has left it's 'calling card', well a few actually. A couple of which, possibly, over time, will be resolved, such as the small gain in weight and libido loss. Though other side effects may take longer to alleviate or minimise, such as the Peripheral Neuropathy and its associated 'friends' - loss of balance etc. But, even now I'm working on those and I'm slowly, but progressively getting the better of them. The confidence within myself, my abilities has not debated. I know **'The Gift'** is still there, still a part of me.

Physically, I have recently been in a position to start toning my upper body and hopefully, with determination, luck and a vision, in the next few months, I will be able to start work on my lower limbs and bring supporting strength and more, back to them.

Mentally, I'm still very much alert, and more than enlightened through the events of the last eight years, and in particular, the last sixteen months. It has been a stressful time for me, and for more than just the cancer. More than anything, I have gained clarity, understanding and compassion from it all.

Because of recent events, I find now, that the goal I seek, to be able to dance again, and through the vision which is so crucial, are achievable, with time. The vision, whilst seemingly unattainable to others, more than helps to spur me on. Without it, I would indeed struggle, and that being at the very least.

To me it's simple enough, without that vision being there constantly, I will not be able to attain the goal. And having that vision, puts a smile on my face when things are not going so good.
Now, that isn't' such a bad thing to visualise, is it?

FEBRUARY 21st 2022

A new year has started to unfold, bringing with it new adventures, and a path, that for a long, long time has not been trod upon. But by the end of the year, a new doorway will be opened and that old path walked again and onto to new adventures.
I can now grip some objects with my fingertips, but still have a lot of difficulty picking up a flat object, like a knife or coinage from a flat surface, but I can, for the most part, circumnavigate those issues. I am steadier on my feet, though still have to pre-think a lot of my steps.
It's surprising how quickly the mind can adapt to correct body posture in an ongoing situation. My weight is up and down, I need the 'down' more regular, though I suspect that this has a lot to do with my ongoing quarterly hormone treatment. As for my libido, well let's just say I feel I have been blessed, once again.

Now back in July 2020, I was strongly advised by clinical staff to seriously look into the wearing of a specialist brand of Orthopaedic shoes. Sadly the styles available were limited, and though I say it myself even at my age, I do like to look 'good'. After a little research. I found an everyday brand, with duel fitting insoles and along with the purchase of a pair of Orthotic insoles, they provided the support and comfort I needed – at a quarter of the price.

And of recent, I have been able to start wearing my leather-soled shoes for short periods once again, what a true joy.

OCTOBER 26th 2022

Because I am now constantly on the quarterly anti-hormone injection Prostap, I'm technically not in remission but on continuous observation. There were side-effects initially, such as erectile dysfunction associated with this drug. But once again as in 2015 I have been 'blessed'. So what the future activities holds in that particular area, is anybody's guess. I have nothing planned or even thought about.

As for the side effects of the Peripheral Neuropathy, I feel generally good, really good.

I am not controlling the pain or discomfort, I'm living with it. Although my turns whilst walking have improved, it will still be a while before I am able to dance 'proper' (ha-ha) again.

But I believe I WILL, because in the recesses of my mind, I NEED to. It is part of the vision and the goal, both of which give me the appetite to succeed.

My voice box will never get stronger and I accept that, but the future is sure looking brighter for everything else including my regular PSA blood checks. For over the last two years and a half years since Chemo treatment finished they have consistently shown a 'negative' reading.

And so, no matter how it was, and still is being achieved, I'm ready to, very shortly, take on the new path to which I am looking forward to,

~ October 26th 2022

A (sad) End Note:

It was on February 13th 2023 that I belatedly learnt of the passing of someone whom I had not seen since around 1970. I was not only in shock, but terribly saddened as well.

I had only found out by chance she was on Facebook in 2014. I contacted her and became friends. I never mentioned about my Cancers to her, in truth there was no reason to. To find out she died from Cancer on April 29th 2021, was a horrible coincidence.
My mind went back to the Lady I mentioned in the Cancer Update #8.
Could that person I saw have been Lynn?

I could not say for certain at the time as it had been fifty years since I last saw her, people change physically over that long period and I was not close enough.

From what I was to learn from Lynn's Niece over the next couple of days, there is no doubt that it was indeed Lynn, whom I saw.
It appears Lynn had been in the midst of starting her treatment when I saw her, and whilst I was finishing mine.

Lynn Cohen, I will always remember your wide smile, blonde tresses and almost Doe-like eyes, and yes, those long legs of yours.
On seeing a photo of your Niece there is indeed a strong Family resemblance. She looks so much like you from way back then.
Lay your head forever on your pillow, my lovely Lady.

~ February 20th 2023

And so, this really has become a never-ending story.
And it will merely continue with another page
in another Chapter, that is yet to be written.
For this is Kismet.

*And yet, for a very small number of people,
it has already become, so more than that.*

Acknowledgements

To Athena and Christina: We have known each other since our teens, and Athena's deep and lasting affection for my late Brother.
We had some great times together, both in the past such as those hilarious 'Treasure Hunts' in our cars and in more recently times, dining out and causing mini riots, a spot of DIY with 15kg sledge hammers and renovating the renovations over four years in three houses.
You both were custodians of the unfinished original manuscript – and having read it, gave me your very blunt personal opinions. And, seriously, I fully appreciated your deep concerns as well as your smiles.
I love you both and always will, my two adorable twins from way back when.

To Jools: A World apart in status and wealth, and yet joined together in dance, in friendship, in laughter and even in sorrow over the many years.
Your sometimes, unexpected honesty being so refreshingly welcome. Though not always well received by others, due to your bluntness. And yet, you proved time and time again to be diplomatic both in business and your personal life.
A walking contradiction.
You became the catalyst to the opening up of the revelations that led me to find answers to questions I had sought, and to a deeper inner knowledge.
May our friendship remain as it is now, full of interest and laughter. Yes, we are different, yet so much alike in many ways.

To Jennifer: We became friends in a rather unorthodox way, and I am so glad we did. You had become a calming light in many things and a Sage in others. You also gave me your candid opinion on some of the events within the book (which you were the first to read), that you were quite uncomfortable with. I listened to and acknowledged those opinions, because that's what friends do.
It is my wish for that friendship, through any lapses along the way
to continue.

In Memory

For My Mother and Father (Vee and Walt): you both suffered hardships through your youth and then through the Second World War.
You, My Father, dutifully took care of my Mother when she became struck down with a depressive illness, whilst at the same time you made sure both my late brother and I were properly fed and clothed. You never shirked from your duty or your marriage vows.
My Mother never truly recovered from her illness. This put an intolerable strain on the Family, but a family we remained.

For My Brother (Patrick): We were quite different. I, becoming independent mainly due to my Fathers teachings, whilst you seemed to feign responsibility. But at the same time, you became a much respected, untiring stalwart where a particular children's charity was concerned. You were also loved and respected by your work colleagues, as the day of your funeral service would testify.
A Family trait it seems, and without fear of contradiction, the same was witnessed at our Fathers funeral. You passed away two weeks after your marriage, a marriage you could not even remember the following day. You left behind a heartbroken Mother and Brother but our lives forever enriched with the memories, and your legacy.

For Marie: You were always an inspiration.to me, and still are.
As children and early teens, we grew up together, then went our separate ways. Your words and acts of guidance, which were more often friendly lectures, often confused me at times
And later in life, you continued to be loved and admired by so many of your peers and justifiably so, and that was so evident at your memorial service in the University's Great Hall in France.
It has been said, that we would have been a formidable force to be reckoned with, had I chosen to follow you in your chosen field. I am not sure about that observation, and though it was not to be, it brought a loving, and knowing smile to my face. Such is fate.
With your sudden passing, which still hurts so deep, you never got to see the fruition of your wisdom within the pages of this book, or maybe you already have?
In me, in your Family, you are still very much with us, overseeing our lives, even our mistakes, and smiling.